CW01184072

The Garden Almanac
2025

Quarto

First published in 2024 by Frances Lincoln,
an imprint of The Quarto Group.
One Triptych Place
London, SE1 9SH,
United Kingdom
T (0)20 7700 6700
www.Quarto.com

Design Copyright © 2024 Quarto
Text Copyright © 2024 Zia Allaway and Guy Barter
Illustrations on pages 8, 26, 44, 64, 82, 102, 122, 142, 160, 178, 198, 216 © 2024 Angie Lewin

Cover illustrations by Angie Lewin

Zia Allaway and Guy Barter have asserted their moral right to be identified as the Author of this Work in accordance with the Copyright Designs and Patents Act 1988.

All rights reserved. No part of this book may be reproduced or utilized in any form or by any means, electronic or mechanical, including photocopying, recording or by any information storage and retrieval system, without permission in writing from Frances Lincoln.

Every effort has been made to trace the copyright holders of material quoted in this book. If application is made in writing to the publisher, any omissions will be included in future editions.

A catalogue record for this book is available from the British Library.

ISBN 978-0-7112-9397-7
Ebook ISBN 978-0-7112-9398-4

10 9 8 7 6 5 4 3

RHS Books Publisher: Helen Griffin
RHS Head of Editorial: Tom Howard
RHS Books Editor: Simon Maughan
RHS Senior Wildlife Specialist: Helen Bostock
Authors: Zia Allaway and Guy Barter
Designer: Sarah Pyke
Publisher: Philip Cooper
Commissioning Editor: Alice Graham
Editorial Director: Nicky Hill
Editor: Katerina Menhennet
Senior Designer: Isabel Eeles
Production Controller: Rohana Yusof

The RHS would like to acknowledge:
James Lawrence for the Seasonal planting ideas
Helen Bostock for consulting on the wildlife pages
Fiona Davison for consulting on the Horticultural Heroes entries
Beth Marshall (the gut-health gardener) for the Fermentation recipes

MIX
Paper | Supporting responsible forestry
FSC® C118234
www.fsc.org

Printed in Bosnia and Herzegovina

The Royal Horticultural Society is the UK's leading gardening charity dedicated to advancing horticulture and promoting good gardening. Its charitable work includes providing expert advice and information in print, online and at its five major gardens and annual shows, training gardeners of every age, creating hands-on opportunities for children to grow plants and sharing research into plants, wildlife, wellbeing and environmental issues affecting gardeners. For more information visit www.rhs.org.uk or call 020 3176 5800.

RHS

Royal Horticultural Society

The Garden Almanac 2025

The month-by-month guide to your best ever gardening year

Zia Allaway and Guy Barter

FRANCES LINCOLN

Introduction	6
January	8
February	26
March	44
April	64
May	82
June	102
July	122
August	142
September	160
October	178
November	198
December	216
RHS Gardens to Visit	234
Index	236

Introduction

Welcome to the 2025 edition of the *RHS Garden Almanac*, a celebration of the growing year and all it has to offer. This colourful month-by-month guide includes invaluable advice on what to sow, plant and grow throughout the year, written by the Royal Horticultural Society's experts and horticulturists. The book also includes ideas on how to garden sustainably and reduce your carbon footprint, together with simple tips on how to save money.

Wildlife watching has been shown to benefit our mental health, and the pages on birds, insects and animals offer an insight into the creatures you may spot in your garden or the surrounding countryside. You can also delve deeper into the lives of key horticultural heroes who have impacted the world of plants and gardening.

The almanac includes average monthly rainfall figures for all areas of the UK, as well as sunrise and sunset times, to help you plan your garden's irrigation needs and monitor the light levels that affect plant growth. Moonrise and set times are also listed, since moonlight can influence the activity of garden wildlife, including some herbivorous insects that feed more heavily when nights are brighter.

You will also find inspirational seasonal projects for each month, designed to enhance your garden and support the wildlife living there, and delicious ferment recipes, which will help you to make the most of your produce, while improving your gut health. Keep the book to hand throughout the seasons to enjoy your plants, crops, and garden wildlife throughout 2025.

Moon phases

A Moon cycle, or lunation, is the time it takes for the Moon to travel through all of its lunar phases, and it lasts about 29½ days. Half of the Moon's surface is always illuminated by the Sun, but the surface area we can see changes as the Moon orbits the Earth. The eight phases in a lunar month are divided into four primary and four intermediate phases, as follows:

1. **NEW MOON** Primary phase, when the Moon is between the Sun and the Earth and cannot be seen because the whole surface is in shadow.

2. **WAXING CRESCENT MOON** Intermediate phase: the right half can be seen in the UK and in the Northern Hemisphere.

3. **FIRST QUARTER MOON (HALF MOON)** Primary phase: the right half of the Moon is illuminated in the UK and Northern Hemisphere.

4. **WAXING GIBBOUS MOON** Intermediate phase: the right half is illuminated in the UK and Northern Hemisphere.

5. **FULL MOON** Primary phase: the Moon and the Sun are on opposite sides of the Earth and the whole Moon is illuminated.

6. **WANING GIBBOUS MOON** Intermediate phase: the left half is lit in the UK and Northern Hemisphere.

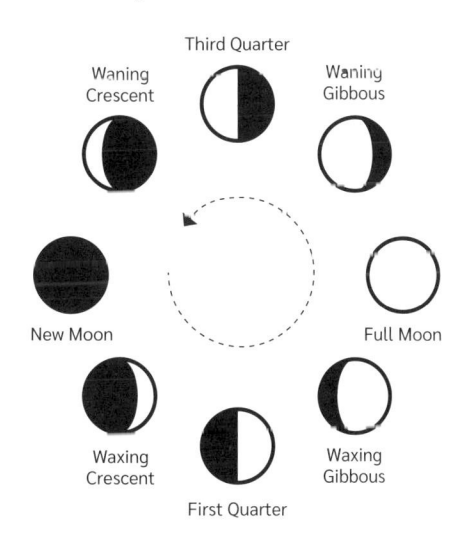

7. **THIRD QUARTER MOON (HALF MOON)** Primary phase: the left half is lit in the UK and Northern Hemisphere.

8. **WANING CRESCENT MOON** Intermediate phase: the left half is lit in the UK and Northern Hemisphere.

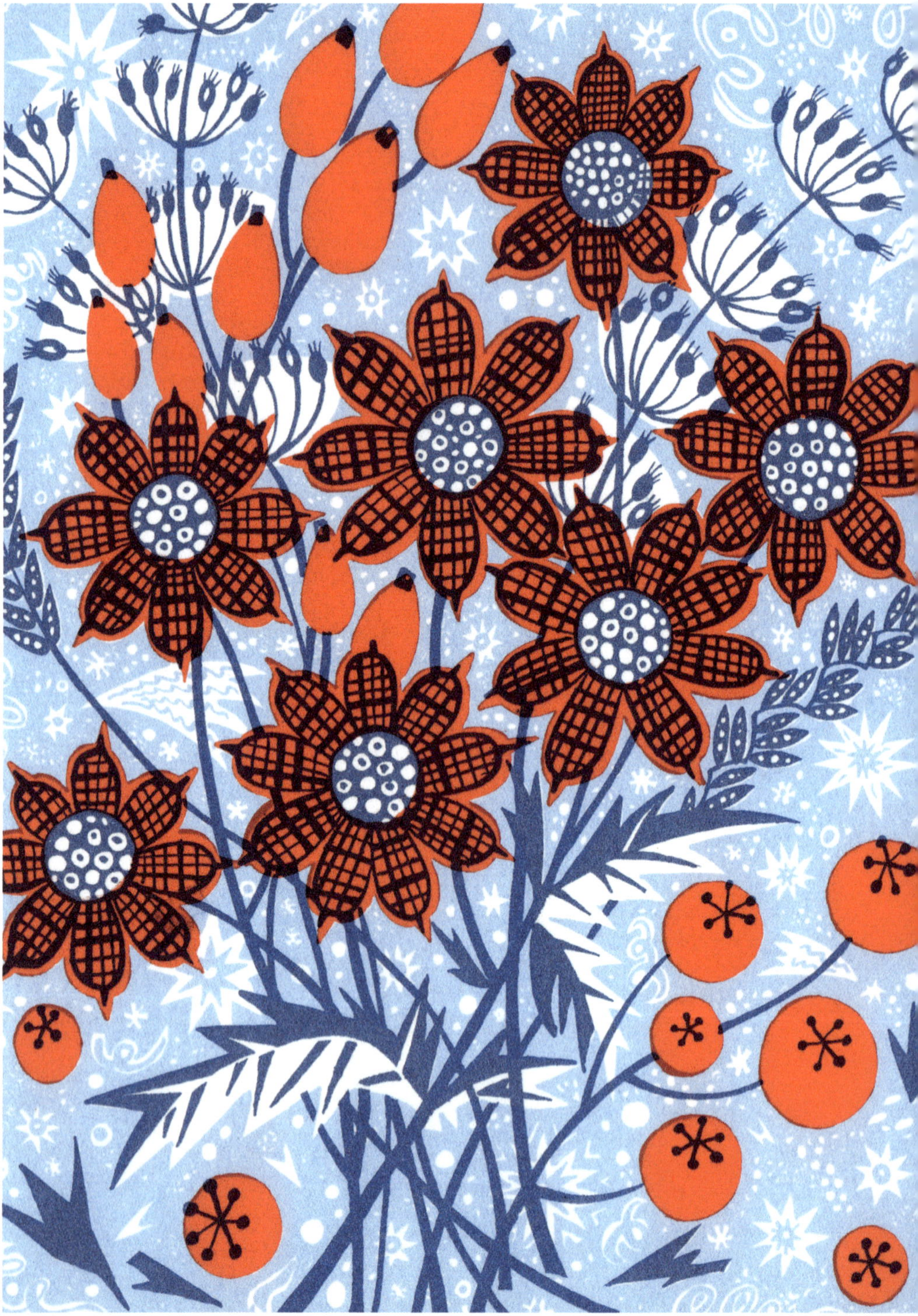

January

Even in the depths of a cold dark winter, gardens have the power to lifts our spirits with their precious gifts. Evergreens glisten under veils of ice, while stands of scarlet and gold dogwood blaze a trail under moody skies. Winter flowers also abound, with witch hazel and sweet box braving the harsh conditions to produce their perfumed blooms, and dainty snowdrops peeping above the bare earth.

KEY EVENTS
New Year's Day, 1 January
Twelfth Night, 5–6 January
St Hilary's Day, 13 January (*said to be the coldest day of the year*)
Burns Night, 25 January
Lunar New Year, 29 January (*Year of the Snake*)
Big Garden Birdwatch, 25–26 January

What to do in January

Short days, often accompanied by heavy rain or snow and freezing temperatures, mean there are not many windows of opportunity to venture out into the garden. However, January can also bring periods of dry weather when you can plant bare-root shrubs, trees, roses and perennials, which are all available now. When wintry conditions keep you indoors, enjoy a glimpse of things to come by ordering plants and bulbs for the seasons ahead, and use this time to clean your tools, shed and greenhouse.

In the garden

PLANT BARE-ROOT PERENNIALS, which are widely available now. Representing great value for money, they will arrive in segments, each with some buds and roots. Plant them as soon as possible in beds, if the soil is not frozen or waterlogged, or in pots, and they will soon put on growth as temperatures rise. Perennials to try include achilleas, aquilegias, astilbes, hemerocallis, sedums, stachys and veronica. ❶

POLLARDED TREES and shrubs create a graphic effect in the garden, with their clear trunks topped with vase-shaped canopies. This pruning technique also helps to keep fast-growing species such as ash (*Fraxinus*), common lime (*Tilia × europaea*) and elder (*Sambucus*) in check. Begin pollarding in winter when the tree is young and has grown to a desired height. Remove the lower branches, to leave a clear stem of about 1m (3ft), and all the branches above to create a fist-shaped stump on top. In following years, when there has been sufficient regrowth, repeat this cutting method, removing new shoots to keep the trunk clear and taking back all the branches above it to their point of origin. ❷

REMOVE SUCKERS from trees and shrubs. These shoots arise from the roots of the parent plant and can develop into new plants and, in extreme cases, form thickets. Severing suckers at ground level can lead to buds at the base regrowing, so, instead, dig down and pull the suckers from the parent's roots. Avoid using weedkiller, which will polish off the suckers but may also harm the parent plant.

BRUSH SNOW OFF hedges and evergreens, which may break under the weight, and from bird-proof netting in the vegetable garden. ❸

PLANT EARLY-FLOWERING NECTAR PLANTS to sustain bees and other pollinators that will soon be on the wing during mild spells in late winter. Early flowering plants, such as *Viburnum tinus*, *Mahonia* × *media*, deciduous flowering currants (*Ribes*) and Japanese quince (*Chaenomeles*) can be planted during dry periods this month. Willows, with their pollen-rich catkins, are especially valuable, too, with *Salix hastata* 'Wehrhahnii' and male plants of the native *S. lanata* offering great ornamental value into the bargain.

RENOVATE CLIMBING AND RAMBLING ROSES that have become overgrown. They are very robust and will sprout afresh in spring and summer. Start by removing all crossing, dead and weak shoots, then cut out the old gnarled stems. You can leave six or seven sturdy young shoots, or be brave and cut the lot down to 45–60cm (18–24in) – the new growth will soon fill the gaps. ❹

In the fruit & veg patch

SOW HARDY VEGETABLES INDOORS for early crops. With spring almost in sight, start sowing lettuce and broad beans in seed trays or modules and keep them in a heated greenhouse or on a warm windowsill. The seedlings can then be planted outside in March. Outdoor sowing begins in spring, but you can get a head start by preparing the ground now, either digging it over to create loose friable soil or laying organic mulches (see p.29) over the surface to help reduce weed growth.

PLANT GARLIC BULBS in January, selecting a sunny area with free-draining soil, and setting them 15cm (6in) apart, with the tips 2.5cm (1in) below the surface.

CHIT EARLY SEED POTATOES by placing them in egg boxes or seed trays indoors, in an area with moderate light, and with the eyes (sunken areas) facing upwards. They will soon sprout, ready to be planted outside in March. ❺

Indoors

ENSURE LIGHT LEVELS in your home are sufficient for sun-loving houseplants such as cacti and succulents. These plants can cope with quite low temperatures, as long as their compost is kept dry, but may suffer in the low-light conditions in January. Move to a heated conservatory or bright windowsill if they are looking misshapen or lacklustre.

DO NOT FEED your houseplants in winter. They will be either dormant or growing very slowly now and fertilizing them now will not benefit them. Most houseplants also need less water in winter for the same reason.

SWISS CHEESEPLANTS (*MONSTERA*) are easy to grow indoors and enjoy a warm room over winter. Clean their leaves of dust to maximize their ability to photosynthesize when light levels are low in January, and water them just enough to prevent wilting.

MONEY-SAVING IDEA
Sow microgreens in old food trays
Microgreens are the young shoots of herbs, salad crops and brassicas such as radishes, which offer a constant supply of nutrient-packed fresh greens all year round. Minimize the cost by bulk buying microgreens seed or culinary seeds offered at Asian supermarkets. Puncture some drainage holes in the base of empty plastic or foil food trays and fill with seed compost, then water lightly to moisten it. Sow the seed closely on top and cover to the depth recommended on the pack. Place under a grow light, in a warm conservatory or on a sunny windowsill. Keep the compost moist and harvest your microgreens 6–8 weeks later, when they're about 5cm (2in) tall.

Plants of the month

1. Myrtle (*Myrtus communis* 'Variegata')
2. Berried skimmia (*Skimmia japonica* 'Tansley Gem' pictured)
3. Silk tassel bush (*Garrya elliptica*)
4. Sweet box (*Sarcococca confusa*)
5. *Viburnum × bodnantense* (*V. × bodnantense* 'Charles Lamont' pictured)
6. *Erica × darleyensis* (*E. × darleyensis* 'Katia' pictured)
7. *Cyclamen coum*
8. Winter-flowering cherry (*Prunus × subhirtella* 'Autumnalis')
9. Winter-flowering honeysuckle (*Lonicera fragrantissima*)
10. *Helleborus × hybridus* (yellow-flowered hybrid pictured)
11. Hepaticas (*Hepatica acutiloba × nobilis* 'Cremar' pictured)

Project: Make an airplant mobile

Tiny airplants (*Tillandsia*) bring your home to life with their sparkling leaves in shades of green and silver, and bright flowers that appear as if by magic from the foliage bundles. This beautiful chandelier is a great way to display airplants, which survive with no soil or compost – you simply pop them in a tray of tepid rainwater or deionized water (offered in supermarkets and DIY stores for use in steam irons) once a week for 30 minutes, then leave to drain, or mist them every few days. Airplants thrive in temperatures of 15–24°C (59–75°F) and enjoy high humidity levels and filtered sun, so a spot in a kitchen or bathroom would be a good choice of location.

YOU WILL NEED
Flat wire wreath frame
Thin florist wire (stainless steel is best)
Selection of airplants (*Tillandsia species*)
Raffia

1 Lay out your selection of airplants – seven or eight plants will work well. Then carefully wrap the florist wire around the end of each one so that it will be secure when you hang it up. Leave 15–45cm (6–18in) of wire attached to the plant to fix it to the wreath frame. The chandelier looks best when the plants are at different levels, so make the wires various lengths.

2 Wrap the ends of the wires evenly around the wreath frame. Then fix another piece of florist wire or string to the frame so that you can hang it up.

3 Finally, cover the frame with some raffia, and more plants – Spanish moss (*Tillandsia usneoides*) is particularly effective – secured with florist wire.

14 / JANUARY

Looking up

Sunrise and sunset

Many plants are leafless or growing very slowly in January, when the low angle of the sun and short days offer little light for photosynthesis.

	LONDON		EDINBURGH	
DAY	Sunrise	Sunset	Sunrise	Sunset
Wed, Jan 1	8:03:54 am	4:04:28 pm	8:40:54 am	3:52:02 pm
Thu, Jan 2	8:03:45 am	4:05:32 pm	8:40:36 am	3:53:16 pm
Fri, Jan 3	8:03:33 am	4:06:39 pm	8:40:14 am	3:54:34 pm
Sat, Jan 4	8:03:18 am	4:07:49 pm	8:39:47 am	3:55:55 pm
Sun, Jan 5	8:02:59 am	4:09:01 pm	8:39:17 am	3:57:19 pm
Mon, Jan 6	8:02:38 am	4:10:16 pm	8:38:42 am	3:58:46 pm
Tue, Jan 7	8:02:12 am	4:11:33 pm	8:38:04 am	4:00:16 pm
Wed, Jan 8	8:01:44 am	4:12:52 pm	8:37:22 am	4:01:48 pm
Thu, Jan 9	8:01:12 am	4:14:13 pm	8:36:36 am	4:03:24 pm
Fri, Jan 10	8:00:38 am	4:15:36 pm	8:35:47 am	4:05:02 pm
Sat, Jan 11	8:00:00 am	4:17:02 pm	8:34:54 am	4:06:42 pm
Sun, Jan 12	7:59:19 am	4:18:29 pm	8:33:57 am	4:08:25 pm
Mon, Jan 13	7:58:35 am	4:19:57 pm	8:32:57 am	4:10:10 pm
Tue, Jan 14	7:57:48 am	4:21:28 pm	8:31:53 am	4:11:58 pm
Wed, Jan 15	7:56:59 am	4:23:00 pm	8:30:46 am	4:13:47 pm
Thu, Jan 16	7:56:06 am	4:24:34 pm	8:29:36 am	4:15:38 pm
Fri, Jan 17	7:55:10 am	4:26:09 pm	8:28:22 am	4:17:31 pm
Sat, Jan 18	7:54:12 am	4:27:45 pm	8:27:05 am	4:19:26 pm
Sun, Jan 19	7:53:11 am	4:29:23 pm	8:25:46 am	4:21:23 pm
Mon, Jan 20	7:52:07 am	4:31:02 pm	8:24:23 am	4:23:21 pm
Tue, Jan 21	7:51:01 am	4:32:42 pm	8:22:57 am	4:25:20 pm
Wed, Jan 22	7:49:52 am	4:34:23 pm	8:21:29 am	4:27:21 pm
Thu, Jan 23	7:48:41 am	4:36:05 pm	8:19:58 am	4:29:23 pm
Fri, Jan 24	7:47:27 am	4:37:48 pm	8:18:24 am	4:31:26 pm
Sat, Jan 25	7:46:10 am	4:39:32 pm	8:16:47 am	4:33:30 pm
Sun, Jan 26	7:44:52 am	4:41:17 pm	8:15:08 am	4:35:35 pm
Mon, Jan 27	7:43:31 am	4:43:02 pm	8:13:26 am	4:37:41 pm
Tue, Jan 28	7:42:07 am	4:44:48 pm	8:11:42 am	4:39:47 pm
Wed, Jan 29	7:40:42 am	4:46:35 pm	8:09:56 am	4:41:55 pm
Thu, Jan 30	7:39:14 am	4:48:22 pm	8:08:07 am	4:44:03 pm
Fri, Jan 31	7:37:45 am	4:50:09 pm	8:06:17 am	4:46:11 pm

Moonrise and moonset

Moon phases

◗ **THIRD QUARTER** 21 January
● **NEW MOON** 29 January

◐ **FIRST QUARTER** 6 January
○ **FULL MOON** 13 January

DAY	LONDON Moonrise	LONDON Moonset	LONDON Moonrise	EDINBURGH Moonrise	EDINBURGH Moonset	EDINBURGH Moonrise
Jan 1	09:47	17:29		10:30	17:13	
Jan 2	10:11	18:55		10:45	18:48	
Jan 3	10:28	20:22		10:56	20:22	
Jan 4	10:42	21:46		11:03	21:54	
Jan 5	10:55	23:10		11:09	23:24	
Jan 6	11:07			11:15		
Jan 7		00:35	11:20		00:56	11:22
Jan 8		02:01	11:35		02:30	11:30
Jan 9		03:30	11:56		04:07	11:43
Jan 10		04:59	12:25		05:45	12:04
Jan 11		06:22	13:07		07:15	12:39
Jan 12		07:30	14:07		08:26	13:37
Jan 13		08:20	15:21		09:11	14:57
Jan 14		08:54	16:43		09:36	16:27
Jan 15		09:17	18:05		09:51	17:57
Jan 16		09:34	19:23		10:01	19:23
Jan 17		09:46	20:38		10:08	20:44
Jan 18		09:57	21:50		10:13	22:01
Jan 19		10:06	23:00		10:17	23:17
Jan 20		10:16			10:22	
Jan 21	00:10	10:27		00:33	10:27	
Jan 22	01:22	10:39		01:52	10:33	
Jan 23	02:36	10:56		03:12	10:43	
Jan 24	03:51	11:19		04:36	10:58	
Jan 25	05:05	11:52		05:57	11:24	
Jan 26	06:12	12:39		07:08	12:08	
Jan 27	07:06	13:45		08:00	13:16	
Jan 28	07:45	15:04		08:32	14:44	
Jan 29	08:13	16:32		08:51	16:20	
Jan 30	08:33	18:01		09:03	17:58	
Jan 31	08:49	19:29		09:12	19:33	

Average rainfall

In January, the average rainfall in the UK is 166mm (6½in), but evidence suggests that climate change is resulting in wetter winters and heavier downpours.

LOCATION	DAYS	MM	INCHES
Aberdeen	12	68	2.7
Aberystwyth	16	102	4
Belfast	14	88	3.5
Birmingham	13	72	2.8
Bournemouth	13	96	3.8
Bristol	13	82	3.2
Cambridge	10	48	1.8
Canterbury	12	64	2.5
Cardiff	16	127	5.0
Edinburgh	12	65	2.5
Exeter	13	97	3.8
Glasgow	17	147	5.8
Gloucester	13	78	3.0
Inverness	16	118	4.6
Ipswich	11	48	1.8
Leeds	16	109	4.3
Liverpool	13	69	2.7
London	12	70	2.75
Manchester	17	119	4.7
Newcastle upon Tyne	10	45	1.8
Norwich	11	55	2.2
Nottingham	12	59	2.3
Oxford	12	57	2.25
Sheffield	13	75	3.0
Truro	16	109	4.3

Plant an eco-friendly hedge

Hedges make beautiful natural garden boundaries and internal subdivisions that are both wildlife friendly and environmentally sustainable. More durable than fences, they also provide shelter from wind, absorb rainwater and help to prevent flooding, reduce noise and, according to recent RHS research, help to mop up pollution particles. In addition, hedges play an important role in mitigating the effects of climate change and are ideal in small gardens where a tree is not practical or will cast too much shade.

The benefits to wildlife are huge, too. Hedges offer cover and nesting places for birds, and can also provide food, while supporting a wide range of insects, particularly if you use native hedging trees such as hazel or beech. In addition, they create 'wildlife corridors' along which animals such as hedgehogs can travel, shielded from predators.

In tight places, natives, including yew (*Taxus baccata*), hawthorn (*Crataegus monogyna*) and hornbeam (*Carpinus betulus*), can be cut to form narrow hedges 60cm (24in) wide. Box (*Buxus*) also makes a neat hedge, but with box blight and box tree caterpillars now widespread it is not recommended, so opt instead for compact evergreen euonymus or holly.

POLLUTION BUSTERS
RHS research has shown that *Cotoneaster franchetii* is an exceptional plant for reducing pollutants. Its hairy leaves catch airborne particles, and trials showed that in seven days 1m (3ft) of well-managed *C. franchetii* hedge absorbed pollutants equivalent to those emitted during an 800km (500-mile) car journey, making it especially suitable for boundaries near busy roads.

Other hedge plants that capture lower volumes of pollutants include yew, hawthorn and hornbeam – all are good choices for gardens that are adjacent to less heavily used roads.

For the best results, a pollution-busting hedge should be 1.5m (5ft) wide, which is also the optimum size for wildlife benefits. A slimmer hedge in a smaller garden will still offer some protection.

BEST CHOICES FOR WILDLIFE
Wildlife hedges can be composed of a mix of native plants such as dog rose, dogwood, hawthorn, holly, field maple, hazel and spindle bush. Cut your hedge every two or three years, to allow them to grow large enough to produce berries. Similarly, berried non-native plants such as berberis and pyracantha need a light touch when pruning if they are to bear their fruits, loved by birds.

PLANTING A HEDGE

Hedges are easy to create, and plants are not too expensive when bought in winter as young 40cm (16in) bare-root whips (see right below). Prepare the soil by removing competing plants such as couch grass and nettles. Then plant the whips every 40cm (16in), where their close proximity will curb the trees' growth and they will form a dense but manageable hedge. A single row is usually sufficient, but double staggered rows give quicker results. Some weeding and, in dry periods, watering during the first year after planting, will help the plants to establish. You can expect your whips to make a reasonably tall hedge in five to seven years. Larger plants and ready-made hedges are also available but they are more expensive.

SPEED WARNING
Fast-growing plants including cherry laurel (*Prunus laurocerasus*), shrubby honeysuckle (*Lonicera ligustrina* var. *yunnanensis*) and privet (*Ligustrum ovalifolium*) will soon create a leafy hedge, but bear in mind that these will need more frequent cutting. Portugal laurel (*Prunus lusitanica*) is reasonably speedy while requiring less trimming. Conifers such as Leyland cypress (*Cupressus* x *leylandii*) and *Thuja plicata* make lovely hedges but can be difficult to renovate, as regrowth from old wood is unreliable and they can suffer from bare patches.

Top Hawthorn (*Crataegus*) is one of the best hedging plants for capturing pollution particles.
Bottom Planting young bare-root trees, known as 'whips', is the most affordable option.

Edible garden

While January is a quiet month in the edible garden, there are still crops to be sown indoors and outside, as well as stocks of winter vegetables to harvest, most of which can be left in the ground until needed and added to warming dishes such as stews.

Vegetables

SOW INDOORS Broad beans ❶; summer cabbages; lettuces; microgreens (see p.12); peas; radishes; spinach.

PLANT OUTDOORS Asparagus crowns; garlic sets; Jerusalem artichokes; shallots.

HARVEST Brussels sprouts; carrots; celeriac; chard; kale; leeks; lettuce and radishes grown under a cloche or in a cool greenhouse; parsnips; sprouting broccoli; swedes; turnips; winter cabbages and savoys.

Fruit

PLANT OUTDOORS Bare-root hardy fruit trees such as apples, apricots, cherries, nectarines, peaches, pears, plums, quinces.

HARVEST Citrus fruits such as lemons and oranges grown undercover, when ripe, as indicated by the colour of the skin.

HERB OF THE MONTH: PARSLEY
One of the UK's most popular herbs, parsley (*Petroselinum crispum*), is a biennial, which means it grows leaves in the first year after germination and flowers and sets seed in the second. Choose curly- or flat-leaved varieties, and sow seed in pots in late spring or buy young plants in spring or summer. These hardy plants can be kept outside all winter, but crop the leaves lightly during this time. Bring potted plants indoors for winter, where they will continue to provide a small but regular crop on a windowsill. However, the plants will be growing more slowly at this time of year, so ensure you have a line of pots and only harvest a few leaves at a time.

Challenges this month

The cold weather either kills many unwanted creatures or they find quiet areas to hibernate, but houseplants are still vulnerable and should be checked regularly, while outside roe deer and rabbits will stray into gardens to browse on plants.

HOUSEPLANT FLIES, such as sciarid flies or fungus gnats, flying around your house can be alarming, but they do little actual damage to plants. However, the adult flies may also signal the presence of their larvae in damp potting compost, which can eat the roots of seedlings and cuttings, although they rarely affect healthy mature houseplants. Wet roots, especially in winter, can also cause plants to rot, so ensure the compost is not waterlogged and leave it to dry out if it's too damp. Yellow sticky traps can reduce the numbers of adult flies, while biological controls such as nematodes for houseplants and predatory mites in conservatories can also be applied, following the instructions carefully.

SCALE INSECTS feed on houseplants at this time of year and are more of a threat than flies. There are many different species but all suck the sap from plants, causing distorted or poor growth. They look like little, shell-like bumps on stems and the undersides of leaves, and some deposit their eggs under a covering of white waxy fibres. Those that feed on houseplants also excrete sticky honeydew on which black sooty moulds may grow. Inspect your plants regularly, and wipe off any scales you see with a damp cloth.

More widespread populations can be treated with the nematode *Steinernema feltiae*, which is a biological control, or with organic sprays such as natural pyrethrum (e.g. Bug Clear Ultra 2, Neudorff BugFree Bug and Larvae Killer) or plant oils (e.g. Vitax Plant Guard Pest & Disease Control, and Bug Clear Fruit and Veg).

NATIVE ROE DEER are found in rural and suburban gardens near woodland, and eat a wide range of plants, including raspberries, runner beans and roses, to name a few. About the size of a goat, they tend to hide by day, coming out around dusk and dawn. You will need 2m (6ft) fences to keep them out, but. if the cost is too high, choose plants these deer rarely devour, such as daphnes, hellebores, foxgloves, *Skimmia, Choisya*, and *Verbascum*.

Focus on wildlife

Little owl

The UK's smallest owl, this little bird of prey is not much bigger than a song thrush and may be seen in gardens throughout England, Wales and southern Scotland, close to farmland, parks and orchards. While the little owl is not a native, having been introduced to Britain from Continental Europe in the 1870s, it has filled what appears to be an ecological niche with no detrimental effects on wild species. However, populations here and in Europe are on the decline due to habitat loss.

This compact hunter has a brown upper body with white markings and paler underparts with broad brown streaks – both sexes are similar in appearance. Pale eyebrows and dark edges make its piercing, round, yellow eyes stand out against the mottled plumage. The birds' diet consists mainly of small mammals and large invertebrates such as earthworms and beetles, although they also eat small birds, and hunt for prey from a perch on a building or tree.

You may hear their high-pitched, squawking call in autumn and spring, when young birds are searching for breeding territories where, once established, mating pairs will remain throughout the year. Little owls make their nests in April in small cavities in hedgerow trees or old buildings, which the male will guard while the female incubates her clutch of three or four eggs. Once hatched, the chicks fledge after 30–35 days. Little owls have just one clutch of eggs per year.

Spotlight on: Witch hazel (Hamamelis)

Flowering in the depths of winter when little else is in bloom, witch hazel (*Hamamelis*) is prized for its spidery blooms and spicy fragrance, which fills the frosty air. The flowers come in shades of yellow, orange and red, and adorn the bare stems of this large deciduous shrub from December to March. Broad oval green leaves unfurl as the blooms fade, and turn fiery shades of yellow, orange and red in autumn before falling. Grow witch hazel in well-drained, neutral to acid soil in a sunny or lightly shaded, sheltered spot, ideally where the low winter sun catches the flowers. While hardy in most parts of the country, witch hazel may suffer in areas that experience temperatures below −15°C (5°F) in winter.

HAMAMELIS × INTERMEDIA 'JELENA'
This vase-shaped shrub produces clusters of lightly scented, coppery orange flowers on bare stems from January to February, which are ideal for cutting and bringing indoors.
H x S: 4 x 4m (13 x 13ft)

HAMAMELIS × INTERMEDIA 'PALLIDA'
A popular, award-winning variety, 'Pallida' produces large, highly fragrant, sulphur-yellow flowers over a long period from December to March.
H x S: 3 x 3m (10 x 10ft)

HAMAMELIS × INTERMEDIA 'DIANE'
The flowers of this cultivar are a deep red and produce a rich perfume in January and February. It is a great choice for use in floral displays for the home.
H x S: 4 x 4m (13 x 13ft)

HAMAMELIS × INTERMEDIA 'ARNOLD PROMISE'
Loved for its bright yellow flowers that twinkle in the low winter sun, this cultivar also has a rich spicy perfume.
H x S: 3 x 3m (10 x 10ft)

HAMAMELIS × INTERMEDIA 'VESNA'
A little harder to come by, but well worth seeking out, this very fragrant form has rich golden-orange flowers from January to March.
H x S: 3 x 3m (10 x 10m)

Seasonal planting ideas

WINTER SCENT COMBO

WHY IT WORKS
A combination of frosted evergreen foliage and delicious winter scent, this group includes a bright golden-yellow-flowered witch hazel (*Hamamelis*) and the bare fleshy stems of the paperbush (*Edgeworthia*), which adds its own interest, with unusual buds opening to round clusters of small yellow flowers in late winter and early spring. Providing colour, fragrance and structure just when it is most needed, these plants will brighten up the winter months.

WHAT'S GROWING HERE?
Hamamelis × intermedia 'Harry' is a large, upright, deciduous shrub, growing to 4m (13ft), with broad oval leaves that turn orange-red in autumn and large, pale yellow-orange, perfumed flowers in winter and early spring.

Edgeworthia chrysantha 'Grandiflora' is a bushy deciduous shrub, also about 4m (13ft) in height, with rounded flowerheads composed of small, lightly fragrant, yellow flowers that open from hairy buds in late winter and early spring, before the narrowly oval leaves appear.

Mahonia nitens 'Cabaret' is a compact, upright, evergreen shrub, growing to about 1.2m (4ft), with glossy, spiny, dark green foliage. Orange-red buds open to yellow flowers from late summer to autumn, followed by blue-grey berries.

Pinus mugo is a compact, bushy, evergreen conifer that reaches about the same height as the *Hamamelis*. It has dark green needles and small brown cones in autumn and winter.

WHEN TO PLANT
Plant this group in autumn, so the shrubs have time to settle in well before winter. Alternatively, do this in spring and keep the plants well-watered through the first summer. Grow in a sheltered spot in full sun or part shade, and in moist but well-drained soil.

WHERE TO SEE IT
Visit the Winter Walk at RHS Garden Wisley during the cold months to see this stunning combination at its best.

Horticultural heroes

Lancelot 'Capability' Brown · 1716–1783

Lancelot 'Capability' Brown was the most influential landscape architect of his time, and many of the parks he created can still be seen today. A pioneer of the English landscape garden style, Brown's designs typically included rolling hills, grasslands, lakes and woods that represented an idealized pastoral view of the countryside. At the time, this naturalistic approach was considered revolutionary, but by the mid-eighteenth century it was *de rigueur*, as Brown's influence spread far and wide, and rich nobles and even the King rushed to convert their formal patterned gardens into a 'Capability' landscape.

Brown was nicknamed 'Capability' because of the technique he used to sell his designs, persuading clients that their properties had great 'capabilities'. His landscapes include those at Stowe in Buckinghamshire, Croome in Worcestershire and Blenheim Palace in Oxfordshire. At Croome, he even moved an entire village to create uninterrupted views from the remodelled Palladian-style house.

The son of a land agent and a chambermaid, Brown was born in Kirkharle in Northumberland and worked until the age of 16 as an apprentice gardener on the estate where his father was employed. His rise to fame began after he moved to Stowe in 1739 to work for Lord Cobham, where he became head gardener in 1741. His work there included the famous Grecian valley, an Arcadian vision of Ancient Greece, which he installed under the supervision of William Kent, one of the founders of the English landscape garden style.

In 1764, aged 48, Brown was appointed Chief Gardener at Hampton Court Palace by King George III, and, in 1770, he bought his own estate at Fenstanton in Cambridgeshire, where he is buried at the local parish church.

While detractors criticized Brown's style during and after his lifetime, his legacy lives on, a testament to his skill and the longevity of his landscapes, many of which look as spectacular today as they did more than 300 years ago.

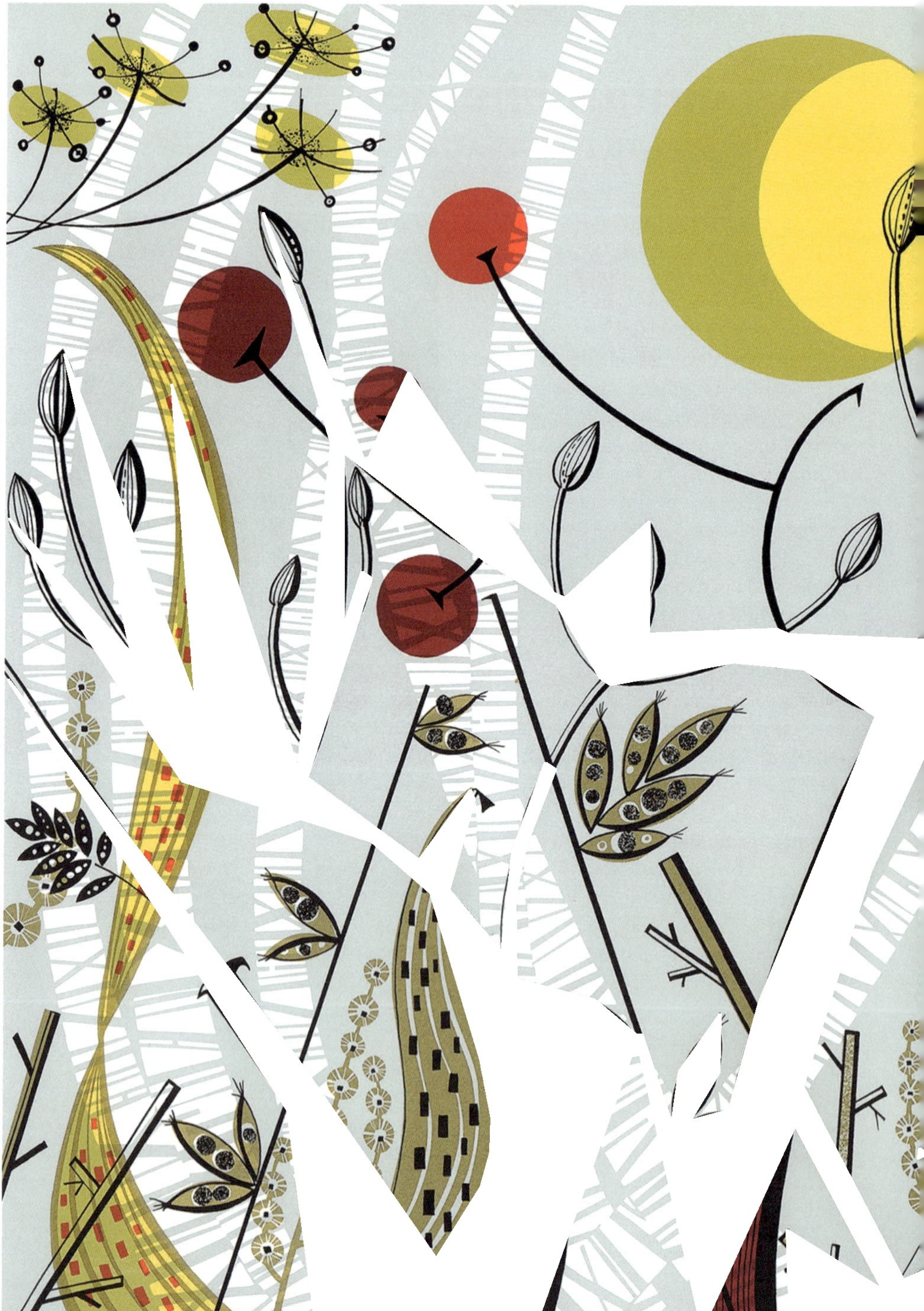

February

As winter draws to a close, the garden begins to stir with early signs of life. Daffodils, hardy cyclamen and crocuses brave the cold, their colourful blooms dancing in the chill air. The heart quickens as buds on trees and shrubs begin to swell, and frogs return to the water to play their amorous games, marking the time when we, too, are looking for romance and anticipating the warmer days to come.

KEY EVENTS
Candlemas Day, 2 February
St Valentine's Day, 14 February
Maha Shivaratri, 26 February
Start of Ramadan, 28 February

What to do in February

With spring just a few weeks away, February is a good time to plant hardy trees, shrubs and perennials, when the weather and soil conditions allow. These plants will soon burst into growth, fuelled by the increased light levels and plentiful soil moisture. It's also your last chance to save money by purchasing cheaper bare-root woody plants, which are available only until the end of the month. Also prune late-flowering clematis that bloom in or after July, cutting all stems to 25cm (10in) from the ground.

In the garden

CUT BACK ORNAMENTAL GRASSES, such as *Miscanthus, Panicum, Hakonechloa* and *Molinia* at the end of February, before they start to regrow. The dead stems of these deciduous grasses are left overwinter to provide structure in the garden and habitats for wildlife. Cutting the old growth down to the ground now allows space for new stems to come through. The old growth on evergreen grasses, such as *Stipa* and *Festuca*, is best combed out now with gloved fingers or a rake. ❶

PLANT LILIES IN POTS in February to provide summer colour and fragrance on a patio or in a border. Asiatic hybrids are the easiest for beginners and should be planted in containers of peat-free multipurpose compost at a depth of twice the height of the bulbs, with the pointed tip facing upwards. Keep the compost moist but never allow it to become wet, and feed the plants when they emerge every fortnight with an organic fertilizer. ❷

SOW HARDY ANNUALS in pots undercover now for earlier flowers. Sow the seed in pots, trays or even guttering, and protect them in an unheated greenhouse or on a window ledge in a cool room indoors. *Orlaya grandiflora, Calendula, Cerinthe major* and scabious are good choices. Pot on the seedlings and plant out in spring when soil temperatures rise. ❸

MULCH BEDS instead of digging, to convert uncultivated ground into a bed or border. Dig out competing plants, then smother grass, other vegetation and bare soil with a layer of cardboard, topped off with 15cm (6in) or more of garden compost, composted manure or soil improver. Sow or plant into this top layer. Over time, the cardboard will rot and the compost will be brought down into the ground by soil organisms to produce a rich, deep root zone.

PLANT SNOWDROPS IN THE GREEN, which will be available now from online suppliers. These winter flowers establish well from bulbs with roots and leaves. Plant them in beds or pots, at the same depth as they were in the ground, where they are to bloom the following year. ❹

FEED ROSES with a general organic-based fertilizer, rich in potassium, to boost growth and flowering, or use one specially formulated for these plants, following the application rates recommended on the packaging.

In the fruit & veg patch

FEED FRUIT TREES AND BUSHES lightly now, using a potassium-rich fertilizer to promote flowering and fruit formation. One feed in February, following the manufacturer's instructions, is usually all that's needed. After fertilizing, add a 5–8cm (2–3in) mulch of garden compost or well-rotted manure.

SOW TENDER VEG such as peppers, aubergines, chillies and tomatoes indoors on a sunny windowsill or in a heated greenhouse. These slow-growing plants benefit from an early start and should produce strong healthy plants to plant in an unheated greenhouse in April or outside after the frosts in May.

Alternatively, buy plug plants or larger plants later in spring.

CUT BACK AUTUMN RASPBERRIES, which crop on new canes that arise after the old ones have been pruned to ground level in February. Summer raspberries fruit on canes that grew in the previous year, and the old fruiting canes are cut in autumn. ❺

POT UP MINT ROOT CUTTINGS. Dig some thick root strands about 6cm (2½in) long, making a horizontal cut at the upper end and an angled cut at the lower end. Pot them up, with the angled end at the bottom, in multipurpose peat-free compost in a tub 45–60cm (18–24in) wide. The original clump will soon recover and both will offer a crop from spring.

Indoors

PRUNE TENDER PERENNIALS AND SHRUBS, such as fuchsias, salvias and pelargoniums. Remove old, dead and diseased stems, then apply an all-purpose organic-based liquid fertilizer to boost growth. Plant outside after frosts.

DO NOT OVERWATER HOUSEPLANTS, which are either dormant or growing very slowly. Water only when the compost feels dry, to prevent disease.

MONEY-SAVING IDEA
Sow your own bedding plants
Buying bedding plants can be pricey, especially if you have lots of pots to fill. An easy and economic option is to sow seeds of bedding dahlias, petunias, cosmos and marigolds, starting them off on a windowsill indoors. Fill a seed tray, or old food tray with drainage holes in the base, with seed compost. Water lightly to moisten it and sow the seeds thinly to the depth recommended on the packet. Cover with a clear lid or recycled clear plastic bag and place on a warm windowsill until the seeds germinate. Remove the lid or plastic and keep the compost moist. When the seedlings have a few leaves, transplant them to individual pots or cell trays to grow on. Plant out after the frosts.

Plants of the month

1. Japanese pink pussy willow (*Salix gracilistyla* 'Mount Aso')
2. Daphne (*Daphne bholua* 'Jacqueline Postill' pictured)
3. Nodding snowflake (*Leucojum aestivum*)
4. Winter aconite (*Eranthis hyemalis*)
5. Forsythia (*Forsythia × intermedia* pictured)
6. Paperbush (*Edgeworthia chrysantha*)
7. Corkscrew hazel (*Corylus avellana* 'Contorta')
8. Early-flowering clematis (*Clematis cirrhosa* var. purpurascens 'Freckles' pictured)
9. Daffodils (*Narcissus*)
10. Crocuses (*Crocus*)
11. *Mahonia × media* 'Winter Sun'

Project: Make an insulation box

Protecting tender plants in a greenhouse can be expensive if you use a fuel-hungry heater to warm the whole structure, but this simple box offers a cost-effective alternative. Providing just enough insulation to keep out all but the worst frosts, it also allows some light to penetrate to the plants inside. Open up the plastic on sunny days to prevent overheating and condensation, which may cause diseases. Pelargonium cuttings, succulents, winter salads, cannas and dahlias will all benefit from this protection, as will seedlings at night (the plastic cuts out too much light for them during the day).

YOU WILL NEED
12–14 bamboo canes
String
Scissors
Recycled bubble plastic
Duct tape

1 Measure eight canes for the uprights and the sides and four longer canes for the front and back to create a rectangular box. Tie the canes together with string in each corner, as shown. For additional strength, fix two more canes diagonally.

2 Cut recycled bubble plastic to size, so you can fit it around the cane box without too much bagginess. Tape into place with duct tape, leaving one side loose for access.

3 Place the box inside the greenhouse, either on the floor if it is going to house heavy pots, or on staging for small plants that may tempt mice or slugs. Help maintain the temperature inside the box on particularly cold nights by covering with an old curtain or towels for additional insulation.

Looking up

Sunrise and sunset

Light levels increase dramatically in February, fuelling rapid plant growth by the end of the month as we approach spring and the beginning of the growing year.

	LONDON		EDINBURGH	
DAY	Sunrise	Sunset	Sunrise	Sunset
Sat, Feb 1	7:36:13 am	4:51:57 pm	8:04:24 am	4:48:20 pm
Sun, Feb 2	7:34:39 am	4:53:45 pm	8:02:29 am	4:50:30 pm
Mon, Feb 3	7:33:04 am	4:55:34 pm	8:00:32 am	4:52:40 pm
Tue, Feb 4	7:31:26 am	4:57:23 pm	7:58:33 am	4:54:50 pm
Wed, Feb 5	7:29:47 am	4:59:12 pm	7:56:32 am	4:57:01 pm
Thu, Feb 6	7:28:06 am	5:01:01 pm	7:54:29 am	4:59:11 pm
Fri, Feb 7	7:26:23 am	5:02:50 pm	7:52:25 am	5:01:22 pm
Sat, Feb 8	7:24:38 am	5:04:39 pm	7:50:19 am	5:03:33 pm
Sun, Feb 9	7:22:52 am	5:06:29 pm	7:48:11 am	5:05:44 pm
Mon, Feb 10	7:21:05 am	5:08:18 pm	7:46:02 am	5:07:55 pm
Tue, Feb 11	7:19:15 am	5:10:08 pm	7:43:51 am	5:10:06 pm
Wed, Feb 12	7:17:25 am	5:11:57 pm	7:41:38 am	5:12:17 pm
Thu, Feb 13	7:15:33 am	5:13:46 pm	7:39:25 am	5:14:28 pm
Fri, Feb 14	7:13:39 am	5:15:35 pm	7:37:09 am	5:16:39 pm
Sat, Feb 15	7:11:44 am	5:17:24 pm	7:34:53 am	5:18:50 pm
Sun, Feb 16	7:09:48 am	5:19:13 pm	7:32:35 am	5:21:00 pm
Mon, Feb 17	7:07:51 am	5:21:02 pm	7:30:16 am	5:23:10 pm
Tue, Feb 18	7:05:53 am	5:22:50 pm	7:27:56 am	5:25:21 pm
Wed, Feb 19	7:03:53 am	5:24:39 pm	7:25:35 am	5:27:31 pm
Thu, Feb 20	7:01:52 am	5:26:27 pm	7:23:13 am	5:29:40 pm
Fri, Feb 21	6:59:50 am	5:28:15 pm	7:20:49 am	5:31:50 pm
Sat, Feb 22	6:57:47 am	5:30:02 pm	7:18:25 am	5:33:59 pm
Sun, Feb 23	6:55:43 am	5:31:50 pm	7:15:59 am	5:36:08 pm
Mon, Feb 24	6:53:39 am	5:33:37 pm	7:13:33 am	5:38:16 pm
Tue, Feb 25	6:51:33 am	5:35:24 pm	7:11:06 am	5:40:25 pm
Wed, Feb 26	6:49:26 am	5:37:11 pm	7:08:38 am	5:42:33 pm
Thu, Feb 27	6:47:19 am	5:38:57 pm	7:06:09 am	5:44:41 pm
Fri, Feb 28	6:45:11 am	5:40:43 pm	7:03:39 am	5:46:48 pm

Moonrise and moonset

Moon phases

◗ **THIRD QUARTER** 20 February
● **NEW MOON** 28 February
◐ **FIRST QUARTER** 5 February
○ **FULL MOON** 12 February

DAY	LONDON Moonrise	LONDON Moonset	LONDON Moonrise	EDINBURGH Moonrise	EDINBURGH Moonset	EDINBURGH Moonrise
Feb 1	09:02	20:55		09:18	21:07	
Feb 2	09:14	22:21		09:24	22:40	
Feb 3	09:27	23:49		09:31		
Feb 4	09:41				00:15	09:38
Feb 5		01:17	10:00		01:52	09:49
Feb 6		02:46	10:25		03:30	10:06
Feb 7		04:10	11:02		05:02	10:36
Feb 8		05:23	11:55		06:19	11:24
Feb 9		06:17	13:03		07:10	12:36
Feb 10		06:55	14:22		07:41	14:03
Feb 11		07:21	15:43		07:58	15:33
Feb 12		07:39	17:03		08:09	17:00
Feb 13		07:53	18:19		08:17	18:23
Feb 14		08:04	19:32		08:22	19:42
Feb 15		08:14	20:44		08:27	20:59
Feb 16		08:23	21:54		08:31	22:15
Feb 17		08:33	23:06		08:35	23:33
Feb 18		08:45			08:41	
Feb 19	00:18	08:59		00:52	08:49	
Feb 20	01:33	09:19		02:14	09:01	
Feb 21	02:47	09:46		03:36	09:21	
Feb 22	03:56	10:26		04:52	09:55	
Feb 23	04:55	11:22		05:52	10:51	
Feb 24	05:40	12:35		06:32	12:10	
Feb 25	06:13	13:59		06:56	13:43	
Feb 26	06:36	15:28		07:10	15:21	
Feb 27	06:54	16:58		07:20	17:00	
Feb 28	07:08	18:28		07:27	18:37	

Average rainfall

The average rainfall in February for the UK is 120mm (4.7in), but note the dramatic differences throughout the country, with regions of high ground in the west receiving almost double that of regions in the east.

LOCATION	DAYS	MM	INCHES
Aberdeen	11	59	2.3
Aberystwyth	14	98	3.8
Belfast	13	70	2.75
Birmingham	10	55	2.2
Bournemouth	11	67	2.6
Bristol	10	58	2.3
Cambridge	9	36	1.4
Canterbury	9	50	2.0
Cardiff	12	93	3.7
Edinburgh	10	53	2.1
Exeter	14	133	5.2
Glasgow	15	115	4.5
Gloucester	11	66	2.6
Inverness	12	61	2.4
Ipswich	9	42	1.6
Leeds	13	89	3.5
Liverpool	12	57	2.2
London	11	51	2.0
Manchester	14	97	3.8
Newcastle upon Tyne	9	41	1.6
Norwich	11	45	1.8
Nottingham	11	50	2.0
Oxford	9	47	1.8
Sheffield	11	67	2.6
Truro	13	83	3.3

Pruning masterclass: when to prune

Many woody plants such as shrubs and trees benefit from pruning. Some are best cut every year, while others may need a prune only once in a while, when they outgrow their space. These guidelines will help you to identify when to prune your plants, but bear in mind that there many exceptions to the rules, so visit the RHS website at rhs.org.uk for more advice about specific specimens.

Good quality secateurs are an essential item for a pruning tool kit.

TIMING IT RIGHT

Pruning deciduous trees and shrubs in winter can be easier than at other times of year because you can see the stem structures more easily. This is also an ideal time to renovate overgrown shrubs or to shape young trees, so that each plant's food reserves in the roots, which are not removed by pruning, can then fuel vigorous regrowth in spring. Plants where this type of regrowth is desired include coppiced or pollarded trees and shrubs (see p.10); autumn-fruiting raspberries that flower on new shoots; blackcurrants, to induce fruit-bearing young growth; and plants that flower in late summer on new shoots produced in the same year, including *Buddleja* and *Hydrangea paniculata*.

However, too much vigorous regrowth on apple and pear trees and large fruit bushes gives rise to lots of new but unproductive stems, so cut back just a few boughs each winter (see pp.226–7).

Trained forms of apples and pears, such as cordons and espaliers, are pruned in summer – removing the leafy stems at this time curbs their vigour and promotes more flower buds to form (see pp.152–3).

Shrubs that bloom in spring or early summer, such as *Philadelphus* and *Weigela*, form flower buds on stems made the previous year, which are removed if they are pruned in winter or early spring. Most are therefore cut back after flowering, cutting out one in three of the oldest shoots near ground level to keep the shrubs youthful and compact. Where plants have become overgrown or severely congested, you can renovate them in winter, but may lose their flowers for a year or two.

Plants at risk of diseases that proliferate during the colder seasons, such as cherries and other *Prunus* species, birches (*Betula*) and walnuts (*Juglans*), are pruned in summer. Wounds heal quickly during the warmer months, helping to prevent silver leaf and other diseases from entering the plant, and there is no risk of the sap bleeding after cutting in spring or infection that can sometimes follow late winter pruning.

Evergreens don't go dormant in winter, and their leaves nourish them until spring, but many still benefit from pruning now and again. Spring-flowering shrubs such as camellias and *Choisya*, for example, are pruned after flowering. Others, including *Garrya*, hollies (*Ilex*) and rhododendrons, are best pruned in March.

FEBRUARY PRUNING GUIDE

PLANT	PRUNING METHOD	NOTES
Buddleja davidii	Cut back to near the framework of permanent shoots	Flowers on new shoots in late summer; prune in late winter/early spring to encourage new shoots
Ceratostigma	As for *Buddleja*	
Clematis, late-summer flowering on new shoots	Cut back to lowest pair of swollen healthy buds	Easy to be caught unawares, as buds develop fast
Deciduous *Ceanothus*	As for *Buddleja*	
Hydrangea paniculata	As for *Buddleja*	
Ilex	Trim to size	Robust evergreens can be pruned in February or March in cold regions
Lavatera	As for *Buddleja*	
Prunus lusitanica	As for *Ilex*	
Rosa	Prune to framework (bush roses) or remove some older shoots on shrub roses.	Pruning depends on form of rose
Wisteria	Shorten young shoots to within two buds of their base	

Edible garden

As temperatures rise, you can sow many hardy crops in an unheated greenhouse or outside in a cold frame or under a cloche. Also continue to plant fruit trees while the cheaper bare-root plants are still available.

Vegetables

SOW INDOORS Indoor aubergines; Brussels sprouts; chillies; cucumber; kale; leeks; lettuces; peppers; radishes; spinach; tomatoes.

SOW OUTDOORS UNDER CLOCHES OR IN A COLD FRAME Bolt-resistant beetroot; broad beans; summer cabbages; lettuces; onions; peas; radishes; spinach; spring onions. ❶

PLANT NOW Asparagus crowns; garlic sets; onion sets

HARVEST NOW Brussels sprouts; cauliflowers (in mild regions); celeriac; chard; kale; leeks; lettuce and radishes grown under a cloche or in a cool greenhouse; sprouting broccoli; swedes; winter cabbages.

Fruit

PLANT NOW Bare-root hardy fruit trees such as apples, cherries, peaches, pears, plums, quinces; rhubarb.

LIFT AND DIVIDE RHUBARB (see p.219)

HARVEST Citrus fruits such as lemons and oranges, when they colour up.

HERB OF THE MONTH: ROSEMARY
This relative of sage (*Salvia rosmarinus*) is an evergreen, sun-loving shrub from the Mediterranean region that's very easy to grow in a free-draining border or a large pot of peat-free soil-based compost. It tolerates temperatures down to −10°C (14°F), or lower if kept dry, and produces aromatic foliage and blue, pollen-rich flowers in late spring. Prune it in late spring; replace old straggly plants. Harvest the leaves lightly in February, when it will be growing very slowly, if at all.

Challenges this month

Temperatures in February are generally still too cold for many creatures to breed rapidly and cause visible feeding damage, but in warm areas such as greenhouses and indoors your seedlings and young plants could succumb to fungal diseases.

DAMPING-OFF DISEASES are fungal and fungus-like diseases that infect and kill germinating seeds and young seedlings grown indoors, which then rot away. To avoid the problem, wash pans, pots, seed trays and propagators with detergent or disinfectant, and use fresh commercial seed compost and tap water to irrigate your seedlings and young plants. Sowing seeds thinly in warm conditions, while not overwatering and improving air circulation, will also reduce the risk.

GLASSHOUSE MEALYBUGS can weaken and stunt the growth of a wide range of plants grown indoors, by sucking the sap from the roots, stems and leaves. They also excrete a sticky honeydew on foliage, which promotes the growth of black sooty moulds. These insects look like little woodlice and feed on cacti and succulents, African violets, bougainvillea, hoya, orchids and other houseplants. The first signs of their presence are often patches of white fluffy wax in the leaf axils or other sheltered places on the plant, which are covering their orange-pink eggs. To prevent problems in the first place, quarantine any new plants for at least a month. Also, remove dead leaves and prunings from the soil, which may be harbouring the bugs or eggs. A ladybird, *Cryptolaemus montrouzieri*, can be released into greenhouses to control mealybugs from May to September. Due partly to their waxy covering, mealybugs are difficult to control with insecticides, but organic sprays may work (see scale insects on p 21).

MOLES are on the move in February, creating their telltale hills in lawns, borders and vegetable plots, while extending their runs and constructing breeding nests, known as 'fortresses'. These little mammals can consume over half their body weight in earthworms and grubs each day. Where possible, moles should be treated as part of the biodiversity that gardens support. However, if they are disrupting your lawn or productive plot, refer to the RHS website for more guidance.

Focus on wildlife

Bluetit

One of our most common native garden birds, the blue tit can be seen all year round flitting between trees and shrubs and eating nutrient-rich suet balls, peanuts and seeds from feeders.

Loved for their brightly coloured plumage and little round bodies, these compact tits are easy to identify, sporting a bright blue cap, dark blue-black eye stripes set against white cheeks, yellow breast and blue-green markings on the wings. Although male birds are brighter in colour than the females, there is little difference between them.

While we think of blue tits as garden birds, their native habitat is deciduous woodland, which offers a home to the large numbers of spring caterpillars they need to feed their chicks at that time of year. However, research shows that offering these little birds a range of foods, such as those listed above, in our gardens throughout the winter and early spring increases their chances of survival.

Blue tits start looking for nesting sites and suitable mates in late winter and early spring. In the wild, they will nest in tree holes but may also take up residence in a cosy nest box in your garden. The female builds the nest alone, with little or no help from the male, using moss from lawns and logs to form a cup, which she then lines with feathers, fur or wool.

In April she lays a clutch of 8–12 eggs, which she broods until they hatch – the male provides some of her food during this time. The chicks will then fledge after 18–21 days.

Unlike many other garden birds, including blackbirds and robins, which may have multiple broods each year, blue tits usually raise just one in spring.

Spotlight on: Dwarf iris (*Iris reticulata*)

Few flowers brave the cold in February but the dainty little *Iris reticulata* is guaranteed to put on a show now, peeping through snow-laden soil to reveal its dainty fragrant blooms. Choose from a range of sumptuous shades, including dark purple, lilac, yellow and pinky red, or opt for a bicoloured form. Each flower is decorated with yellow and white markings on the outer petals (falls), and the blooms are surrounded by linear green leaves. Natives of the mountains of Turkey, Iraq, Iran and Russia, plant these iris bulbs in autumn in free-draining soil at the front of a sunny border, or in a trough or rock garden, where you can enjoy them at eye level and they won't rot.

IRIS 'PIXIE'
The small but beautiful dark violet flowers of this cultivar are set off by white and yellow markings on the outer petals, known as 'falls'.
H x S: 10 x 10cm (4 x 4in)

IRIS 'KATHARINE HODGKIN'
Relatively large, pale blue flowers with intricate dark veins and spots on the falls adorn this award-winning cultivar.
H x S: 12 x 10cm (5 x 4in)

IRIS 'GEORGE'
The dark purple-pink petals and sweetly scented flowers look beautiful in a large pot close to a path where they can be enjoyed up close.
H x S: 15 x 10cm (6 x 4in)

IRIS 'KATHARINE'S GOLD'
The creamy yellow flowers of this cultivar make a striking contrast with the dark purple forms. They bloom from January to March.
H x S: 15 x 10cm (6 x 4in)

IRIS 'HARMONY'
This royal blue-flowered cultivar flowers from late January through to the end of February and its sweet scent can be enjoyed from close range.
H x S: 15 x 10cm (6 x 4in)

Seasonal planting ideas

COLOURFUL CATKINS

WHY IT WORKS
The pink catkins of the 'Mount Aso' willow are picked up in the flowers of the heathers, helping to create this harmonious composition. As well as making a beautiful border, the flowers of these shrubs help to sustain pollinators that emerge in winter and early spring. The heathers also make an effective groundcover on neutral or acid soils, helping to reduce weed growth and retain soil moisture.

WHAT'S GROWING HERE?
Salix gracilistyla 'Mount Aso' is a shrubby willow that reaches about 2.5m (8ft). Eye-catching, upright pink catkins with a silvery sheen appear in late winter and early spring before the slightly bluish leaves, silvery on the underside, unfurl.

Erica × darleyensis f. *albiflora* 'Silberschmelze' is a white, winter-flowering heather. A spreading evergreen shrub, 45cm (18in) high, it produces small, needle-like, green leaves, tipped with cream in spring, and scented, white, urn-shaped flowers from early winter into spring.

Erica × darleyensis 'Ghost Hills' is similar in height and habit to 'Silberschmelze', and will make a wide mat of bright green foliage with purple-pink flowers, darker near the tips, in late winter and early spring.

WHEN TO PLANT
These shrubs are best planted in autumn, to allow them to settle in well before winter, or plant in spring and water well through their first summer.

WHERE TO SEE IT
This colourful combination of willow and heathers can be seen in the winter border at RHS Garden Harlow Carr.

Horticultural heroes

Gertrude Jekyll · 1843–1932

British horticulturist, garden designer and artist Gertrude Jekyll is celebrated for her naturalistic plantings and painterly style. She created more than 400 garden designs in the UK, Europe and America, many in partnership with the architect Sir Edwin Lutyens. Both were advocates of the Arts & Crafts movement, which was a reaction against what followers believed to be the degradation of the decorative arts, after the rise of factory-made items.

Jekyll chose each plant in her designs for its colour, structure and habit, as well as its suitability to the site and soil, ideas she expanded in her ground-breaking book *The English Flower Garden*, written in collaboration with her friend, the influential plantsman William Robinson (see p.101). In the book, the pair explored ways of creating naturalistic gardens using swathes of hardy perennials – an idea that's still popular today.

Gertrude Jekyll was born in 1843 in London, to Captain Edward Jekyll, an officer in the Grenadier Guards, and his wife Julia. When Jekyll was five, the family moved to Bramley House in Surrey and it is here that her love of plants began. In 1861, aged 18, she returned to London to study at the South Kensington School of Art, where she also took classes in botany and the science of colour, exploring theories that influenced her work as a painter and garden designer.

Following the death of her father in 1876, her mother built a house on Munstead Heath, near Godalming in Surrey, where Jekyll's design of the garden led to her move from art into horticulture. As well as designing gardens, including Hestercombe House in Somerset, Woolverstone House in Suffolk and the Manor House in Upton Grey, Hampshire, she also ran a successful nursery near her home in Surrey and bred many new plants, while filling the rest of her time writing books and magazine features.

In 1897, she was awarded the Victoria Medal of Honour by the Royal Horticultural Society and the Veitch Memorial Medal in 1929. Jekyll's work is still highly influential today, with many gardeners emulating her famous flower-filled borders.

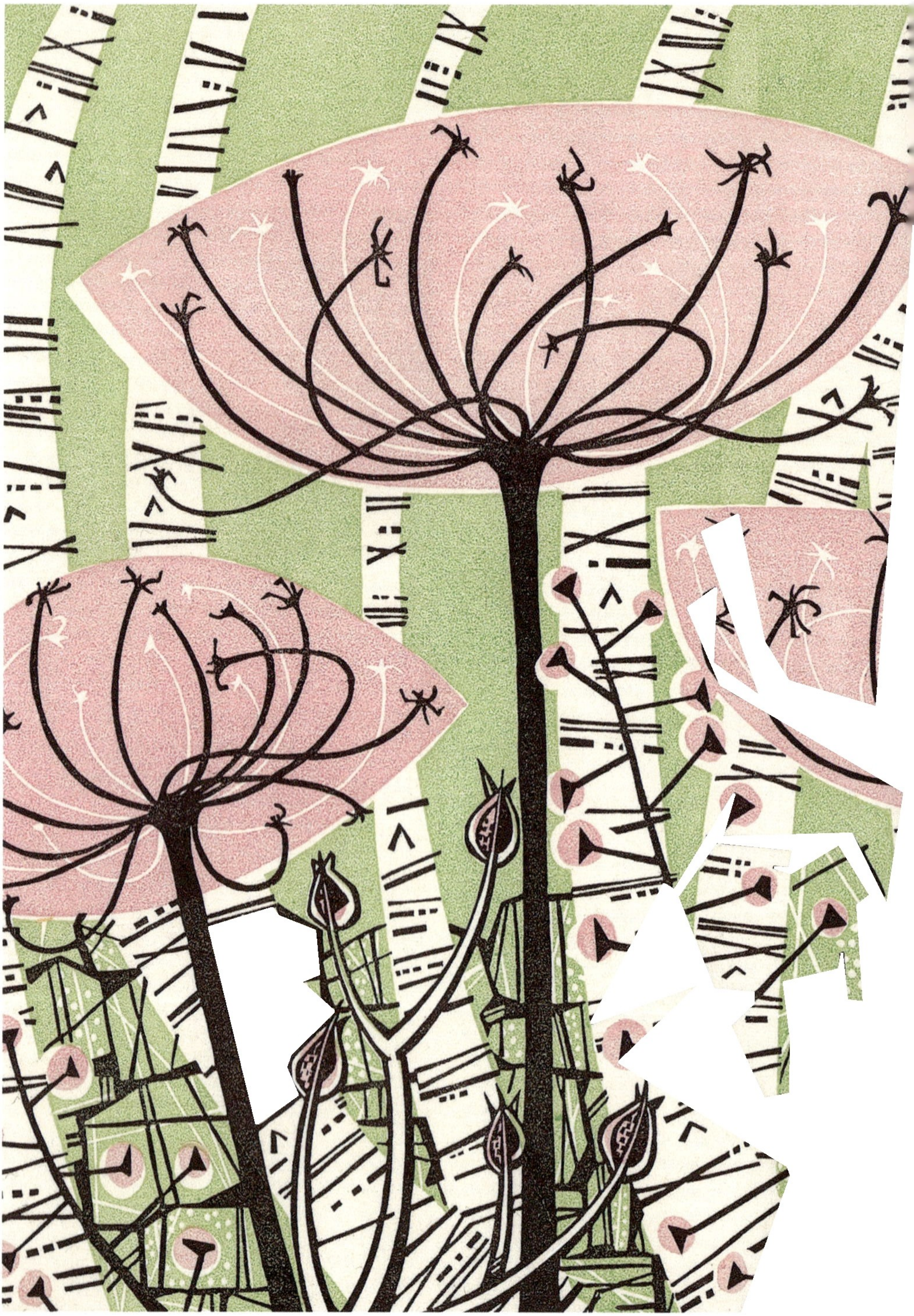

March

The arrival of spring heralds a flurry of activity in the garden. Increasing light levels accelerate plant growth, transforming barren soil into carpets of foliage and flowers. Little white windflowers flutter in the breeze and nectar-rich pulmonarias play host to early-flying bees, while trees join in the show, their flower-filled canopies shimmering like confetti.

KEY EVENTS
St David's Day, 1 March
First day of meteorological spring, 1 March
Shrove Tuesday, 4 March
Masi Magam, 12 March
St Patrick's Day, 17 March
Vernal equinox, 20 March
Eid al-Fitr, 31 March
End of Ramadan, 30 March

What to do in March

The main season for planting and seed sowing outdoors in both the flower and productive garden begins in March, but, while the longer days accelerate germination and growth rates, heavy rain, frost or even snow can temporarily bring plants to a halt. Meanwhile, sowing seed indoors continues apace, and you can also catch up on pruning late summer-flowering shrubs and climbers that were missed last month (see pp.36–7). Weeding is another essential task – hoeing or digging out unwanted plants while they are young and easier to remove.

In the garden

SOW HALF-HARDY ANNUALS INDOORS from seed, to fill summer pots and borders. French marigolds (*Tagetes*) and cosmos are easy to grow, as are helichrysum and statice (*Limonium sinuatum*) – the latter two are both suitable for drying. Also try silvery dusty miller (*Jacobaea maritima*, syn. *Senecio cineraria*), ideal for edging and hanging baskets, and tall spider flower (*Cleome*) for a border. Sow in warmth on a sunny windowsill or in a heated greenhouse, and pot up the seedlings when they have a few leaves. Plant outside when all risk of frost has passed. ❶

FEED POTTED DAFFODILS with tomato organic-based fertilizer every fortnight to help build up the bulbs for next year. Also apply 35g per square metre (1oz per square yard) of general organic-based fertilizer to daffodils in beds, leaving the rain to wash it down to the roots. Allow the foliage to die down naturally after flowering, but deadhead the blooms to prevent plants making seed. ❷

DIVIDE PERENNIALS to reinvigorate old clumps and make new plants. Lift plants with a fork and sever the rootballs with a knife, or, for large clumps, plunge two forks back-to-back in the middle and ease them away from each other. Choose sections of healthy growth from the edges to replant or pot up. ❸

RAKE OUT LAWN MOSS, which grows at lower temperatures and light levels than grass and can smother it in early spring. Gently removing the moss with a lawn rake will keep it under control. You could also use these mossy fragments elsewhere to create a Japanese-style feature and suppress weed germination. In a shaded area, remove unwanted plants, stones and surface debris, and rake the soil. Scratch the surface lightly and press the moss fragments into the soil, then water well. ❹

PLANT PINEAPPLE LILY (*EUCOMIS*) BULBS for spectacular summer flowers that resemble the fruit after which they are named. Plant the bulbs in a sunny spot in well-drained soil, or in a pot filled with peat-free compost, 15cm (6in) below the surface.

ADD BARLEY STRAW or introduce more floating plants to suppress algae growth in garden ponds.

In the fruit & veg patch

PLANT OUT HARDY VEGETABLES sown indoors in winter, when the soil is moist but not frozen. From late March onwards, sow directly into the ground carrots, broad beans, lettuce, parsnips, peas, radish, spinach and spring onions.

PLANT EARLY POTATOES from seed potatoes chitted in January or February (see p.12), when the shoots are 5cm (2in) long. In cities and Southern areas of the UK, planting outdoors in March is feasible, but elsewhere plant in tubs or growbags and store in a frost-free shed, greenhouse or conservatory. In April, place the containers outside, but keep your potato plants protected with horticultural fleece until mid-May.

SOW TOMATOES indoors on a sunny windowsill or in a heated greenhouse. Try sweet cherry types such as 'Sungold', 'Sweet Million' and the grape–sized, blight-resistant 'Celano'.

SOW SALAD CROPS in a warm, sunny, sheltered spot outdoors. This will deliver two crops – one from thinning the seedlings and another when the plants mature. Good choices include coriander, lamb's lettuce, mizuna, and pak choi.

PLANT STRAWBERRIES at the beginning of the month from cold-stored runners (bare-root plants), known as '60-day strawberries'. These specially treated plants are designed to deliver a crop in just two months, or a little longer in cooler weather. Once the strawberries have been harvested, the plants can be kept and grown as usual in future years.

Indoors

PLANT POLIANTHES TUBERS indoors in pots of houseplant compost and place in a warm room with plenty of sunlight, such as a conservatory or windowsill. Water the plants lightly, making sure that the compost is never wet or becomes waterlogged, and you will be rewarded with deliciously scented flowers in summer.

CLEAN DUST from large-leaved houseplants with tepid water, which will allow them to photosynthesize more efficiently now that they are coming back into growth. Also increase watering in March.

MONEY-SAVING IDEA
Take dahlia cuttings
To increase your stocks of dahlias for free, pot up firm healthy tubers in trays of peat-free multipurpose compost, with the buds at the top exposed. Water and place in a light, frost-free place. After a few weeks, new shoots will begin to sprout. Leaving some shoots on the original plant, remove the others with a sharp knife, cutting them where they emerge from the tuber. Remove the lowest pair of leaves and plant in pots of compost. Set in a warm, light, frost-free place, and plant out after the frosts.

Plants of the month

1. Species tulips
   (*Tulipa humilis* pictured)
2. Scillas (*Scilla siberica* pictured)
3. Flowering quince
   (*Chaenomeles speciosa* 'Nivalis' pictured)
4. Pieris (*Pieris* 'Forest Flame' pictured)
5. Camellia (*Camellia* × *williamsii* 'Leonara' pictured)
6. Star magnolia
   (*Magnolia stellata*)
7. Dog's tooth violet
   (*Erythronium* 'Pagoda' pictured)
8. Bergenia (*Bergenia cordifolia* 'Purpurea' pictured)
9. Wallflower (*Erysimum* 'Apricot Twist' pictured)
10. Aubrieta (*Aubrieta deltoidea* pictured)
11. Marsh marigold
    (*Caltha palustris*)

MARCH / 49

Project: How to capture rainwater

As water resources come under increasing pressure from climate change and population growth, installing a water butt or two is a great way to store the free stuff that falls from the sky for use on your plants. Local councils and water companies often sell (and deliver) affordable water butts, or you can buy them from DIY stores. To maximize your storage, try linking two or more butts. Some come fitted with taps and pre-drilled holes, but you need to drill to fit others yourself, so make sure you have the right tools for this job.

YOU WILL NEED
2 water butts and stands
Screwdriver, bits and screws
Hacksaw
Diverter kit (if not supplied)
Corrugated pipes (if not supplied with the butts)

1 Each water butt should have two points on either side at the top, where corrugated pipes can be attached. Drill holes where necessary and push or screw the pipes into place.

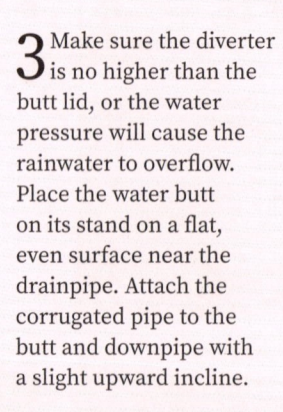

2 Using a hacksaw, remove a section of drainpipe to fit a diverter, which may come with the butt as part of the kit.

3 Make sure the diverter is no higher than the butt lid, or the water pressure will cause the rainwater to overflow. Place the water butt on its stand on a flat, even surface near the drainpipe. Attach the corrugated pipe to the butt and downpipe with a slight upward incline.

4 Position your second water butt next to the first, making sure they are level. Fix more corrugated pipe between the top of each butt so water can flow from one to the other.

50 / MARCH

Looking up

Sunrise and sunset

The beginning of spring heralds longer days, allowing more time for the numerous jobs in the garden, while British Summer Time begins on the last weekend of March.

DAY	LONDON Sunrise	LONDON Sunset	EDINBURGH Sunrise	EDINBURGH Sunset
Sat, Mar 1	6:43:02 am	5:42:29 pm	7:01:09 am	5:48:55 pm
Sun, Mar 2	6:40:52 am	5:44:15 pm	6:58:38 am	5:51:02 pm
Mon, Mar 3	6:38:41 am	5:46:00 pm	6:56:06 am	5:53:09 pm
Tue, Mar 4	6:36:30 am	5:47:45 pm	6:53:34 am	5:55:15 pm
Wed, Mar 5	6:34:19 am	5:49:30 pm	6:51:01 am	5:57:21 pm
Thu, Mar 6	6:32:06 am	5:51:14 pm	6:48:28 am	5:59:27 pm
Fri, Mar 7	6:29:54 am	5:52:58 pm	6:45:54 am	6:01:32 pm
Sat, Mar 8	6:27:40 am	5:54:42 pm	6:43:19 am	6:03:37 pm
Sun, Mar 9	6:25:26 am	5:56:26 pm	6:40:44 am	6:05:42 pm
Mon, Mar 10	6:23:12 am	5:58:10 pm	6:38:09 am	6:07:47 pm
Tue, Mar 11	6:20:58 am	5:59:53 pm	6:35:33 am	6:09:51 pm
Wed, Mar 12	6:18:42 am	6:01:36 pm	6:32:57 am	6:11:56 pm
Thu, Mar 13	6:16:27 am	6:03:19 pm	6:30:20 am	6:14:00 pm
Fri, Mar 14	6:14:11 am	6:05:02 pm	6:27:43 am	6:16:03 pm
Sat, Mar 15	6:11:55 am	6:06:44 pm	6:25:06 am	6:18:07 pm
Sun, Mar 16	6:09:39 am	6:08:26 pm	6:22:29 am	6:20:10 pm
Mon, Mar 17	6:07:22 am	6:10:08 pm	6:19:51 am	6:22:13 pm
Tue, Mar 18	6:05:06 am	6:11:50 pm	6:17:13 am	6:24:16 pm
Wed, Mar 19	6:02:49 am	6:13:32 pm	6:14:35 am	6:26:19 pm
Thu, Mar 20	6:00:32 am	6:15:14 pm	6:11:57 am	6:28:22 pm
Fri, Mar 21	5:58:15 am	6:16:55 pm	6:09:19 am	6:30:25 pm
Sat, Mar 22	5:55:58 am	6:18:36 pm	6:06:41 am	6:32:27 pm
Sun, Mar 23	5:53:40 am	6:20:18 pm	6:04:02 am	6:34:29 pm
Mon, Mar 24	5:51:23 am	6:21:59 pm	6:01:24 am	6:36:32 pm
Tue, Mar 25	5:49:06 am	6:23:40 pm	5:58:45 am	6:38:34 pm
Wed, Mar 26	5:46:49 am	6:25:21 pm	5:56:07 am	6:40:36 pm
Thu, Mar 27	5:44:32 am	6:27:02 pm	5:53:29 am	6:42:38 pm
Fri, Mar 28	5:42:15 am	6:28:43 pm	5:50:51 am	6:44:40 pm
Sat, Mar 29	5:39:58 am	6:30:23 pm	5:48:12 am	6:46:42 pm
Sun, Mar 30*	6:37:41 am	7:32:04 pm	6:45:34 am	7:48:44 pm
Mon, Mar 31	6:35:25 am	7:33:45 pm	6:42:57 am	7:50:46 pm

*Note: hours shift because clocks change forward 1 hour.

Moonrise and moonset

Moon phases

◐ **THIRD QUARTER** 22 March
● **NEW MOON** 29 March

◑ **FIRST QUARTER** 6 March
○ **FULL MOON** 14 March

DAY	LONDON Moonrise	Moonset	Moonrise	EDINBURGH Moonrise	Moonset	Moonrise
Mar 1	07:20	19:57		07:33	20:13	
Mar 2	07:33	21:27		07:40	21:51	
Mar 3	07:47	22:59		07:47	23:31	
Mar 4	08:05			07:57		
Mar 5		00:31	08:28		01:12	08:11
Mar 6		01:59	09:01		02:49	08:36
Mar 7		03:16	09:49		04:12	09:19
Mar 8		04:16	10:53		05:11	10:24
Mar 9		04:58	12:08		05:47	11:46
Mar 10		05:27	13:28		06:07	13:15
Mar 11		05:46	14:48		06:19	14:42
Mar 12		06:01	16:04		06:27	16:06
Mar 13		06:13	17:18		06:33	17:25
Mar 14		06:22	18:29		06:37	18:42
Mar 15		06:32	19:40		06:41	19:59
Mar 16		06:41	20:51		06:46	21:16
Mar 17		06:52	22:03		06:51	22:35
Mar 18		07:05	23:17		06:58	23:56
Mar 19		07:22			07:08	
Mar 20	00:31	07:46		01:18	07:24	
Mar 21	01:42	08:20		02:36	07:51	
Mar 22	02:45	09:08		03:42	08:36	
Mar 23	03:35	10:12		04:29	09:44	
Mar 24	04:11	11:30		04:58	11:09	
Mar 25	04:38	12:55		05:16	12:44	
Mar 26	04:57	14:23		05:27	14:20	
Mar 27	05:12	15:52		05:35	15:57	
Mar 28	05:26	17:22		05:42	17:34	
Mar 29	05:38	18:53		05:48	19:13	
Mar 30*	06:52	21:27		06:55	21:55	
Mar 31	07:08	23:03		07:04	23:39	

*Note: hours shift because clocks change forward 1 hour.

Average rainfall

In March, the average rainfall in the UK is 108mm (4¼in). Lower levels of precipitation and high winds mean that new and young plants may be vulnerable to drying out this month, so prepare to water them during prolonged dry spells.

LOCATION	DAYS	MM	INCHES
Aberdeen	11	54	2.1
Aberystwyth	13	74	2.9
Belfast	13	71	2.8
Birmingham	10	51	2.0
Bournemouth	10	62	2.4
Bristol	10	53	2.0
Cambridge	8	33	1.3
Canterbury	7	39	1.5
Cardiff	12	85	3.3
Edinburgh	10	48	1.9
Exeter	12	112	4.4
Glasgow	14	97	3.8
Gloucester	11	51	2.0
Inverness	12	53	2.0
Ipswich	8	37	1.5
Leeds	12	77	3.0
Liverpool	11	53	2.1
London	9	43	1.7
Manchester	13	90	3.5
Newcastle upon Tyne	8	39	1.5
Norwich	9	46	1.8
Nottingham	10	45	1.8
Oxford	9	43	1.7
Sheffield	11	60	2.4
Truro	12	69	2.7

New ways with lawns

Closely mown lawns are unbeatable for walking on, and for playing games and entertaining, but, if you have more than you need for these activities, there is scope to grow a richer mix of wildlife-friendly grasses and flowers that will draw a whole range of insects and birds to your garden.

LET THE GRASS GROW
By allowing your lawn to grow uncut until September, the grasses in it can flower and set seed, providing birds with invaluable food in winter. Flowers in the lawn such as clovers and daisies will flourish, too, bearing flowers that are appreciated by bees, butterflies and other pollinators.

You can mow paths through larger areas of long grass to get up close and enjoy the wildlife that's attracted to the plants. Then, in September, mow the whole area to curb any tussocks and woody plants such as oak seedlings from establishing, without harming the wildlife. Weedkillers and fertilizers are counterproductive, since they have an adverse effect on insects and wildlife.

MAKE A FLOWER MEADOW
Meadow flowers such as cowslips and ragged robin thrive in poor soil with a low nutrient content. If your soil is nutrient-rich, you can allow the grass

The native meadow at RHS Garden Rosemoor draws in a host of pollinators to feed on the wildflowers.

to grow, then mow and remove the cuttings over a few years to reduce its fertility, or strip off the turf, either across the whole lawn or in sections. The soil you expose will provide the conditions needed for meadow flower seeds to germinate and thrive, while reducing the vigour of the competing grasses. Turn the surplus turves upside down and leave them in a shady spot to rot down. Once decomposed, they make fertile soil, ideal for adding to raised beds in the vegetable garden or for improving flower borders. Sow meadow flower seeds when the soil is warm and moist, before mid-May, choosing a mixture suited to your soil type and light levels. These mixes should contain some less vigorous native grasses, as well as flowers. Inserting plug plants into closely mown grass in spring can also be effective, as long as the soil is not too fertile.

BRIGHT CORNFIELD MIXES
Colourful cornfield annuals, such as the common poppy and cornflowers, do not make satisfactory, long-term meadows but they can create pretty, pollen-rich flowering areas if you resow the seed every year or, with luck, they may self-seed.

Some cornfield-style mixtures also contain cultivated plants such as California poppies (*Eschscholzia californica*) and cosmos, which are more spectacular and flower for longer than native wild plants.

Top Poppies and other cornfield annuals may need to be sown every year to guarantee a colourful display.
Bottom Leaving the lawn grass to grow longer will make a new habitat for wildlife, including bees, butterflies and birds.

Edible garden

It's time to start sowing a wide range of tender crops indoors, and hardy types outside, now that light levels and temperatures are rising. The last winter crops will also be ready to harvest, if you were able to leave some in the ground earlier in the year.

Vegetables

SOW INDOORS Outdoor aubergine; cabbages; cauliflowers; celeriac; celery; chillies; courgettes; indoor cucumbers; kohlrabi; leeks; lettuces ❶; peppers; outdoor tomatoes, turnips.

SOW OUTDOORS, UNDER CLOCHES OR IN COLD FRAMES Bolt-resistant beetroot ❷; broad beans; broccoli; carrots; chard; leeks; lettuce; onions; parsnips; peas, including mange-tout and sugar snap; radishes; rocket; salad crops (see p.12); spinach; spring onions; turnips.

PLANT OUT broad beans; early potatoes; hardy plants sown indoors in February or bought in, including asparagus crowns; garlic sets, onion sets and shallots; lettuce; peas; radishes; spinach; spring onions.

HARVEST NOW Brussels sprouts; cauliflowers ❸; chard; kale; leeks; lettuce; radishes; spring cabbages; purple and white sprouting broccoli.

Fruit

PLANT NOW Bare-root and potted hardy fruit trees such as apples, cherries, medlars, mulberries, pears, plums, quinces; apricot and peach trees in a sheltered spot; blackberry and raspberry canes; strawberries from runners.

HARVEST Rhubarb. ❹

> **TOP TIP**
> **Sowing little and often**
> Sowing seed in small batches every few weeks is known as 'successional sowing' and helps to prevent gluts, while providing you with a stream of fresh produce over a longer period. Ideal candidates for successional sowing are crops prone to bolting, such as lettuces, radishes, spring onions, coriander and spinach.

HERB OF THE MONTH: DILL
This delicious herb has a citrussy flavour and is easy to grow from seed. Sow dill (*Anethum graveolens*) in pots of peat-free seed compost indoors in March and transplant outside into a sunny bed as temperatures warm up. Alternatively, sow the seed directly in the ground from April. This tall annual produces an abundance of soft feathery leaves and domed clusters of small yellow flowers that attract bees and other pollinators. Sow small batches from now until midsummer for a harvest up to the frosts in autumn.

🍲 Try delicious ferments

Fermentation is a traditional preservation technique, and many fermented foods such as cheese and yogurt may already be a familiar part of your diet. Ferments are widely thought to help boost gut health and in this book we have six delicious recipes for you to try (see pp.76, 96, 116, 136, 172 and 192). Before you start, take a look through these tips and the items you will need.

The 'lactic acid fermentation' used in the recipes in the book involves submerging vegetables in salty brine, which prevents the development of micro-organisms that will cause them to spoil, while promoting those that are good for gut health. Microbes that naturally exist on the plants then break down carbohydrates such as sugars and convert them into lactic acid, which is responsible for preserving the vegetables and giving the ferments a delicious sour tang. Kobumcha (see p.76) also uses yeasts and other bacterium to produce alcohol and acetic acid that act as preservatives. Your ferments should last for at least three months in the fridge.

HOW MUCH SALT?
You can change the quantities of produce used in the recipes, but you will then need to recalculate how much salt to add. For every 100g (3.5oz) of produce, you will require 2–3g (0.07–0.1oz) of salt. For example, if you have 1kg (35oz) of sliced cabbage and carrot to ferment, you will need to add 20–30g (0.7–1oz) of salt.

FERMENTATION TIMES
The time it takes for produce to ferment is dependent on the temperature – in warmer conditions, the process will be quicker. After the first few days, taste the ferment every day or two until it reaches the degree of sourness you prefer. The fermentation process does not end once in the fridge, either – cold temperatures simply slow it down and you will find the flavours continue to evolve over time.

YOU WILL NEED
These items, together with bowls, knives and a chopping board, are all you require.

Wide mouthed kilner jars with lids.

Airlocks are one-way valves that allow carbon dioxide to escape from the jars during fermentation, while ensuring oxygen cannot enter, to prevent the ferment from spoiling.

Glass weights are used to submerge the ingredients under the brine, creating an oxygen-free environment that prevents the ferments from rotting.

A mandolin is a useful tool for slicing vegetables finely, which allows salt to quickly penetrate.

A wooden tamper helps pack the ingredients tightly into the kilner jars.

Electric scales allow you to measure precise amounts of salt.

Challenges this month

With spring in the air, slugs and snails become active again and start to breed, some species munching on tender young plants and crops. At this time of year, keep on top of weeding, removing perennials and annuals before they become a nuisance.

SLUGS AND SNAILS can be beneficial, with many species offering an invaluable service by helping to break down rotting vegetation, but a few are attracted to seedlings and young crops. The best approach is to grow plants on to a larger size before planting out. Recent RHS research has found that barriers and traps do little to deter these molluscs. Where there is no other option, and as a last resort, consider slug pellets containing ferric phosphate. Almost as effective are nematode preparations, which can be watered around vulnerable plants from March, when the soil temperatures are warm enough for these biological controls to work.

PERENNIALS such as ground elder, bramble and couch grass can overtake a bed and spread rapidly during spring and early summer, so now is the time to dig them out before they become large and resistant clumps. Try to remove as much of the root system as possible, since these tough perennials will regenerate from even a tiny fragment. Also rake bare ground to stimulate annual weeds to germinate. Hoeing off seedlings now will limit the need to weed later in the year.

BRACKEN can be troublesome in rural gardens and may pose a health risk if you inhale the spores that are released in late summer. The best time to remove this large native fern is in late winter or early spring by cutting, digging out and burning the plants. Repeat this process again later in spring to eliminate them.

RABBITS eat vegetables, young plants and the bark from trees and shrubs, exposing them to infection. Most troublesome in rural gardens, these mammals are very difficult to control, as they tunnel under fences and walls to get to the goodies in your garden. To protect your plants, install 'rabbit fencing' at least 90cm (3ft) high and bury the lower section of wire mesh 15cm (6in) deep in the soil and sloping outwards. Also fit gates with weighted wire mesh at the base.

Focus on wildlife

Great spotted woodpecker

There are three species of woodpecker found in the British Isles, but the one you are most likely to see is the great spotted woodpecker, which comes to feast on fat balls and peanuts offered in garden feeders. This starling-sized, black, white and red bird is larger than the rare lesser spotted woodpecker, which looks similar but is only the size of a sparrow. You may also spot the green woodpecker in rural gardens. The largest of the species, it has yellow and green plumage with a red cap and a laughing cry.

The great spotted woodpecker is a colourful character, easily identified by its distinctive, black and white plumage on the back and red undertail. The males also have a red rectangle on the nape, which is absent on females. These birds have powerful beaks, which they use to make holes in tree bark, from which they extract beetles, caterpillars and spiders. In spring, they will also eat the chicks and eggs of smaller birds that nest in tree cavities.

The drumming sound heard in woodlands in spring is the male hammering against dead trees to proclaim ownership of his territory. This would cause brain damage in most birds, but woodpeckers are protected by their specially adapted, shock-absorbing skull.

Woodpeckers also use their beaks to excavate nesting holes in trees, in which the female lays between four and six eggs. She generally incubates the brood, while both parents bring food to the chicks, which fledge about three weeks after hatching. Young birds all have a red cap and, for this reason, they can be confused with lesser spotted woodpeckers, but the latter are much smaller in comparison and do not have a distinctive white mark on their shoulders. While great spotted populations are increasing, the lesser spotted woodpecker is on the red list, and numbers have fallen by 73 per cent over the last 25 years.

Spotlight on: Early spring-flowering clematis (*Clematis armandi*)

Few climbers are in bloom in March but the evergreen clematis *C. armandi* and *C. × cartmanii* help to fill the gap. *C. armandi* produces large, almond-scented, white or pink flowers on long twining stems covered with lance-shaped, dark green foliage. It will quickly climb up through a tree or cover wires on a fence or wall, but often loses its lower leaves, so plant a shrub or perennials in front to disguise the bare stems. *C. × cartmanii* is a compact form, hardy to −7°C (19°F), that bears an abundance of starry white flowers in spring. Both prefer cool roots and well-drained soil and are best planted in a sheltered spot, protected from cold winds. Prune after flowering.

CLEMATIS 'APPLE BLOSSOM'
An award-winning cultivar with richly scented, pale pink flowers and mid-green leaves that are bronze-tinged when new foliage unfurls in spring.
H x S: 5 x 3m (16 x 10ft)

CLEMATIS ARMANDI
The fragrant, star-shaped, creamy white flowers of the species are hard to beat, while the handsome new leaves that appear in spring are bronze-tinted.
H x S: 5 x 3m (16 x 10ft)

CLEMATIS × CARTMANII 'AVALANCHE'
Masses of white flowers with yellow centres open in March over evergreen foliage. This compact climber is ideal for a large pot or plant it in the ground.
H x S: 2 x 2m (6.5 x 6.5ft)

CLEMATIS 'HENDERSONII RUBRA'
This cultivar is loved for its deep pink buds that open to reveal lightly scented flowers, which appear in abundance in early spring.
H x S: 5 x 5m (16 x 16ft)

CLEMATIS ARMANDI 'SNOWDRIFT'
An abundance of pure white, slim-petalled flowers with a strong perfume appear on this elegant cultivar from March to May.
H x S: 5 x 3m (16 x 10ft)

Seasonal planting ideas

PERFECT PARTNERS

WHY IT WORKS
This simple scheme combines two classic, early-flowering plants – daffodils and hellebores – that herald the promise of spring. Both provide early season colour and thrive in part shade under deciduous trees and shrubs before they come into leaf. The hellebores flower for a long period from late winter and have the additional benefit of attracting early flying pollinators.

WHAT'S GROWING HERE?
Helleborus × hybridus is a semi-evergreen perennial, which grows to around 40cm (16in) in height. It produces divided, glossy, dark green leaves and branched stems of bowl-shaped flowers in a range of colours, including white, pink, green, yellow and purple, while some also feature spots on the inner petals. The variety and unpredictability of flower colour provides additional interest.

Narcissus 'Jack Snipe' is a popular dwarf daffodil, growing to just 20cm (8in) in height, with narrow, dark green leaves and small nodding flowers, with reflexed, creamy white petals and short, bright yellow trumpets.

WHEN TO PLANT
Plant the daffodil bulbs in autumn at a depth of two to three times the height of the bulb. Hellebores are also best planted at the same time, which will allow them to establish before flowering in early spring.

WHERE TO SEE IT
The Winter Garden at RHS Garden Rosemoor is home to this beautiful border, while similar combinations are on display at all the RHS gardens throughout March.

Horticultural heroes

Sir Joseph Banks · 1743–1820

The English scientist, botanist and explorer Sir Joseph Banks travelled the world discovering and describing the new plants he found, most of which still grace our gardens today. He sourced about 110 new genera and 1,300 new species, while some 80 species bear his name, including *Banksia integrifolia*, a tender protea from Australasia, and the beautiful pale yellow *Rosa banksiae* 'Lutea'.

Joseph Banks was born in 1743 in Lincolnshire, the son of William Banks, a wealthy landowner. He was educated at Eton College and the University of Oxford, where he studied natural history. After his father died, Banks inherited Revesby Abbey in Lincolnshire, which made him one of the richest men in England, and he used his wealth to finance plant-hunting expeditions. Aged just 23, he travelled to Newfoundland and Labrador in Canada, and in 1768 he joined the crew of HMS *Endeavour*, captained by James Cook, for a gruelling, three-year expedition to the South Pacific, visiting Brazil, Tahiti, New Zealand, Australia and Java en route. A trip to Iceland followed, and on his return he became president of the Royal Society. He also advised King George III on the expansion of the Royal Botanic Gardens, Kew, and was instrumental in making it the world's leading botanical garden with the plants he, and other botanists commissioned by him, had collected. He amassed a huge library and a herbarium at his home in Soho Square in London and was one of the founding members of the Royal Horticultural Society.

In many ways, Banks was a horticultural hero, responsible for broadening our knowledge and understanding of plants and their survival strategies. However, like many of his contemporaries, he was an outspoken supporter of slavery for much of his life, only opposing it in later years on economic grounds. He also lobbied to make Botany Bay in Australia a penal colony for British convicts.

Banks died in 1820 and left his collections and library to Robert Brown, his librarian and an eminent natural scientist. In 1827 they were transferred to the British Museum, where they remain to this day.

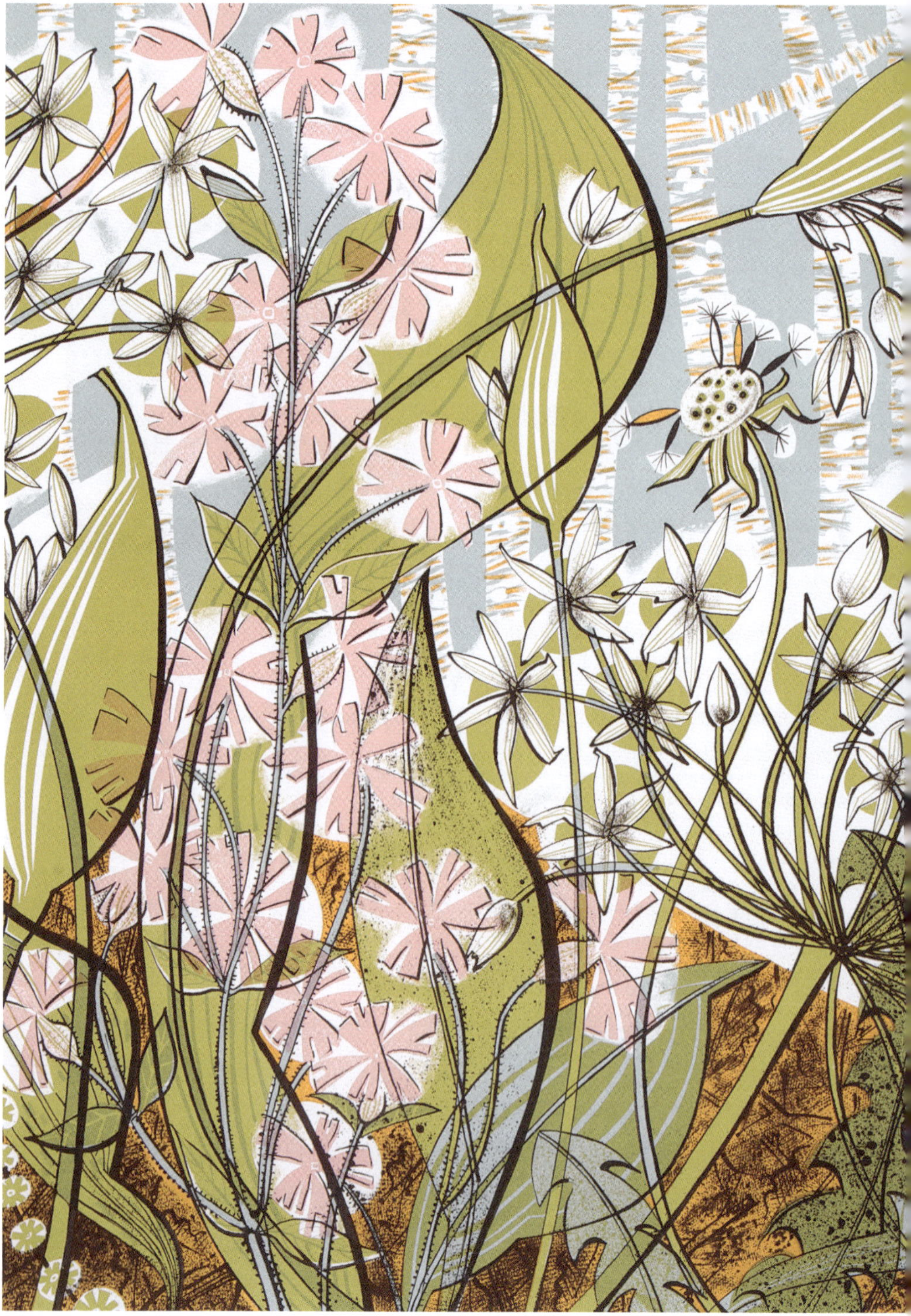

April

As temperatures rise and the days lengthen, plants appear to double in size with each passing hour, challenging the gardener to keep up. Planting and sowing fill every spare moment, but there's always time to pause and enjoy April's abundance. Jewels abound, with tulips in regal shades and magnolias' flowers set out on bare stems like vases, while birds swoop and dive in a quest to feed their young.

KEY EVENTS
Good Friday, 18 April
Easter Day, 20 April
Passover, 12–20 April
St George's Day, 23 April

What to do in April

Planting now will deliver quick results, as crops, flowers and shrubs are growing apace, energized by warm spring sunshine and high soil moisture levels. However, April can be a capricious month, with long periods of drought or weeks of torrential rain, so, depending on the conditions, you may have to water new plants regularly or pause planting altogether until drier conditions return. The timing of seed sowing outside is also affected by prevailing weather conditions, though April is usually one of the best months for establishing both crops and flowers.

In the garden

PRUNE EVERGREENS when you see new growth emerging. Trim Mediterranean shrubs such as lavender and rosemary to new shoots but avoid cutting back into lifeless older wood. Heathers (*Calluna*) also flower on new shoots and can be pruned now. Larger spring-flowering shrubs such as *Camellia* require little pruning, but you can shorten all the shoots after flowering to restrict their size. ❶

PLANT SUMMER BULBS such as gladioli in any fertile soil or a container, setting them 12cm (5in) deep and 10cm (4in) apart. Place in a sunny spot outside from mid-April, and stake taller varieties. To extend the flowering period, plant bulbs in succession every two weeks until June. Try the pink and cream 'Robinetta'; the tall red 'Vivaldi'; red-purple 'Plum Tart'; and the fiery orange-red 'Atom'. ❷

SOW BEE-FRIENDLY ANNUALS outside in a sunny bed or border, where they will bloom in late summer, after many native flowers are over. California poppy (*Eschscholzia californica*), cornflowers (*Centaurea cyanus*), cosmos, annual mallow (*Malva trimestris*), nasturtiums and single-flowered pot marigolds (*Calendula*) are all easy to grow from seed. ❸

STAKE TALL PLANTS that are vulnerable to toppling in summer storms or under the weight of their flowerheads. Insert canes or fencing pins, used for safety fences, combined with string and netting, or buy proprietary plant supports to keep the stems upright. ❹

FEED POTTED SEEDLINGS six weeks after transplanting them, when the roots can be seen through the drainage holes at the bottom. Feed initially every fortnight with an organic seaweed fertilizer, then, as the plant grows, increase to weekly doses until the pot fills with roots.

In the fruit & veg patch

PLANT MAINCROP POTATOES, the leafy stems of which will emerge after the worst of the frosts (although gardeners should be on their guard until early June). Enrich the soil with well-rotted manure and plant the tubers so they are covered by about 8cm (3in) of soil. Allow 75cm (30in) between rows and about 30cm (12in) between tubers.

APRIL / **67**

PROTECT APPLE BLOSSOM from late frosts with sacking or fleece if your trees are small enough to cover. Or, in gardens prone to spring frosts, try very late-flowering apples such as 'Mother' or 'Suntan', which should fare better.

TRY UNUSUAL BEAN/SEED CROPS such as chickpeas, lentils and soya. Sow in cell trays to plant out from mid-May. While they will deliver a good harvest after a long hot summer, if the weather is cool and wet they should still provide tasty green seeds in late summer. ❺

GLOBE ARTICHOKES are undemanding in all but the coldest parts of the UK. Sow seeds now and set out the plants about 70cm (28in) apart in a sunny bed in midsummer. Reliable cultivars include 'Imperial Star', 'Green Globe' and 'Romanesco'.

PLANT BLUEBERRIES IN POTS of peat-free, ericaceous (acidic) compost. Ideally grow at least two different varieties, since cross-pollination will increase the numbers of fruits. Try combining 'Spartan', 'Hardyblue' and 'Chandler'.

Indoors

RESUME WATERING HOUSEPLANTS regularly, now that they are in full growth again. However, take care not to overwater them, which may lead to root and stem rot. Plant them in pots with drainage holes and never allow them to sit in wet compost.

DIVIDE CONGESTED PLANTS, such as calatheas (*Goeppertia*), fiddle-leaf figs (*Ficus lyrata*) and peace lilies (*Spathiphyllum*), that produce clusters of stems from the base. Water, remove the plant from its pot, and gently pull the rootball apart or cut through it to create sections, each with leaves and roots. Replant in pots of fresh compost.

MONEY-SAVING IDEA
Grow your own pomegranates
Pomegranates (*Punica granatum*) are delicious but pricy. These self-fertile shrubs are quite easy to care for and some are hardy to −15°C (5°F). For a reliable crop in the UK, it's best to grow a dwarf variety in a pot of peat-free, loam-based compost in a greenhouse or conservatory, since plants need a long hot period for the fruits to form. Water regularly and feed annually in March with an all-purpose organic-based fertilizer and monthly from May with a high-potassium feed.

Plants of the month

1. Pulmonaria (*Pulmonaria angustifolia* 'Blaues Meer' pictured)
2. Trillium (*Trillium sessile* pictured)
3. Barronwort (*Epimedium perralderianum* pictured)
4. Flowering currant (*Ribes sanguineum* 'Brocklebankii' pictured.)
5. Californian lilac (*Ceanothus* 'Cascade' pictured)
6. Aquilegia (*Aquilegia skinneri* pictured)
7. Cowslip (*Primula veris*)
8. Euphorbia (*Euphorbia amygdaloides* var. *robbiae* pictured)
9. Snake's head fritillary (*Fritillaria meleagris*)
10. Crab apple (*Malus* 'Scarlett' pictured)
11. Bluebell (*Hyacinthoides non scripta*)

APRIL / 69

Project: Make a bath bog garden

Unless you have naturally damp conditions in your garden, it can be difficult to successfully grow moisture-loving plants, such as candelabra primulas and rodgersias. A great solution is to plant them in a large container, such as a tin bath, that's not quite watertight but retains enough moisture to keep the plants healthy – it will also help to contain vigorous plants such as the decorative horsetail *Equisetum hyemale*. Set in sun or light shade and, in summer, use water from a butt to keep the compost moist; rain in winter should keep it wet enough.

YOU WILL NEED
Tin bath – minimum size about 60 x 30 x 30cm (24 x 12 x 12in)
Screwdriver
Gravel or shingle
Aquatic compost
Selection of moisture-loving perennials

1. Make a few holes in the tin bath with a screwdriver to allow some water to flow through, then add a 10cm (4in) layer of coarse gravel to the base.

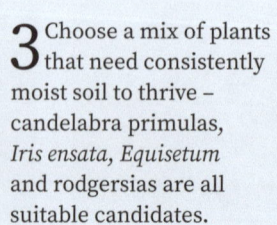

2. Top up with aquatic soil, which is specially made for water and bog plants. Fill the bath to about 10cm (4in) below the rim, to leave space for water to accumulate and drain into the compost, without spilling over the sides.

3. Choose a mix of plants that need consistently moist soil to thrive – candelabra primulas, *Iris ensata*, *Equisetum* and rodgersias are all suitable candidates.

Looking up

Sunrise and sunset

The sun is now rising high in the sky. The extra hours of light power rapid growth and the garden is sparkling with plants' bright, almost luminous, new foliage.

	LONDON		EDINBURGH	
DAY	Sunrise	Sunset	Sunrise	Sunset
Tue, Apr 1	6:33:08 am	7:35:25 pm	6:40:19 am	7:52:48 pm
Wed, Apr 2	6:30:52 am	7:37:06 pm	6:37:42 am	7:54:50 pm
Thu, Apr 3	6:28:37 am	7:38:46 pm	6:35:05 am	7:56:52 pm
Fri, Apr 4	6:26:21 am	7:40:27 pm	6:32:28 am	7:58:54 pm
Sat, Apr 5	6:24:06 am	7:42:08 pm	6:29:51 am	8:00:56 pm
Sun, Apr 6	6:21:52 am	7:43:48 pm	6:27:15 am	8:02:58 pm
Mon, Apr 7	6:19:38 am	7:45:29 pm	6:24:39 am	8:05:01 pm
Tue, Apr 8	6:17:24 am	7:47:09 pm	6:22:04 am	8:07:03 pm
Wed, Apr 9	6:15:11 am	7:48:50 pm	6:19:29 am	8:09:05 pm
Thu, Apr 10	6:12:58 am	7:50:30 pm	6:16:55 am	8:11:07 pm
Fri, Apr 11	6:10:46 am	7:52:11 pm	6:14:21 am	8:13:10 pm
Sat, Apr 12	6:08:34 am	7:53:52 pm	6:11:47 am	8:15:12 pm
Sun, Apr 13	6:06:23 am	7:55:32 pm	6:09:15 am	8:17:14 pm
Mon, Apr 14	6:04:13 am	7:57:13 pm	6:06:42 am	8:19:17 pm
Tue, Apr 15	6:02:03 am	7:58:53 pm	6:04:11 am	8:21:19 pm
Wed, Apr 16	5:59:54 am	8:00:34 pm	6:01:40 am	8:23:22 pm
Thu, Apr 17	5:57:46 am	8:02:14 pm	5:59:10 am	8:25:25 pm
Fri, Apr 18	5:55:39 am	8:03:55 pm	5:56:40 am	8:27:27 pm
Sat, Apr 19	5:53:33 am	8:05:35 pm	5:54:12 am	8:29:30 pm
Sun, Apr 20	5:51:27 am	8:07:16 pm	5:51:44 am	8:31:33 pm
Mon, Apr 21	5:49:22 am	8:08:56 pm	5:49:17 am	8:33:35 pm
Tue, Apr 22	5:47:19 am	8:10:37 pm	5:46:51 am	8:35:38 pm
Wed, Apr 23	5:45:16 am	8:12:17 pm	5:44:26 am	8:37:41 pm
Thu, Apr 24	5:43:14 am	8:13:57 pm	5:42:02 am	8:39:43 pm
Fri, Apr 25	5:41:14 am	8:15:37 pm	5:39:39 am	8:41:46 pm
Sat, Apr 26	5:39:14 am	8:17:17 pm	5:37:17 am	8:43:48 pm
Sun, Apr 27	5:37:16 am	8:18:57 pm	5:34:56 am	8:45:50 pm
Mon, Apr 28	5:35:19 am	8:20:36 pm	5:32:36 am	8:47:52 pm
Tue, Apr 29	5:33:23 am	8:22:16 pm	5:30:18 am	8:49:54 pm
Wed, Apr 30	5:31:28 am	8:23:55 pm	5:28:01 am	8:51:56 pm

Moonrise and moonset

Moon phases

◐ **THIRD QUARTER** 21 April
● **NEW MOON** 27 April

◑ **FIRST QUARTER** 5 April
○ **FULL MOON** 13 April

	LONDON			EDINBURGH		
DAY	Moonrise	Moonset	Moonrise	Moonset	Moonrise	Moonset
Apr 1	07:29			07:17		
Apr 2		00:37	07:59		01:23	07:37
Apr 3		02:02	08:43		02:57	08:14
Apr 4		03:11	09:43		04:07	09:13
Apr 5		03:59	10:57		04:50	10:32
Apr 6		04:32	12:17		05:14	12:01
Apr 7		04:54	13:36		05:28	13:29
Apr 8		05:09	14:53		05:37	14:53
Apr 9		05:22	16:07		05:44	16:12
Apr 10		05:32	17:18		05:48	17:30
Apr 11		05:41	18:29		05:53	18:46
Apr 12		05:51	19:39		05:57	20:02
Apr 13		06:01	20:51		06:02	21:20
Apr 14		06:13	22:04		06:08	22:40
Apr 15		06:29	23:18		06:17	
Apr 16		06:50		00:02	06:31	
Apr 17	00:30	07:20		01:22	06:54	
Apr 18	01:36	08:03		02:32	07:32	
Apr 19	02:30	09:00		03:25	08:30	
Apr 20	03:10	10:11		04:00	09:48	
Apr 21	03:39	11:31		04:21	11:17	
Apr 22	04:01	12:56		04:34	12:49	
Apr 23	04:17	14:21		04:43	14:23	
Apr 24	04:31	15:48		04:50	15:57	
Apr 25	04:43	17:17		04:56	17:32	
Apr 26	04:56	18:48		05:03	19:11	
Apr 27	05:11	20:23		05:10	20:55	
Apr 28	05:29	22:01		05:21	22:42	
Apr 29	05:55	23:34		05:38		
Apr 30	06:34				00:25	06:08

Average rainfall

In April, the average rainfall in the UK is 70mm (2¾in). While the picture in different areas and from year-to-year is very changeable, be prepared to water young plants during warm dry spells, and lay mulches to trap soil moisture.

LOCATION	DAYS	MM	INCHES
Aberdeen	8	38	1.5
Aberystwyth	11	63	2.5
Belfast	11	60	2.4
Birmingham	10	56	2.2
Bournemouth	10	58	2.2
Bristol	10	48	1.9
Cambridge	8	38	1.5
Canterbury	8	45	1.8
Cardiff	11	72	2.8
Edinburgh	9	41	1.6
Exeter	12	94	3.7
Glasgow	12	66	2.6
Gloucester	11	69	2.7
Inverness	10	41	1.6
Ipswich	8	35	1.4
Leeds	11	66	2.6
Liverpool	10	50	2.0
London	9	50	2.0
Manchester	12	68	2.7
Newcastle upon Tyne	8	39	1.5
Norwich	9	39	1.5
Nottingham	9	48	1.9
Oxford	9	49	1.9
Sheffield	10	59	2.3
Truro	11	66	2.6

Edible garden

While sowing and planting continue apace in April, this time of year is known as the 'hunger gap' because there are only a handful of fruit and vegetables ready to harvest in mid-spring, now that the winter crops are all over.

Vegetables

SOW INDOORS IN A SHADED GREENHOUSE Outdoor aubergines; Brussels sprouts; cabbages for summer and autumn, and for storing, including red cabbages ❶; cauliflowers; celeriac; celery; kohlrabi; leeks; outdoor peppers; tomatoes. In the second half of the month: cardoons; courgettes; cucumbers; edible flowers; French and runner beans; globe artichokes; marrows, pumpkins, summer and winter squash; sweetcorn (see p.86).

SOW OUTDOORS Artichokes; beetroots; broad beans; broccoli (calabrese); carrots; chard; leeks, lettuce; onions; parsnips; peas, including sugarsnaps and mangetout; radishes; rocket; salad crops (see p.12); spinach; spring onions; turnips.

PLANT OUT Hardy plants sown indoors in March, including asparagus, cabbages, cauliflowers, celeriac, celery, kohlrabi, and lettuces; globe and Chinese artichokes; onion sets; shallots; maincrop potatoes. ❷

HARVEST NOW Asparagus ❸; chard; kale ❹; lettuce; radishes; shrubby herbs; spinach; spring cabbages; purple and white sprouting broccoli; spring onions.

Fruit

PLANT NOW Potted fruit trees and bushes; blackberry and raspberry canes ❺; strawberry plants.

HARVEST Rhubarb.

TOP TIP
Bridging the hunger gap
With the scarcity of crops ready to be harvested in April, consider growing a few microgreens on the windowsill (see p.12), together with lettuces and radishes under a cloche or in a cold frame to provide a small harvest of fresh leaves. Also, resist the temptation to harvest all of your winter crops earlier in the year, and leave a supply of greens to pick now.

HERB OF THE MONTH: THYME
This dual-purpose, evergreen herb provides leaves for the kitchen and nectar-rich summer flowers adored by bees and other pollinators. Thyme (*Thymus*) prefers free-draining soil and a sunny site, although it will also grow in part shade. It spreads to form a leafy groundcover once established. There is a wide choice of thymes to choose from, many with hints of lemon or orange flavours, while the foliage can be green, gold or variegated. You can harvest the leaves year-round, but limit pickings in winter, when the plant is growing slowly.

APRIL / 75

Ferment recipe

RHUBARB KOMBUCHA

Kombucha is a delicious, refreshing, fizzy drink made from tea fermented with a culture of bacteria and yeast. While expensive to buy, it's very easy to make at home for a fraction of the price. You can also flavour it with fruits, such as rhubarb, and herbs.

STAGE 1: MAKING THE KOMBUCHA BREW

1. Put the teabags or loose leaf tea (in a tea infuser) in a large bowl and add the granulated sugar and boiled water. Stir well. Brew for 20–30 minutes, remove the tea and leave to cool.

2. Once the tea is cool, transfer it to the large 2.5-litre (5-pint) jar. Add the scoby (lightest side upwards) and 125ml (4 fl. oz) of starter liquid that will have been delivered with your scoby.

3. Cover the jar with the muslin cloth and leave for 7–10 days.

STAGE 2: THE SECOND FERMENTATION

4. After the kombucha has brewed, roughly chop the rhubarb and bring to the boil in a saucepan with the water and caster sugar. Simmer for 10–15 minutes until the rhubarb is soft. Strain the liquid into a container and leave to cool. Use the remaining stewed rhubarb however you fancy.

5. Pour your kombucha into the glass bottles, reserving 125ml (4 fl. oz) of the liquid as a starter for your next brew, and leaving room at the top for your rhubarb infusion.

6. Add the rhubarb infusion and seal the bottles. Leave to ferment for a second time at room temperature for 1–3 days. This is when your kombucha will get fizzy. 'Burp' your bottles daily, to avoid a build-up of gas and a kombucha explosion! You can store the bottles in the fridge for a few months, remembering to burp them now and again.

YOU WILL NEED
- 2.5-litre (5-pint) glass jar/container
- Muslin cloth and rubber band, to cover the top of the jar
- Large and small heatproof bowls/containers
- 2 x 1-litre (2-pint) swing-top glass bottles

INGREDIENTS
- A kombucha culture (or scoby). This is a starter culture of live yeast and bacteria. You can buy a scoby online to get you started
- 6–8 tea bags (or 3–4 teaspoons of loose tea with a tea infuser). Do not use fruit or herbal teas
- 170g (6oz) granulated sugar
- 2 litres (4 pints) boiled water
- 500g (1lb) rhubarb stems (leaves removed as these are poisonous)
- 2 tbsp cold water
- 100g (3oz) caster sugar

Challenges this month

Slugs and snails continue to inhabit the garden this month (see p.59), while aphids also start to feed on young plants and buds, so keep your eyes peeled for damage. The soil is too cold for many fungal diseases, but take action to prevent clubroot now.

CLUBROOT is a fungal disease that affects the roots of brassicas such as Brussels sprouts, cabbages, swedes, turnips and cauliflowers. It causes the roots to become swollen and distorted, resulting in stunted growth. Try resistant cultivars of affected crops, especially on allotments, where this disease can be very prevalent. Alkaline soils inhibit clubroot and adding a handful of garden lime (wear protective gloves) in each planting hole can help to supress it. Crop rotation, allowing at least two years between cabbage family crops, is also helpful.

JAPANESE KNOTWEED (*Reynoutria japonica*) is a rampant perennial with spreading roots, bamboo-like stems and large, heart shaped leaves. It will quickly overcome a garden and may affect your property price and saleability, since mortgage lenders could withhold funds if it is found. It is also illegal to allow the plant to spread into wild areas or neighbouring gardens. Look out for young plants and act immediately, treating them with weedkiller, or hire a qualified professional company, who can offer insurance-backed guarantees of efficacy. You will need permission from Natural England or the Environment Agency to treat it with chemicals in sites of special scientific interest or if plants are by water. If digging out Japanese knotweed, take it to a recycling facility that holds a permit for this plant or burn *in situ*. For more guidance, visit rhs.org.uk/weeds/japanese-knotweed/.

APHIDS feed on lush young growth, sucking the sap from foliage, which causes distortion and can spread plant viruses. They also excrete sticky honeydew on which harmless, black, sooty moulds grow. In spring, spray with a hose to remove them. Aphids' natural enemies include ladybirds, and lacewing and hoverfly larvae, which keep them in check in summer. Parasitic microwasps such as *Aphidius* and *Aphelinus*, whose larvae eat aphids, and native, two-spot ladybirds and their larvae are available online for use in greenhouses.

Focus on wildlife

Newt

There are three species of newt native to the UK: the rare great crested newt, the palmate newt and the smooth newt, which is the most common type found in our gardens.

The great crested newt is the largest of the species, and can reach up to 17cm (7in) in length. It is almost black with white spots and has a bright orange belly. The male also sports a wavy crest along its body and tail to lure a female during the breeding season. The smooth newt (pictured) is grey-brown, with an orange belly, and black spots all over its body. It grows to about 10cm (4in) in length, and the male has a smooth crest running along the length of its body and tail during the breeding season. The smaller palmate newt looks very similar to the smooth newt, but has a peachy yellow belly, marked with a few spots on it. During the breeding season, the male develops distinctive black webbing on its hind feet.

Many garden ponds provide homes for newts, and recent studies suggest that they are now an important stronghold for these amphibians, helping to sustain them following the decline of rural wetlands. All three species breed in late spring and then spend the summer and autumn on land in woodlands, hedgerows, boggy areas and grasslands. In winter, they find cover underground among tree roots, under logs and in cracks in old walls, but will come out on warmer days to forage.

During the breeding season, both males and females take to the water, where the female lays individual eggs, which she wraps in pond plant leaves. These hatch into larvae, known as newt tadpoles, which then develop into juveniles (efts) that leave the pond, together with the adults, in summer.

Adults and juveniles eat frogspawn and tadpoles, small fish and other water invertebrates. They also feast on insects, caterpillars and slugs when they move from the water to land, and are therefore useful in protecting crops and ornamental plants in the garden.

Spotlight on: Spring-flowering anemones (*Anemone*)

Decorating gardens with their saucer- or star-shaped blooms and divided or ferny foliage, anemones can be grown in most sheltered gardens. The UK native wood anemone (*A. nemorosa*) likes cool dappled shade, as its name suggests, but the more flamboyant Mediterranean types such as *A. coronaria* are sun-lovers, while the diminutive *A. blanda* will grow in sun or part shade. All anemones prefer well-drained soils, and the Mediterranean species may also need some winter protection in harsh or wet winters and in cold areas of the country. Buy the dry rhizomes or tubers in autumn and soak them in water overnight before planting to encourage shoots to form. Try the sun-lovers in pots that can be moved to a protected site if need be.

ANEMONE APENNINA
This little plant produces nodding, deep blue, star-shaped flowers over divided ferny foliage, and flowers for many weeks from March to May.
H x S: 20 x 15cm (8 x 6in)

ANEMONE NEMOROSA
The wood anemone creates a carpet of elegant, white, saucer-shaped flowers in March and April above deeply cut leaves. *A.n.* 'Allenii' has clear, pale lavender-blue petals tinged pink on the reverse.
H x S: 15 x 15cm (6 x 6in)

ANEMONE CORONARIA DE CAEN GROUP
The florist's anemone is hard to resist, with its bright jewel-coloured blooms in shades of purple, red, cerise and white, which appear on tall stems over divided foliage in March and April.
H x S: 25 x 20cm (10 x 8in)

ANEMONE BLANDA
Plant this diminutive anemone at the edges of trees and shrubs or the front of a sunny border to form a colourful carpet of violet-blue, pink or white, daisy-like flowers and divided foliage. The inexpensive tubers can be planted *en masse* for year-on-year sustainable colour.
H x S: 15 x 10cm (6 x 4in)

Seasonal planting ideas

POTS OF COLOURFUL TULIPS

WHY IT WORKS
Few plants signify spring more than tulips, and the cultivars in this combination are no exception. Their flowers open to form a classic goblet shape, reflecting the outline of their terracotta pots, while the different colours and petal edges make an eye-catching display. The arrangement of pots also accentuates the colour contrasts, from dark red on either side to pink in the middle, with a pop of white on one side. For personal wellbeing, this scheme provides a stunning addition to a spring patio, deck or step by the front door, helping you to celebrate spring and offering the promise of warmer weather to come.

WHAT'S GROWING HERE
These tulips grow to around 45–50cm (18–20in) in height and flower in April and May.

Tulipa 'Jan Reus' produces glaucous, lance-shaped leaves and dark crimson flowers, while the pink petals of 'Fancy Frills' have frilly edges and fade to paler pink then white at the base. 'Purissima' has similar foliage to 'Jan Reus', the golden base of its clear white flowers creating a torch-like effect – it is also long-flowering and may bloom in March in warm years. The pinkish-purple tulip at the back is 'Passionale', which sports a deep purple flame on each of the petals.

WHEN TO PLANT
Tulips are best planted in October or November. Space the bulbs more closely in pots than you would in the ground, perhaps only 2.5cm (1in) apart, to give a fuller flowering effect the following spring. Fill the pots with a free-draining mix of three parts peat-free compost to one part grit, and plant your tulips at a depth of three times the dry bulbs' height. Once flowering has finished, consider moving the containers out of view and allow the plants to die back naturally before replanting them in your borders in autumn.

WHERE TO SEE IT
This combination was snapped in the Cottage Garden at RHS Garden Rosemoor in Devon, where you can enjoy a wealth of spring bulbs throughout the gardens from late January to May.

Horticultural heroes

Wangarĩ Muta Maathai · 1940–2011

Scientist, environmentalist and Nobel Prize winner Wangarĩ Muta Maathai was the founder of The Green Belt Movement, which encouraged women to plant trees to help mitigate the effects of deforestation in her Kenyan homeland and throughout Africa.

Born in the village of Ihithe in Kenya in 1940, in her twenties Maathai became one of the first Kenyans selected to study in the United States under a scholarship scheme set up by John F. Kennedy. After gaining a degree and masters in Biological Sciences, she returned to her homeland, where she became the first woman to earn a PhD from the University of Nairobi.

Maathai joined the National Council of Women of Kenya in 1976 and was its chair from 1981 to 1987. During that time, she introduced the idea of planting trees with women's groups to help conserve the environment and improve their quality of life, establishing The Green Belt Movement in Kenya and, later, throughout Africa. Through the scheme, Maathai assisted women in planting more than 20 million trees, and in 2004, she was the first black woman to receive the Nobel Peace Prize.

Her campaigns against land-grabbing and support for women's rights often brought her into conflict with the Kenyan government, and she was arrested on many occasions. However, in 2002, after running for Parliament as the candidate for the National Rainbow Coalition and winning with 98 per cent of the vote, she was appointed Assistant Minister in the Ministry for Environment and Natural Resources for President Mwai Kibaki's government – a post she held until November 2005.

A formidable force for good, Maathai's campaigns have shaped environmental policies in Africa and helped to improve the lives of women. Her legacy lives on today, and The Green Belt Movement continues to work at grassroots, national and international levels to promote environmental conservation, build climate resilience and empower people, especially women and girls, while helping to foster sustainable livelihoods.

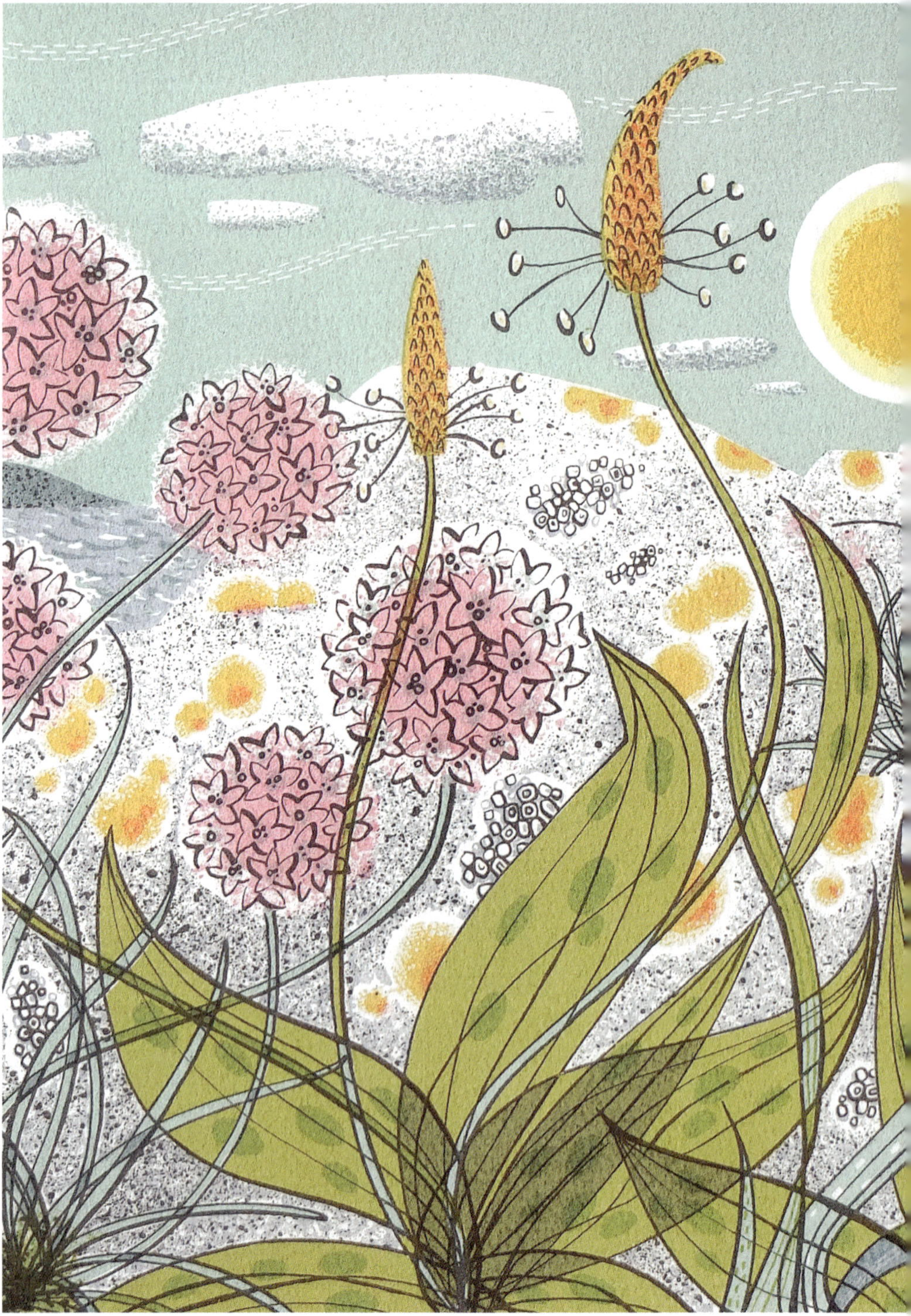

May

Long warm days stretch before us as spring moves into summer, and the sun, rising to a chorus of birdsong, transforms the morning sky into ribbons of pink and gold. A month of feasts and festivals, May is a time to celebrate all that nature has to offer, while gardeners are busy sowing and planting, preparing rich bounties to enjoy in the months that follow.

KEY EVENTS
May Day Bank Holiday, 5 May
RHS Chelsea Flower Show, 20–24 May
Spring Bank Holiday, 26 May
Ascension Day, 29 May

What to do in May

The soil in May is warm and primed for seeds to germinate. All new and young plants, including trees, shrubs and perennials, as well as crops in the fruit and vegetable garden, will need watering regularly during dry periods. Also continue to weed beds and borders and deadhead spring bulbs, such as tulips and camassias, and spring bedding plants after the flowers fade. When the frosts have passed at the end of the month, plant out tender annuals and crops after hardening them off first (see below).

In the garden

COVER SPARE GROUND with plants to prevent weed growth in the gaps. Start by hoeing off any weeds and sow closely spaced rows of hardy annuals such as love-in-a-mist (*Nigella*), pot marigolds (*Calendula*) and nasturtiums (*Tropaeolum majus*). Or use the space for perennials.

ACCLIMATIZE SEEDLINGS to outdoor temperatures a couple of weeks before the last frosts. Known as 'hardening off', simply move seedlings and young plants grown indoors out into the garden by day, bringing them back inside at night, until all risk of frost has passed. Alternatively, leave them outside covered with a double layer of horticultural fleece in the first week, and a single layer during the second. ❶

PLANT WILD FLOWERS to offer a feast for pollinators and support insect larvae. Sow seeds of annuals such as cornflower, common poppy, corn marigold and corncockle in gaps in borders, or insert young plug plants into meadow grass. Perennial wild flowers are often more successful on poor soil, where competition from grasses is not as great, so remove the topsoil or turf before sowing or planting (see also pp.54–5). ❷

ENCOURAGE TULIPS TO FLOWER next year by removing the seedpods and allowing the foliage to die back naturally to feed the bulbs. Then lift and dry the bulbs in a warm shed and replant in autumn in quiet sunny areas where they will flower again, albeit not as profusely as in their first season. ❸

PLANT OUT SUMMER BEDDING and bulbs such as begonias at the end of the month, after the frosts. Remove spent winter flowers from containers, planting any primulas temporarily in a spare corner to reuse the following autumn. To save money, mix the old potting compost with equal proportions of fresh material and add snapdragons (*Antirrhinum*), *Bacopa*, *Calibrachoa*, petunias, verbena and zinnias in sunny spots; begonias, busy Lizzies (*Impatiens*) and *Calceolaria* in part shade; and drought-tolerant gazanias, osteospermums and pelargoniums in hot spots and hanging baskets. ❹

TRY THE CHELSEA CHOP to prevent perennials such as asters, heleniums and sedums from flopping in late summer. Shorten all the stems by about half, or remove one in three stems, to increase the length of the flowering display – the severed stems will regrow and flower later. ❺

In the fruit & veg patch

MAKE THE MOST OF YOUR SPACE by 'intercropping' – sowing speedy herbs, salads leaves, spring onions, beetroots and radishes in between rows of slow-growing vegetables such as Brussels sprouts, peas and beans. These small crops can be harvested before the larger crops shade them out.

SOW RUNNER BEANS *in situ* when the soil is warm and moist but not waterlogged. Erect wigwams or lines of canes, allowing 30cm (12in) between each cane, and sow a couple of beans next to each one. ❻

SOW TWO SWEETCORN seeds in biodegradable paper pots and keep in a warm bright place until they germinate, then remove the weakest seedling. Once roots penetrate the sides of the pots, plant out into fertile soil in a sunny spot in a square formation to aid wind pollination, rather than in long rows. Allow 40cm (16in) between plants and 50cm (20in) between rows.

MULCH STRAWBERRIES with straw after the frosts have passed. Bare soil retains warmth and can release it at night early in the month to protect the flowers, while the straw keeps soil from splashing onto and spoiling the fruits.

SOW BUTTERNUT SQUASHES in early May. Sow one seed per 9cm (3½in) pot and set indoors on a warm windowsill. Plant out in June in fertile soil and full sun, allowing about 1m (3ft) between plants. Recommended varieties include 'Harrier' and 'Hawk'.

Indoors

REPOT HOUSEPLANTS if growth is poor and the roots are congested. Water well, before repotting into a container one size larger than the original. Only succulents can withstand sunny, south-facing windows now, so give other plants some shade.

RESUME FEEDING your houseplants. Most need a dose of houseplant fertilizer about once a fortnight, but visit the RHS website for specific plants' needs.

MONEY-SAVING IDEA
Make biodegradable pots
With seed sowing well underway, a cost-effective way of raising your plants is in recycled toilet roll tubes. Make four 2cm (¾in) cuts up the sides, to create four flaps. Fold them in on each other and tuck the ends under, to create the base. Then fill with seed compost. The cardboard will keep the compost moist and when the seedlings are ready to plant out you can pop the whole tube in the ground or in pots, where it will biodegrade as the roots grow out into the surrounding soil or compost.

Plants of the month

1. Scented-leaved pelargonium (*Pelargonium* 'Lady Plymouth' pictured)
2. Allium (*Allium hollandicum* 'Purple Sensation' pictured)
3. Tulips (*Tulipa* 'Pretty Princess' pictured)
4. Osteospermum (*Osteospermum* 'Lady Leitrim' pictured)
5. *Wisteria* (*Wisteria floribunda* 'Yae-kokuryu' pictured)
6. Diascia (*Diascia* LITTLE TANGO pictured)
7. Lily of the valley (*Convallaria majalis*)
8. Bearded iris (*Iris* 'Benton Lorna' pictured)
9. Rhododendron (*Rhododendron* 'Cool Haven' pictured)
10. Camassia (*Camassia leichtlinii* subsp. *suksdorfii* Caerulea Group pictured)
11. Mexican fleabane (*Erigeron karvinskianus*)

Project: Make a flavour station

Planting up a few pots of herbs to set by the kitchen door will provide you with fresh leaves to hand throughout the year. Most herbs require a sunny spot, but a few, including mint, chives, parsley and oregano, also do well in part shade. Choose a range of hardy herbs that will sail through winter, together with annuals such as basil and coriander. Herb pots with holes in the sides look attractive but need careful watering to ensure moisture reaches all the plants. Pot up mint in its own container to prevent it swamping its neighbours.

YOU WILL NEED
Selection of pots with drainage holes in the bottom
Peat-free John Innes No. 2 compost
Horticultural grit
Selection of herbs

1 Fill each pot with a 2:1 mix of potting compost and horticultural grit, up to about 5cm (2in) from the rim.

2 Plant each herb in its own pot or include two or three with similar needs in a larger one. Plant at the same depth as in the original pots, and leave a gap between the top of the compost and the rim for water to collect when irrigating.

3 Add a layer of horticultural grit on top of the compost, to help lock in moisture and prevent the lower leaves of the herbs sitting on wet soil and rotting.

CARE TIPS
- Take only a few leaves from each plant at any one time, and harvest evergreens sparingly in winter, when they are semi-dormant.
- If your herbs start to lose their vigour, either repot them into larger containers of fresh compost or transfer them into the garden (keep mint in a pot).
- You can also divide vigorous herbs with roots that have filled their pots, in early spring.

Looking up

Sunrise and sunset

Strong sun and long hours of daylight help to warm the soil, but clear nights can still bring late frosts, although in most parts of the UK these are rare by the end of May.

	LONDON		EDINBURGH	
DAY	Sunrise	Sunset	Sunrise	Sunset
Thu, May 1	5:29:35 am	8:25:34 pm	5:25:45 am	8:53:57 pm
Fri, May 2	5:27:43 am	8:27:12 pm	5:23:31 am	8:55:58 pm
Sat, May 3	5:25:53 am	8:28:50 pm	5:21:17 am	8:57:59 pm
Sun, May 4	5:24:04 am	8:30:28 pm	5:19:06 am	9:00:00 pm
Mon, May 5	5:22:16 am	8:32:06 pm	5:16:56 am	9:02:00 pm
Tue, May 6	5:20:30 am	8:33:43 pm	5:14:47 am	9:03:59 pm
Wed, May 7	5:18:46 am	8:35:19 pm	5:12:41 am	9:05:58 pm
Thu, May 8	5:17:03 am	8:36:55 pm	5:10:36 am	9:07:57 pm
Fri, May 9	5:15:22 am	8:38:31 pm	5:08:32 am	9:09:54 pm
Sat, May 10	5:13:43 am	8:40:05 pm	5:06:31 am	9:11:52 pm
Sun, May 11	5:12:06 am	8:41:40 pm	5:04:31 am	9:13:48 pm
Mon, May 12	5:10:30 am	8:43:13 pm	5:02:33 am	9:15:44 pm
Tue, May 13	5:08:56 am	8:44:46 pm	5:00:38 am	9:17:38 pm
Wed, May 14	5:07:25 am	8:46:18 pm	4:58:44 am	9:19:32 pm
Thu, May 15	5:05:55 am	8:47:49 pm	4:56:53 am	9:21:25 pm
Fri, May 16	5:04:28 am	8:49:19 pm	4:55:03 am	9:23:17 pm
Sat, May 17	5:03:02 am	8:50:48 pm	4:53:17 am	9:25:07 pm
Sun, May 18	5:01:39 am	8:52:16 pm	4:51:32 am	9:26:56 pm
Mon, May 19	5:00:18 am	8:53:43 pm	4:49:50 am	9:28:44 pm
Tue, May 20	4:58:59 am	8:55:08 pm	4:48:10 am	9:30:31 pm
Wed, May 21	4:57:42 am	8:56:33 pm	4:46:33 am	9:32:16 pm
Thu, May 22	4:56:28 am	8:57:56 pm	4:44:59 am	9:33:59 pm
Fri, May 23	4:55:16 am	8:59:18 pm	4:43:27 am	9:35:41 pm
Sat, May 24	4:54:07 am	9:00:38 pm	4:41:58 am	9:37:21 pm
Sun, May 25	4:53:00 am	9:01:57 pm	4:40:32 am	9:38:59 pm
Mon, May 26	4:51:56 am	9:03:15 pm	4:39:09 am	9:40:36 pm
Tue, May 27	4:50:54 am	9:04:30 pm	4:37:49 am	9:42:10 pm
Wed, May 28	4:49:55 am	9:05:44 pm	4:36:32 am	9:43:42 pm
Thu, May 29	4:48:59 am	9:06:56 pm	4:35:18 am	9:45:11 pm
Fri, May 30	4:48:05 am	9:08:06 pm	4:34:07 am	9:46:39 pm
Sat, May 31	4:47:14 am	9:09:15 pm	4:33:00 am	9:48:04 pm

Moonrise and moonset

Moon phases

◑ **THIRD QUARTER** 20 May
● **NEW MOON** 27 May
◐ **FIRST QUARTER** 4 May
○ **FULL MOON** 12 May

DAY	LONDON Moonrise	LONDON Moonset	LONDON Moonrise	EDINBURGH Moonrise	EDINBURGH Moonset	EDINBURGH Moonrise
May 1		00:54	07:28		01:50	06:58
May 2		01:53	08:40		02:46	08:13
May 3		02:32	10:01		03:17	09:42
May 4		02:58	11:23		03:35	11:12
May 5		03:16	12:42		03:46	12:39
May 6		03:30	13:57		03:53	14:00
May 7		03:41	15:09		03:59	15:18
May 8		03:50	16:19		04:03	16:34
May 9		04:00	17:29		04:07	17:50
May 10		04:10	18:40		04:12	19:07
May 11		04:21	19:53		04:18	20:26
May 12		04:36	21:07		04:26	21:48
May 13		04:56	22:20		04:39	23:08
May 14		05:23	23:28		04:59	
May 15		06:02		00:22	05:32	
May 16	00:25	06:55		01:21	06:24	
May 17	01:09	08:01		02:01	07:36	
May 18	01:42	09:18		02:25	09:01	
May 19	02:05	10:39		02:41	10:30	
May 20	02:22	12:02		02:51	12:01	
May 21	02:36	13:25		02:58	13:31	
May 22	02:49	14:49		03:05	15:02	
May 23	03:01	16:16		03:11	16:36	
May 24	03:14	17:47		03:17	18:14	
May 25	03:31	19:22		03:27	19:58	
May 26	03:52	20:58		03:40	21:44	
May 27	04:24	22:26		04:03	23:20	
May 28	05:11	23:37		04:42		
May 29	06:17				00:32	05:48
May 30		00:26	07:37		01:15	07:14
May 31		00:58	09:01		01:38	08:48

90 / MAY

Average rainfall

The average rainfall in the UK in May is 91mm (3½in). However, precipitation can be very variable this month, with drought one year, followed by torrential downpours the next. Climate change is also making the weather more difficult to predict.

LOCATION	DAYS	MM	INCHES
Aberdeen	10	54	2.1
Aberystwyth	10	62	2.4
Belfast	11	60	2.4
Birmingham	10	61	2.4
Bournemouth	8	49	1.9
Bristol	10	58	2.3
Cambridge	7	43	1.7
Canterbury	8	50	2.0
Cardiff	11	78	3.0
Edinburgh	10	48	1.9
Exeter	10	80	3.1
Glasgow	12	69	2.7
Gloucester	11	65	2.6
Inverness	11	56	2.2
Ipswich	7	39	1.5
Leeds	11	64	2.5
Liverpool	10	52	2.0
London	9	51	2.0
Manchester	11	66	2.6
Newcastle upon Tyne	9	41	1.6
Norwich	8	47	1.9
Nottingham	9	50	2.0
Oxford	10	57	2.2
Sheffield	9	54	2.1
Truro	10	58	2.3

Natural plant protection

You may not be aware that an invisible army of tiny creatures, together with beneficial fungi and bacteria, are continuously working in the garden on your behalf to protect your plants by helping to keep other organisms or insect populations in balance.

To maintain this natural system, it is important to refrain from using insecticides and fungicides, which may offer relief from unwanted insects and diseases in the short term, but can also undermine your battalion of helpers, which do the job with no ill effects to the environment.

WHO'S ON YOUR TEAM?
Many beneficial organisms are microscopic but sharp-eyed gardeners may see adult ladybirds and their larvae (pictured), and the larvae of both lacewings and hoverflies, munching on aphids, or sickly caterpillars that have fallen prey to tiny parasitoid wasps. Birds are your friends, too, adeptly picking off caterpillars to feed to their young in spring, while ground beetles and spiders also prey on insects that can damage plants. Perhaps surprisingly, tiny money spiders are particularly useful, snaring aphids, small flies and springtails in their sticky webs and attacking them with venomous fangs. Bats are often overlooked but they play an important role, eating nocturnal insects such as codling moths (see p.173).

Ladybird larvae, which look quite unlike the adults, are friendly bugs that feast on aphids.

MAKE A HOME FOR PREDATORS
To encourage these beneficial organisms and enhance their effectiveness, try mimicking the natural environments

where they have evolved to thrive. Try companion planting, mixing plants prone to aphids, such as roses, with nectar-rich flowering perennials visited by hoverflies and lacewings (look out for the Plants for Pollinators logo on plant labels). Another idea is to plant clover between your crops, the flowers of which attract insect predators. Providing a refuge such as a log pile for ground beetles, and mulching rather than digging, which disrupts natural communities of soil-dwelling organisms, are other good strategies.

As well as enhancing biodiversity in beds and borders, the wider gardenscape has an important effect, too. Ideally, include some native trees and shrubs, together with areas of longer grass, and tolerate a few patches of nettles and other so-called weeds. These interventions help to increase populations of natural predators, parasitoids and beneficial pathogens that prevent unwanted organisms. Also avoid leaving large areas of soil unplanted for long periods, which will encourage competitive plants to take hold. Sow a cover crop (see p.170) or tolerate plants such as dandelions and herb robert between ornamental plants to support beneficial creatures.

Encourage hoverflies with pollen-rich plants, as the larvae of some species help to keep aphid populations in check.

BUYING IN HELP

Many natural predators can be released into greenhouses to control unwanted aphids, red spider mite and whitefly, and, if introduced early enough, they can give full control. You can buy a range of biological controls from specialist online suppliers. Outdoors, the value of beneficial organisms is dependent on environmental factors such as the weather conditions, and the numbers of unwanted and helpful organisms visiting the garden at any one time. While this makes natural controls rather unpredictable, they are often highly effective, and it's usually best to wait and see how problems resolve themselves before reaching for artificial methods. More often than not, natural controls kick in before significant harm is done.

Edible garden

Fast-growing crops such as lettuces, radishes and spring onions are ready to harvest in May, together with some crops sown last year. The first of the strawberries also offer a sweet treat now, with others to follow in the summer months ahead.

Vegetables

SOW INDOORS Butternut squash (see p.86); calabrese; courgettes; cucumbers; marrows, pumpkins, summer and winter squash; peppers; sprouting broccoli; sweetcorn (see p.86).

SOW OUTDOORS Artichokes; beetroots; broad beans; broccoli; calabrese; carrots; Florence fennel; French beans; lettuce; parsnips; peas; radishes; rocket; runner beans; salad crops; spinach; spring onions; turnips; winter crops such as late winter cabbages and savoys, cauliflowers and sprouting broccoli.

PLANT OUT Hardy plants sown indoors in March, including Brussels sprouts, cabbages ❷, cauliflowers, celeriac, celery, kohlrabi, lettuces; maincrop potatoes. After the last frosts from mid-May or crops grown under cloches: courgettes; marrows, pumpkins, summer and winter squash; outdoor cucumbers; outdoor tomatoes ❶; sweetcorn.

HARVEST NOW Chard; lettuce; radishes ❸; spring cabbages; spring cauliflowers; spring onions; shrubby herbs; spinach; turnips.

> **TOP TIP**
> **Growing a Mediterranean feast**
> While some tender veg will grow happily outside after the frosts have passed, providing a warmer greenhouse environment for tomatoes, peppers and aubergines often results in an earlier and heavier crop. If you don't have space for a greenhouse, consider a small, wall-mounted growing structure – models of different sizes are available online.

HERB OF THE MONTH: GREEK BASIL
Regular basil can be a little tricky to grow as it needs ample light and warmth, but this bushy variety (*Ocimum minimum*), with its smaller and slightly sweeter leaves, is generally less demanding. Sow seed indoors from March to June on a windowsill or in a heated greenhouse, or buy a few young plants. Once the seedlings have some leaves, transplant each to a small pot to grow on, then move to a larger container or plant outside in a bed after the frosts have passed. Keep plants just moist and avoid watering the leaves. You can extend the harvesting period by growing three or four plants, picking a few leaves from one, then leaving it to recover while you harvest another.

Fruit

PLANT NOW Potted fruit trees and bushes such as blueberries and blackberries; long cane raspberries to crop later this year; 60-day strawberry plants for later summer strawberries.

HARVEST Rhubarb; first early strawberries in late May.

Ferment recipe

FENNEL, ASPARAGUS AND ORANGE PICKLE

This pickle is based on the delicious flavours of fennel, asparagus and orange salad, and works really well as a ferment – you can still taste all the flavours, but with a tangy edge. Asparagus is delicious eaten fresh, so you may find it difficult to save any for preserving, but at least this way you can enjoy it for longer.

INGREDIENTS
400g (14oz) Florence fennel bulbs (about 2 bulbs)
800g (1lb 12oz) cabbage (about one head)
300g (10½oz) asparagus spears
2 tbsp salt
1 orange (juice and zest)

1. Slice the Florence fennel and cabbage very finely. A mandolin is the quickest and easiest way to do this.

2. Slice the asparagus spears into small chunks.

3. Rub the salt into the sliced vegetables thoroughly until they are glistening with moisture.

4. Stir in the orange juice and zest.

5. Pack all the ingredients tightly into kilner jars with a tamper. Submerge the ingredients under the brine with a glass weight and seal with an airlock (see page 58).

6. Leave to ferment at room temperature for 5–7 days or until you are happy with the sourness of the flavour.

7. Remove the airlock, seal with the jar lid and store in a cool place. It will keep in the fridge for at least three months.

Challenges this month

Continue to inspect plants for slugs, snails and aphids, removing them by hand wherever possible. This month, be on the look out for beetles, a few of which can be harmful, and keep an eye on the weather forecasts for late frosts.

ALGAE in ponds turns them green and reduces the oxygen in the water, which can harm pondlife. It starts to spread as temperatures warm up in May, but small amounts can be beneficial, providing shelter and hiding places for aquatic creatures, so do not worry too much about it unless it is creating a large, impenetrable mat. Placing barley or lavender straw in a net into a pond in March often helps to prevents algae, while growing more floating plants such as waterlilies can help to shade it out. Preventing any garden organic matter or fertilizer from getting into the pond will also help to keep algae under control.

LATE FROSTS can affect the top growth of potato plants, and while it seldom kills the tubers – the plants regrow from underground stems – the size of the crop may be lower than usual. Dahlias also regrow when damaged by a light frost, which acts like 'pinching' out the shoot tips, promoting bushier growth and more flowers. However, cucumbers, courgettes, petunias and other tender plants will probably have to be replaced, so keep an eye on the weather forecast and cover susceptible plants with newspaper, cloches or a double layer of fleece at night during early and mid-May.

BEETLES are appearing in gardens now. Little black pollen beetles that feed on flowers do no significant harm. Pea and bean weevils nibble leaves but, again, have little effect on growth or crop size. However, scarlet lily beetles will cause damage and, unless they are removed quickly, these beetles can spoil lilies.

Colourful orange, black and white asparagus beetles lay eggs on new spears, but these can be rubbed off before cooking, while viburnum beetle larvae eat holes in the leaves in spring and can be removed by hand, or left for birds and ground beetles to keep them in check. Plants usually recover from this damage as the year progresses.

Focus on wildlife

Ladybird

There are more than 3,000 different species of ladybird worldwide, over 40 of which are found in the UK. They are members of the beetle family, and most have red wing-cases decorated with black spots, although there are also native yellow, orange, beige and black species, each with a different number of spots. A newcomer to our shores is the harlequin ladybird, which has more than 100 different colour patterns. Slightly larger than natives, research is ongoing as to the threat, if any, this interloper poses to indigenous species.

The most common ladybirds found in our gardens are the seven-spot and two-spot red species, which you will see feasting on aphids and scale insects on your plants. Others also eat aphids, helping to keep their populations in check, while a few feed on mildews, and the 24-spot species eats plants, but none of them cause any problems in the garden.

Ladybirds ward off predators with their bright colours and by squirting out a yellow toxic substance called 'reflex blood' that has a foul smell.

Adult ladybirds sometimes overwinter in large groups in sheltered areas such as in leaf litter, grass tussocks, bark crevices and buildings, emerging in spring to mate and lay batches of up to 40 eggs. These then hatch into larvae that look quite unlike the adults, with their bullet-shaped, black, grey or yellow bodies, some marked with orange spots or patterns (see p.92). The larvae also eat aphids, so check online to see what they look like, and take care not to harm them. Each larva goes on to develop into a pupae before emerging as an adult in mid- or late summer.

The best way to encourage these gardeners' friends is to avoid using pesticides, and to leave plant stems uncut over winter, to act as shelter for the adults.

Spotlight on: Viburnum (*Viburnum*)

These useful shrubs include evergreens and deciduous plants, with some towering types growing to the size of small trees and others offering excellent groundcover. Many have wonderfully fragrant flowers, too, and a few, including *V. tinus* and *V. × bodnantense*, bloom through winter and offer sustenance to pollinators flying at this time of year. Some viburnums also produce colourful fruits in autumn, loved by birds and other wildlife. Grow these shrubs in sun or part shade on reasonably fertile, moist but free-draining soil, and plant more than one for cross-pollination to guarantee autumn fruits. Choose from these award-winners and combine a few to decorate your garden all year round.

VIBURNUM PLICATUM F. TOMENTOSUM 'MARIESII'
The tiered branches of this deciduous form are decorated in May with white lacecap flowers set off by deeply veined, dark green leaves that turn red-purple in autumn.
H x S: 3 x 4m (10 x 13ft)

VIBURNUM CARLESII 'AURORA'
This deciduous viburnum produces pinky red flower buds that open to reveal highly fragrant, pale pink flowers in April and May. The green leaves also offer good autumn colour.
H x S: 2 x 2m (6 x 6ft)

VIBURNUM × BODNANTENSE 'DAWN'
Dense clusters of fragrant, dark pink flowers appear on the bare stems of this deciduous shrub from November to March. The dark green leaves turn bronze in autumn.
H x S: 3 x 2m (10 x 6ft)

VIBURNUM OPULUS 'COMPACTUM'
The compact guelder rose produces flat heads of lacecap, creamy white flowers in spring, followed in autumn by bright red berries, loved by birds. The green leaves also turn red in autumn.
H x S: 1.5 x 1.5m (5 x 5ft)

VIBURNUM DAVIDII
This evergreen shrub forms a dome of veined, dark green leaves and is grown more for its metallic turquoise-blue autumn fruits than its white spring flowers. Plant two shrubs in autumn to ensure one is a female, fruit-bearing form. It also prefers slightly acid soil.
H x S: 1 x 1m (3 x 3ft)

MAY / 99

Seasonal planting ideas

SPRING SYMPHONY

WHY IT WORKS
Fresh spring foliage alongside sweetly fragrant lily of the valley (*Convallaria*) flowers appeal to the senses in this stunning combination. The reddish-brown *Rodgersia* stems and leaves are at their most vivid at this time of year, and the rich colour is picked up in the midribs (known as rachis) of the male fern (*Dryopteris*), with a carpet of white bells set against blue-green leaves filling the space below. This scheme will enliven a slightly shaded border with moisture-retentive soil, and the interest extends into summer, when the *Rodgersia* flowers open.

WHAT'S GROWING HERE?
Rodgersia pinnata 'Chocolate Wing' is a clump-forming herbaceous perennial, with distinctive palmate leaves that emerge purplish-bronze and turn green as they mature. Reddish-brown stems hold pale pink plumes of star-shaped flowers from June to August, when they reach a height of around 1m (3ft).

Dryopteris affinis, known as the scaly male fern, is a robust semi-evergreen that forms a rosette of erect fronds, 1.2m (4ft) in length. The leafy fronds are bright yellow-green when they unfurl in spring and later turn a darker rich green, with dense reddish-brown scales on the stems.

Convallaria majalis, better known as lily of the valley, is a bulbous perennial, about 25cm (10in) in height, that forms spreading colonies of paired elliptical leaves that set off the classic bell-shaped, fragrant white flowers in late spring.

WHEN TO PLANT
This combination can be planted in autumn or early spring. Try to avoid planting in summer, when warmer, drier conditions make establishment harder. These plants prefer humus-rich, fertile and reliably moist soils and a position in light or part shade, with shelter from cold drying winds.

WHERE TO SEE IT
RHS Garden Harlow Carr plays host to this beautiful combination in May.

Horticultural heroes

William Robinson · 1838–1935

One of the most influential gardeners and horticultural writers of his time, William Robinson helped to spearhead a revolution in garden design, advocating a naturalistic approach where plants take the lead, and rejecting the formal bedding schemes that were the fashion in the late nineteenth century.

Born in Ireland in 1838, Robinson studied horticulture at the National Botanic Gardens at Glasnevin near Dublin. After working at a number of large Irish estates, he moved to England in 1861 to take up a post at Regent's Park. Visits to the countryside instilled his love of native plants and shaped the ideas outlined in his ground-breaking book, *The Wild Garden*, published in 1870. In it, he proposes that gardens should mimic wild landscapes, with native and exotic hardy plants chosen for their suitability to the site and soil, as well as for colour and form. He also popularized the idea of mixed borders filled with shrubs and perennials.

In 1871, Robinson launched *The Garden*, a weekly journal that allowed him to explore naturalistic principles in greater detail and to reach a wider readership. Then, in 1893, Robinson published what was to become his most influential book, *The English Flower Garden*, inspired by cottage gardens. In later editions, he included contributions from his friend Gertrude Jekyll (see p.43), with whom he worked for more than 50 years. Robinson describes the gardener as a 'true artist' who delights 'in natural form and beauty of flower and tree' and rejects the 'barren geometry' of formal schemes.

In 1884, Robinson bought Gravetye Manor in Sussex, where he used the 80 hectares (200 acres) of land to put his theories to the test. The gardens included coppiced woodland underplanted with spring bulbs and edged with perennials and shrubs. Closer to the house, he planted mixed borders, a walled kitchen garden and a water garden, featuring one of the largest collections of waterlilies in Europe.

Robinson's ideas were to influence garden styles throughout the twentieth century, and they continue to inform the designs of many contemporary gardens today.

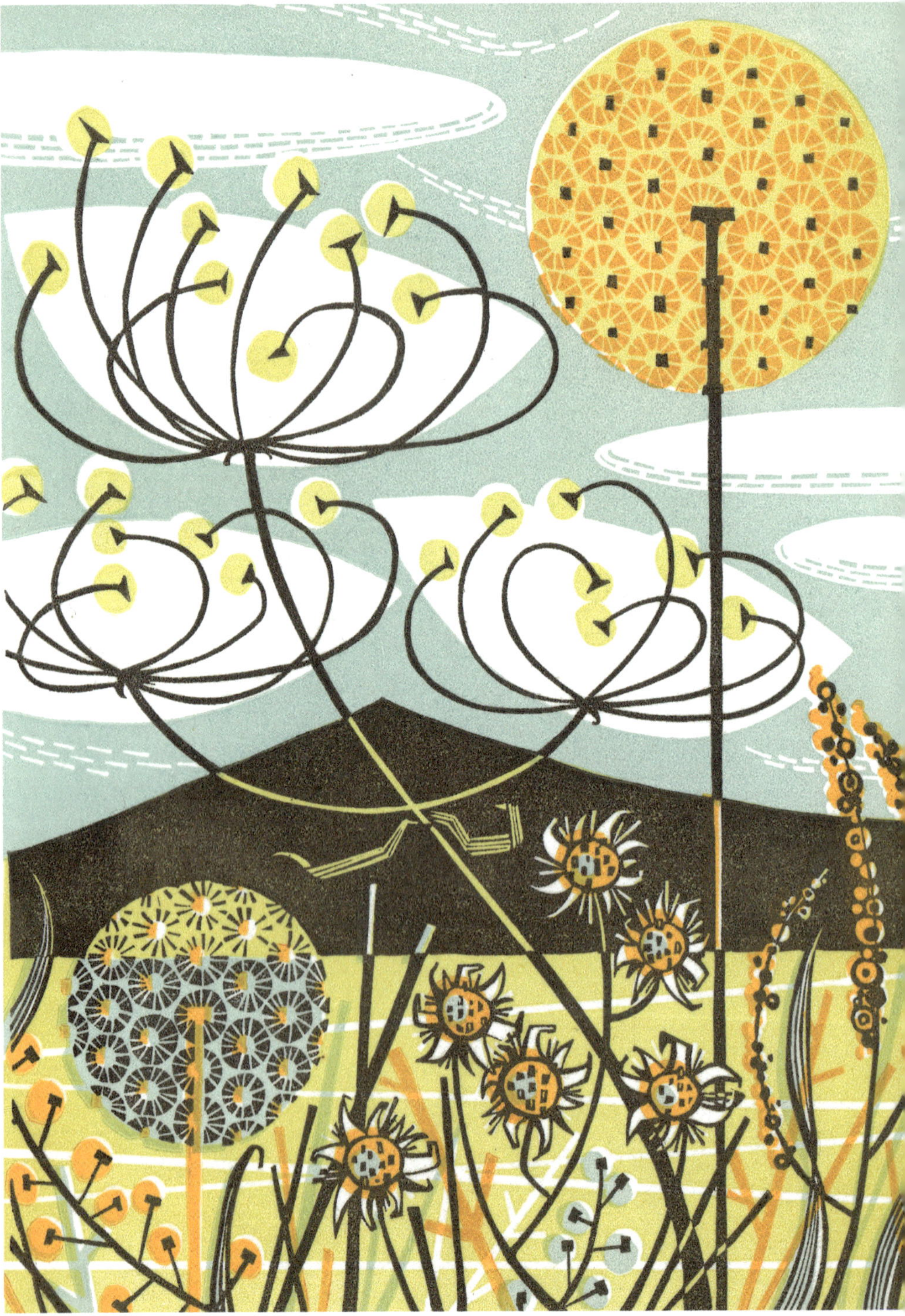

June

An explosion of colour ushers in the lazy days of summer, when gardeners can relax a little and enjoy the fruits of their labour. Bees are kept busy, though, serenading us with their reassuring hum as they work from bloom to bloom, gathering stores of pollen and nectar. Roses are June's stars – their buds, held tight, unfurl now to reveal satin-petalled blooms and wafts of sweet perfume.

KEY EVENTS
Shavuot, 1–3 June
Eid al-Adha, 6 June
Whit Sunday, 8 June
Father's Day, 15 June
Windrush Day, 22 June
Midsummer's Day, 24 June

What to do in June

Now that the frosts have passed, it's time to plant out tender ornamentals and crops, watering both regularly during dry periods to ensure their roots establish well. You can also sow tender crops in situ *and keep weeds at bay by hoeing between productive plants. Spring-flowering shrubs will be ready to prune (see pp.112–13), while deadheading repeat-flowering roses over the coming months will prolong the display.*

In the garden

PINCH OUT TIPS OF PERENNIALS and annuals such as asters, dahlias, chrysanthemums, cosmos, phlox and zinnias. Using a finger and thumb, remove the soft tips, which will encourage sideshoots to grow, resulting in shorter, bushier plants that need less staking. This also delays flowering, so try pinching some plants of each type, and leave others to extend your display. Do not pinch out delphiniums, campanulas or sunflowers where you want just one large flower per stem. ❶

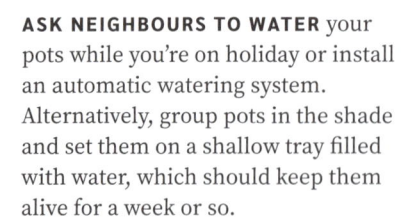

ASK NEIGHBOURS TO WATER your pots while you're on holiday or install an automatic watering system. Alternatively, group pots in the shade and set them on a shallow tray filled with water, which should keep them alive for a week or so.

FEED POT-GROWN PLANTS every fortnight to improve growth and flowering. Start with a balanced general-purpose organic-based fertilizer until flowering starts, then switch to a high-potassium tomato feed. To make your own liquid fertilizer, see pp.132–3. ❷

LEAVE LAWNS TO GROW LONGER during warm dry weather to reduce drought-stress; longer grass has a deeper root system that can tap into moisture lower down in the soil. Set the mower height to remove no more than a third of the grass blades, and leave the clippings *in situ* to form a mulch over the soil, which will also reduce water loss and help keep the lawn green. ❸

SOW AUTUMN BEDDING such as violas and primulas in pots and trays undercover. The resulting young plants will be ready to plant out in autumn and flower over winter and the following spring. ❹

WEED REGULARLY by hoeing as shallowly as possible to avoid bringing up seeds, then use a trowel or gloved hand to pull up weeds growing close to ornamental plants. Finally, use a trowel and border fork to dig out deep-rooted plants such as brambles and horsetails. You can leave some self-sown plants to flower in inconspicuous places to support pollinators, but remove them before they set seed. ❺

In the fruit & veg patch

EARTH UP POTATOES to increase your crop. Every week, rake up soil to form a ridge that covers the stems and foliage to protect the swelling tubers from sunlight, which will make them green and unpalatable. The soil covering also helps to protect the potato plants from blight spores.

JUNE / 105

SOW CORIANDER in batches from spring to late summer. This easy annual thrives in any garden soil in full sun, but it will flower and set seed quickly in hot, dry weather. Therefore, sow seeds regularly for a constant supply. 'Calypso' and 'Confetti' are slower to flower.

SOW SALAD LEAVES, including lettuce, chard, rocket and spinach, in shallow pots filled with a peat-free multipurpose potting compost. Sow seeds about a finger width apart, to make the most of your space and minimize water needs.

SOW CARROTS, RADISHES AND BEETROOT thinly with two finger widths between each seed, having watered the soil the previous day. Cover carrots and radishes with fleece or insect-proof mesh to fend off root flies. Harvest beetroots when they are the size of golf balls.

Indoors

TAKE HOUSEPLANT CUTTINGS, to increase your stock. Remove a couple of leaves from *Sansevieria* and *Streptocarpus* plants and cut into horizontal strips,

> **MONEY-SAVING IDEA**
> Pot up supermarket salad leaves
> As temperatures rise in summer, it can be more difficult to grow lettuces, since germination rates decrease in hot weather. One solution is to buy a tray of supermarket salad leaves, comprising lots of small seedlings. Water well and gently tease apart the seedlings, then repot them in a larger container or small individual pots of peat-free multipurpose compost to grow on into larger plants. Keep the lettuces in a part-shaded spot and water regularly. Pick the leaves as needed.

inserting them on their cut ends, up to a third deep, in houseplant potting compost – roots will grow from the buried edges. For more begonias, lay a leaf face down and make several cuts at right angles to each vein. Place the leaf, face up, on a tray of potting compost, using paperclips to keep the cut edges in contact with the compost. Roots should soon form. ❻ ❼

BRING HOUSEPLANTS OUTSIDE when nights are warm enough. Many will survive temperatures of 10°C (50°F) or lower when acclimatized, but some are more tender, so check each individual plant's needs before moving them.

Plants of the month

1. Daylily (*Hemerocallis* 'Bibury' pictured)
2. Abutilon (*Abutilon* 'Wakehurst' pictured)
3. Astrantia (*Astrantia* 'Buckland' pictured)
4. Lupin (*Lupinus* 'Persian Slipper' pictured)
5. Penstemon (*Penstemon* 'Rich Ruby' pictured)
6. Philadelphus (*Philadelphus* 'Lemoinei' pictured)
7. Deutzia (*Deutzia* × *rosea* YUKI CHERRY BLOSSOM pictured)
8. Honeysuckle (*Lonicera periclymenum* 'Serotina' pictured)
9. Love-in-a-mist (*Nigella damascena*)
10. Byzantine gladiolus (*Gladiolus communis* subsp. *byzantinus*)
11. Eryngium (*Eryngium alpinum* pictured)

Project: Make a hedgehog hideout

Once a common sight in the countryside and domestic gardens, the UK hedgehog population is estimated to have declined by a third since 2000, so it's increasingly important to help protect these beautiful nocturnal creatures and provide them with a suitable habitat. They are also gardeners' allies, eating insects and other small creatures, including unwanted ones, and helping to maintain a healthy ecosystem. Make a home for hedgehogs in your garden with this simple shelter, which will provide a safe place for them to sleep during the day and to hibernate during the winter months.

YOU WILL NEED
Old bricks
Straw
Prunings and leaves from the garden
4–5 short planks of recycled wood
Recycled bin liner or plastic bag

1 Choose a quiet area of the garden that does not get waterlogged, such as under a tree or large shrub, and level the ground. Set out the bricks to form a G-shaped enclosure, as shown. Add a second course on top, staggering the bricks, so the structure is tall enough for a hedgehog to access it, and has an entrance hole measuring about 12 x 15cm (5 x 6in).

2 Loosely pack the enclosure with straw and dried leaves, then cover it with the planks of wood. Lay an old bin liner or recycled plastic bag over the top, to keep out the rain.

3 Finally, add some shrub prunings and leaves on top to keep the plastic in place, and then wait for your night-time visitors to take up residence.

108 / JUNE

Looking up

Sunrise and sunset

The summer solstice on 21st June marks the longest day of the year. The garden is at its peak now, with colourful flowers and crops spilling out of beds and borders.

	LONDON		EDINBURGH	
DAY	Sunrise	Sunset	Sunrise	Sunset
Sun, Jun 1	4:46:26 am	9:10:21 pm	4:31:56 am	9:49:26 pm
Mon, Jun 2	4:45:41 am	9:11:25 pm	4:30:55 am	9:50:46 pm
Tue, Jun 3	4:44:59 am	9:12:27 pm	4:29:58 am	9:52:03 pm
Wed, Jun 4	4:44:20 am	9:13:27 pm	4:29:05 am	9:53:17 pm
Thu, Jun 5	4:43:43 am	9:14:25 pm	4:28:15 am	9:54:28 pm
Fri, Jun 6	4:43:10 am	9:15:20 pm	4:27:28 am	9:55:36 pm
Sat, Jun 7	4:42:40 am	9:16:13 pm	4:26:46 am	9:56:41 pm
Sun, Jun 8	4:42:12 am	9:17:03 pm	4:26:07 am	9:57:43 pm
Mon, Jun 9	4:41:48 am	9:17:51 pm	4:25:32 am	9:58:41 pm
Tue, Jun 10	4:41:27 am	9:18:36 pm	4:25:01 am	9:59:36 pm
Wed, Jun 11	4:41:09 am	9:19:19 pm	4:24:34 am	10:00:28 pm
Thu, Jun 12	4:40:54 am	9:19:59 pm	4:24:11 am	10:01:16 pm
Fri, Jun 13	4:40:42 am	9:20:36 pm	4:23:51 am	10:02:00 pm
Sat, Jun 14	4:40:33 am	9:21:10 pm	4:23:36 am	10:02:41 pm
Sun, Jun 15	4:40:27 am	9:21:41 pm	4:23:25 am	10:03:18 pm
Mon, Jun 16	4:40:25 am	9:22:10 pm	4:23:18 am	10:03:51 pm
Tue, Jun 17	4:40:25 am	9:22:35 pm	4:23:14 am	10:04:20 pm
Wed, Jun 18	4:40:29 am	9:22:58 pm	4:23:15 am	10:04:46 pm
Thu, Jun 19	4:40:35 am	9:23:17 pm	4:23:20 am	10:05:07 pm
Fri, Jun 20	4:40:45 am	9:23:34 pm	4:23:28 am	10:05:24 pm
Sat, Jun 21	4:40:58 am	9:23:47 pm	4:23:41 am	10:05:38 pm
Sun, Jun 22	4:41:14 am	9:23:57 pm	4:23:50 am	10:05:47 pm
Mon, Jun 23	4:41:32 am	9:24:04 pm	4:24:18 am	10:05:53 pm
Tue, Jun 24	4:41:54 am	9:24:08 pm	4:24:43 am	10:05:54 pm
Wed, Jun 25	4:42:19 am	9:24:09 pm	4:25:11 am	10:05:51 pm
Thu, Jun 26	4:42:46 am	9:24:07 pm	4:25:43 am	10:05:44 pm
Fri, Jun 27	4:43:17 am	9:24:02 pm	4:26:19 am	0:05:33 pm
Sat, Jun 28	4:43:50 am	9:23:53 pm	4:26:59 am	10:05:18 pm
Sun, Jun 29	4:44:26 am	9:23:41 pm	4:27:42 am	10:04:59 pm
Mon, Jun 30	4:45:04 am	9:23:26 pm	4:28:28 am	10:04:37 pm

Moonrise and moonset

Moon phases

● **NEW MOON** 25 June
◐ **FIRST QUARTER** 3 June

○ **FULL MOON** 11 June
◑ **THIRD QUARTER** 18 June

	LONDON			EDINBURGH		
DAY	Moonrise	Moonset	Moonrise	Moonrise	Moonset	Moonrise
Jun 1		01:20	10:24		01:52	10:19
Jun 2		01:36	11:42		02:01	11:44
Jun 3		01:48	12:57		02:08	13:04
Jun 4		01:58	14:08		02:13	14:21
Jun 5		02:08	15:18		02:17	15:37
Jun 6		02:18	16:29		02:22	16:53
Jun 7		02:29	17:41		02:27	18:12
Jun 8		02:42	18:54		02:35	19:33
Jun 9		03:00	20:08		02:46	20:54
Jun 10		03:25	21:18		03:04	22:11
Jun 11		04:00	22:20		03:32	23:16
Jun 12		04:49	23:08		04:19	
Jun 13		05:53	23:44	00:01	05:26	
Jun 14		07:08		00:30	06:49	
Jun 15	00:10	08:28		00:47	08:17	
Jun 16	00:28	09:50		00:59	09:47	
Jun 17	00:43	11:12		01:07	11:16	
Jun 18	00:56	12:34		01:13	12:44	
Jun 19	01:07	13:57		01:19	14:14	
Jun 20	01:20	15:23		01:25	15:47	
Jun 21	01:34	16:53		01:33	17:25	
Jun 22	01:53	18:26		01:44	19:08	
Jun 23	02:19	19:57		02:02	20:48	
Jun 24	02:57	21:16		02:32	22:11	
Jun 25	03:54	22:15		03:24	23:07	
Jun 26	05:08	22:55		04:43	23:39	
Jun 27	06:33	23:21		06:16	23:57	
Jun 28	07:59	23:40		07:51		
Jun 29	09:22	23:53			00:08	09:20
Jun 30	10:39				00:15	10:44

Average rainfall

June is one of the driest months of the year, with a UK average rainfall of 82mm (3.2in). You will need to water annual crops and new plants and flowers regularly, ideally harvesting supplies from water butts attached to downpipes (see p.50).

LOCATION	DAYS	MM	INCHES
Aberdeen	12	69	2.7
Aberystwyth	11	81	3.2
Belfast	11	69	2.7
Birmingham	10	68	2.7
Bournemouth	8	53	2.1
Bristol	10	56	2.2
Cambridge	9	49	1.9
Canterbury	8	45	1.8
Cardiff	10	74	2.9
Edinburgh	10	66	2.6
Exeter	9	83	3.3
Glasgow	12	68	2.7
Gloucester	10	71	2.8
Inverness	12	62	2.4
Ipswich	8	51	2.0
Leeds	11	80	3.1
Liverpool	10	64	2.5
London	9	58	2.3
Manchester	13	83	3.3
Newcastle upon Tyne	10	56	2.2
Norwich	10	63	2.5
Nottingham	10	67	2.6
Oxford	8	50	2.0
Sheffield	9	75	3.0
Truro	10	63	2.5

Pruning masterclass: early summer

Pruning during the summer months has a couple of benefits. Firstly, it removes foliage from plants, thereby reducing their food resources, which can result in a significant reduction in their overall size. In contrast, pruning in winter, when a plant's food reserves are safely stored in the roots, results in vigorous regrowth come spring (see pp.36–7), which may only marginally reduce the plant's size. Secondly, the warm temperatures help cuts to heal more swiftly, reducing the risk of infection.

However, before you start, remember to check plants for nesting birds and delay pruning until all chicks have fledged.

CUTTING BACK EVERGREENS
Most evergreens can be pruned once temperatures and light levels rise in spring and early summer. Shorten all shoots to some extent, as any left unpruned will suppress the regrowth of those you have cut back. Regrowth from old wood can be slow but, by late summer, enough leaves should have formed to sustain the plant, though rhododendrons and *Garrya* are notably slow to regrow. Later-flowering evergreens such as Mexican orange blossom (*Choisya*) and camellias are pruned in summer, after their spring flowers have faded.

Prune evergreens such as *Choisya* in summer after the flowers have faded.

TRIM EARLY-FLOWERING SHRUBS
Spring- and early summer-flowering deciduous shrubs such as *Deutzia*, *Forsythia*, *Philadelphus* and *Weigela* are pruned as soon as possible after flowering. As ever when pruning, remove dead, weak, crossing and rubbing shoots, as well as diseased ones, before tackling the remaining stems. Remove one in three shoots near ground level, taking out the tallest, oldest stems

to keep the shrub compact, while leaving the rest to flower the following year. In the absence of timely pruning, many spring- and early-summer flowering shrubs can become excessively large and ungainly, and may die sooner than those that are cut back regularly. However, if you have an overgrown specimen, it should respond well to renovation in winter, when you can cut all the shoots back to near ground level. Just bear in mind that this often means you will lose the flowers for several years, with lilacs (*Syringa*) especially slow to bloom again after renovation.

PRIORITIZE *PRUNUS*

Trees in the cherry genus (*Prunus*), including plums, damsons and ornamental cherries, are susceptible to the highly destructive silver leaf fungus disease, whose airborne spores peak from late summer into winter. Pruning these trees from mid-spring until midsummer, when spores are few and wounds heal fast, minimizes the risk of infection from this deadly tree disease.

Top right Plum trees and other *Prunus* species are pruned in summer to help prevent silver leaf disease.
Middle Wayward stems of *Weigela*, which flower in late spring, can be cut back now to reduce the overall size of the plant.
Bottom Deutzias such as this *D.* × *hybrida* 'Mont Rose' are best pruned in summer after flowering.

Edible garden

The first fresh peas and early potatoes will be ready to harvest this month, together with other crops sown earlier in the year. Continue to sow and plant edibles, to provide a continuous feast throughout the summer and into autumn.

Vegetables

SOW INDOORS Calabrese; cucumbers ❶ to plant in the greenhouse in July; spring cauliflowers.

SOW OUTDOORS Beetroots; carrots; chicory and endive; Chinese cabbage; courgettes; cucumbers including gherkins; Florence fennel; French beans; herbs including coriander, basil, parsley; kohlrabi, lettuce; mustard greens; pak choi; peas; pumpkins; radishes; rocket; runner beans; salad crops; spinach; spring onions; sprouting broccoli; turnips; winter squash.

PLANT OUT Plants sown indoors in April and May, including artichokes, Brussels sprouts, cabbages, cauliflowers, celeriac, celery, courgettes, kohlrabi, lettuces, marrows, outdoor cucumbers, outdoor tomatoes, squash, sweetcorn. ❷

> **TOP TIP**
> **Feed sparingly**
> Recent research shows crops that are not mollycoddled with excessive water and fertilizer may actually produce more health-promoting phytochemicals, which can prevent ill health. Try experimenting with a few plants, providing fewer feeds and reducing water given, to see which crops thrive on a little less.

HARVEST NOW Broad beans ❸; chard; first early potatoes; herbs; lettuces; peas; radishes; spinach; spring cabbages; spring cauliflowers; spring onions; turnips.

Fruit

PLANT NOW Potted fruit trees and shrubs such as blueberries ❹; strawberry plants.

HARVEST Black, red and white currants; gooseberries; rhubarb; strawberries.

HERB OF THE MONTH: CHIVES
Chives (*Allium schoenoprasum*) are very easy to grow and these hardy perennials will pop up each year after initial planting. Buy young plants or sow seed in spring and plant in beds or pots in a sunny or partly shaded area. You can harvest the tangy, hollow, grass-like leaves as needed; more will appear until the plants die down in autumn. You can also make new plants every few years by dividing established clumps of chives in the spring.

Ferment recipe

KIMCHI WITH CHIVE FLOWERS

No year of fermentation recipes would be complete without kimchi. Traditional recipes usually include fish sauce, but this one is vegan and uses soy sauce instead. Many recipes also include spring onions, but chive flowers work equally well – the blooms have a similar oniony flavour, and they add an interesting texture and look really pretty.

INGREDIENTS
2 Chinese cabbages
4 tbsp salt
5 garlic cloves
2.5cm (1in) piece of ginger
2 tbsp soy sauce
1–2 tbsp gochugaru (Korean red chilli pepper flakes, or you can substitute with chilli flakes)
2 tsp caster sugar
30–40 chive flowers

1. Remove the stems, then chop the Chinese cabbages into small chunks.

2. Place the cabbage in a large bowl and rub in the salt thoroughly. The cabbage will quickly start releasing moisture. Cover it with a plate to keep it submerged under the brine and leave it for about 8 hours (or overnight).

3. Rinse the cabbage thoroughly and leave to drain.

4. Chop and crush the garlic and ginger, using a pestle and mortar or a blender, and place in a large bowl. Mix in the soy sauce, gochugaru and sugar.

5. Add the chive flowers and mix all the ingredients together in the bowl.

6. Pack the ingredients into wide-mouthed kilner jars. Place glass weights on the top to keep the fermented ingredients submerged under the brine.

7. Seal the jars with airlocks (see page 58) and leave for 3–5 days. Kimchi is usually slightly quicker to ferment than some other ferments. Taste regularly until it reaches the desired level of fiery pickliness you require.

Challenges this month

Developing tree fruits can play host this month to various insects, including the apple sawfly and pear midge, while aphids and capsid bugs may continue to cause problems for soft-stemmed plants such as perennials and bedding.

APPLE SAWFLY'S caterpillar-like larvae feed on apple fruitlets from late spring to early summer, and the affected fruits usually drop off in June, when you will see scarring and entry holes in them. Checking fruit in late spring and thinning those with symptoms will reduce populations and create more air and light around the remaining apples. Also avoid cultivars that are susceptible to apple sawfly, including 'Worcester Pearmain', 'Charles Ross', 'James Grieve' and 'Ellison's Orange'. Encouraging predators of sawfly, such as birds and ground beetles, into the garden will also limit numbers. Fruits suffering from 'maggoty' flesh later in summer also feature holes, but this problem is due to codling moth (see p.173).

PEAR MIDGE larvae also lead to fruits dropping in early summer. These creamy white maggots are the offspring of gall midges. They burrow into young fruits, causing them to turn black at the opposite end to the stalk, and then fall. Remove fruits showing signs of pear midge before the larvae enter the soil to pupate. Hoeing the soil around the base of the tree in June and July can also kill off some pupae and expose them to natural predators such as birds, hedgehogs and ground beetles.

CAPSID BUGS, like aphids (see p.77), suck the sap from a wide range of plants. The adults look like large green or brown aphids, but do not congregate together in colonies. Symptoms include misshapen leaves peppered with brown-edged holes, while affected flower buds may fail to develop or open unevenly.

Apple capsid (*Plesiocoris rugicollis*) feeds on young fruitlets, causing bumps or raised corky growths on the mature fruit, but they do not affect the taste of the crops or their storage life. In most cases, the damage should be tolerated as plants recover, while natural predators such as birds, hedgehogs and ground beetles will keep the bugs in check. Removing dead vegetation in late winter may destroy overwintering sites for the tarnished capsid bug.

Focus on wildlife

Damselfly

There are 17 species of damselfly in the UK, and these colourful insects are guaranteed to brighten up your garden during the summer months.

The various species sport bodies in a range of shimmering shades, from metallic green and bright turquoise to red, dark blue and black, with some also decorated with stripes or patterns. Their eyes are set on each side of a rectangular head, and they close their two pairs of wings, which are of equal size, when resting. These characteristics distinguish them from their larger cousins, the dragonflies, which have eyes that meet in the middle of the head, and wings of different sizes that are held open when resting.

Most garden ponds attract damselflies from early May to September, with most seen during July and August flying over water in search of small insects to eat and a suitable mate.

Damselflies only live as flying adults for a few days, although some may survive for up to two weeks, during which time they mate, when you will see them flying along in tandem (see picture, top right). The females then lay their eggs in or near water. The eggs hatch after a few weeks, and the larvae feed on live prey such as tadpoles or even small fish. As the larvae grow, they cast off their skins many times, until the final moult when the winged adult emerges. The larvae stage can last several weeks or even months, and 95 per cent of the damselfly life cycle is spent underwater.

You can attract these beautiful insects into your garden by providing them with a water source with plants nearby, where the adults can rest and hide from predators. A few large stones in a sunny spot will also offer perches on which they can warm themselves. Never use pesticides, which can harm both damselflies and their prey.

Spotlight on: Peony (*Paeonia*)

The prima donnas of the early summer border, herbaceous peonies produce huge frilly flowers with a spicy perfume that makes them the star attraction. Choose from white, yellow, apricot, pink, red or bicoloured blooms. Equally impressive are the tree peonies, which are hardy deciduous shrubs that produce large bowl-shaped flowers or small daintier blooms in a similar colour range to the herbaceous plants. The flowering period for all peonies is brief, but they provide an invaluable source of food for pollinators, especially those with single flowers. The deeply cut leaves also help to sustain the show into late summer or early autumn. Plant peonies in full sun or part shade in moist, free-draining soil. Stems weighed down with heavy flowers on herbaceous types may also need staking.

PAEONIA LACTIFLORA 'KELWAY'S GLORIOUS'
Once established, this award-winning herbaceous peony produces an abundance of huge, almost spherical, white, double flowers with some red streaking and a wonderful scent.
H x S: 90 x 60cm (36 x 24in)

PAEONIA LACTIFLORA 'SARAH BERNHARDT'
The large, pale pink, double blooms with a sweet perfume have made this herbaceous peony a florist's favourite. A red variety is also available. The tall stems require staking.
H x S: 100 x 90cm (39 x 36in)

PAEONIA x *LEMOINEI* 'HIGH NOON'
One of the easiest hybrid tree peonies to grow, 'High Noon' produces fragrant, semi-double, yellow flowers with orange centres, among stems of deeply cut foliage.
H x S: 120 x 90cm (4 x 3ft)

PAEONIA LACTIFLORA 'KANSAS'
The large, round, dark reddish-pink blooms, held on straight stems, are ideal for cutting, while the sweet fragrance adds to this herbaceous form's charms.
H x S: 90 x 90cm (3 x 3ft)

PAEONIA DELAVAYI
A more naturalistic looking shrub, this tree peony produces small, dark red blooms which are rather variable and can also be more orange in tone. The deeply divided, staghorn-shaped, green leaves are a feature in themselves.
H x S: 1.5 x 1.5m (5 x 5ft)

JUNE / 119

Seasonal planting ideas

COLOUR CLASH

WHY IT WORKS
With an explosion of colour in shades of red, orange, pink and yellow, these plants bring warmth and excitement to a summer border, the vivid hues really standing out against the dark green yew hedge. The flowers of *Achillea*, *Silene* and *Salvia* also attract pollinators, thereby increasing biodiversity.

WHAT'S GROWING HERE?
Achillea filipendulina 'Cloth of Gold' is a tall robust perennial, about 1.8m (6ft) in height, with divided foliage and large, flat-topped heads of bright yellow flowers throughout summer.

Euphorbia griffithii 'Fireglow' is a perennial that grows to around 75cm (30in) and produces upright stems clothed in narrow, red-tinged leaves and showy orange-red flowers in early summer.

Silene chalcedonica is a tall perennial, up to 1m (3ft) in height, with oval leaves and small, bright vermilion flowers held in compact domed heads.

Salvia microphylla 'Pink Blush' is a subshrub that grows to around 80cm (32in) in height. Airy sprays of deep pink blooms appear over grey-green foliage for many months from June.

Alchemilla mollis is a low-growing perennial, 30cm (12in) in height. Its pale green leaves with scalloped edges are joined by frothy sprays of tiny bright yellow flowers throughout summer.

WHEN TO PLANT
Plant in autumn or early spring. In combination, these plants prefer a sunny aspect on well-drained soils; however, the *Euphorbia* and *Alchemilla* would also be happy in part shade.

WHERE TO SEE IT
This colourful border can be seen at RHS Garden Hyde Hall in June.

Horticultural heroes

Ellen Willmott · 1858–1934

The horticulturist and garden-maker Ellen Willmott was famous during her lifetime for the vast sums of money she lavished on the gardens at Warley Place in Essex and her other properties in Europe, as well as for the plants and flowers named after her.

The eldest daughter of Frederick and Ellen Willmott, she was born in 1858 in Heston, Middlesex. The family then moved to Warley Place in 1875, which she inherited after her father's death in 1892. However, it was the money she had received from her aunt, Countess Helen Tasker, four years earlier, that financed her spectacular gardens.

She employed more than 100 gardeners to care for her properties, which at Warley Place included an alpine gorge, a boating lake, and a fernery in a glass-covered cave. A knowledgeable horticulturist and member of various RHS committees, she is believed to have cultivated more than 100,000 species and cultivars, and sponsored expeditions by eminent plant-hunters including Ernest Henry Wilson, who named *Ceratostigma willmottianum*, *Rosa willmottiae* and *Corylopsis willmottiae* after her.

In 1897, Ellen Wilmott and Gertrude Jckyll (see p.43) were the only women to be awarded the Royal Horticultural Society's Victoria Medal of Honour, but Wilmott's reputation was tarnished when she didn't show up to collect the award. Considered a snub at the time, new research suggests it was due to grief, following a thwarted love affair with Georgiana 'Gian' Tufnell.

Rumours about her prickly character abounded and she was said to carry a pistol, but the legend of her secretly scattering seeds of Miss Willmott's ghost, (*Eryngium giganteum*), the sea holly that bears her name, in other people's gardens is unfounded, according to research by author Sandra Lawrence.

Ellen Willmott ended her life almost bankrupt and, after her death, Warley Place was sold to pay her debts. The house was demolished in 1939, but the gardens survive in part and are now an Essex Wildlife Trust nature reserve.

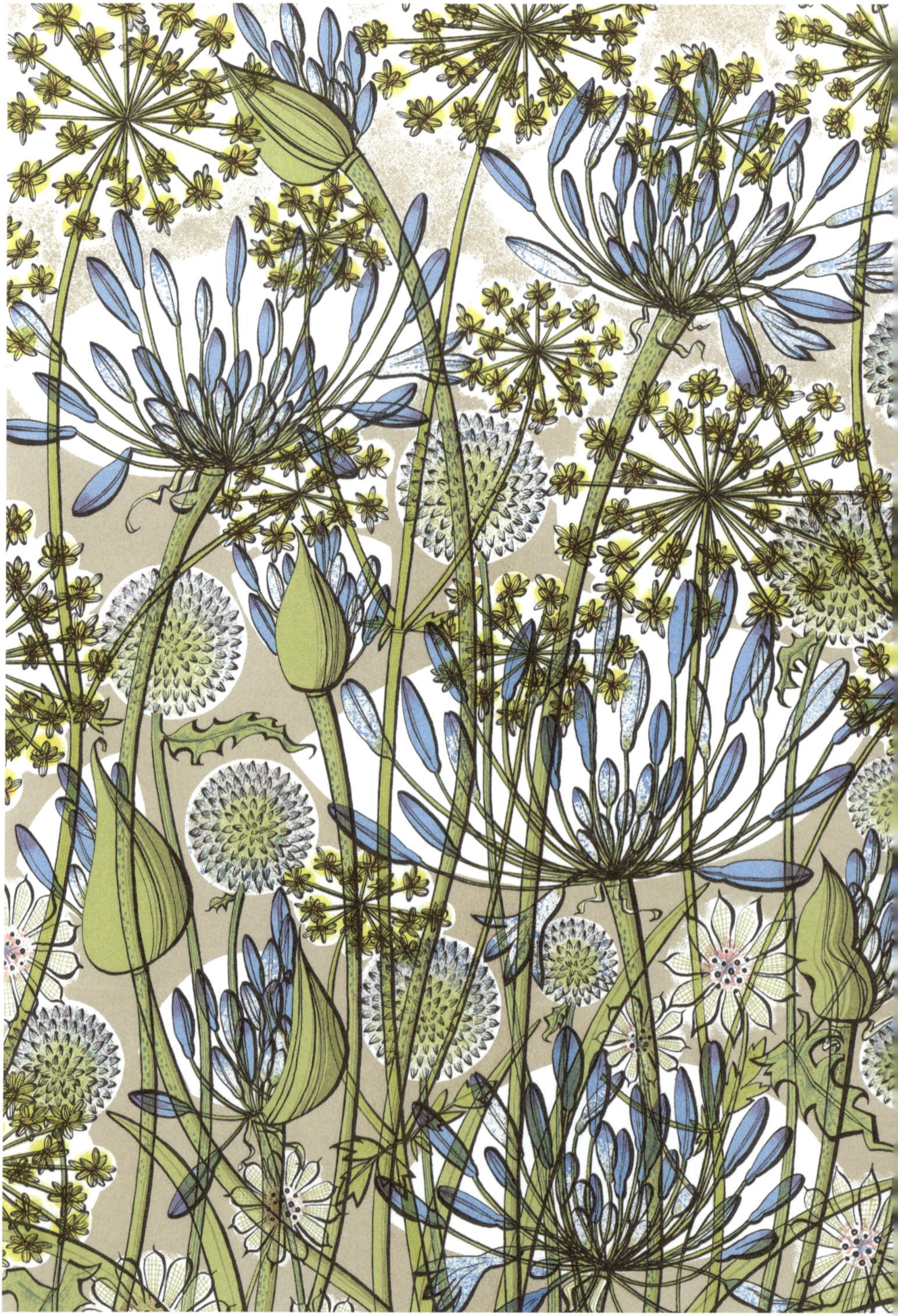

July

With summer in full swing and an abundance of crops to fill our plates, gardeners can also take delight in their flower gardens bustling with blooms. While successional sowing continues apace, and autumn and winter harvests have to be planned, the long evenings offer a moment to unwind, as family and friends arrive to share fresh produce and a tipple to celebrate the treasures the season brings.

KEY EVENTS
RHS Hampton Court Palace Garden Festival, 1–6 July
Battle of the Boyne (Holiday in NI), 12 July (Bank Holiday on 14 July)
St Swithin's Day, 15 July

What to do in July

*Long periods of dry weather are common in July, and the gardener's main job this month is keeping new and potted plants hydrated. Mowing the lawn and weeding, especially between crops, continue throughout the month. Deadheading half-hardy annuals will keep them flowering, while removing spent blooms from perennials such as hardy geraniums and catmint (*Nepeta*) may encourage a second flush. Also top up ponds, ideally with water from a butt, or tap water that's been left to stand for a day.*

In the garden

TAKE HYDRANGEA CUTTINGS to make new plants. Remove 10cm (4in), non-flowering shoots, halve the leaf surface and cut off the soft tip and the leaves on the lower stem. Using a dibber or pencil, insert the cuttings in pots filled with a 50:50 mix of multipurpose peat-free compost and grit, up to the lowest leaf. Water and cover with a recycled plastic bag or place in a propagator. Remove the plastic or lid when the cuttings have rooted. Repot in spring. ❶

SOW POLLINATOR-FRIENDLY BIENNIALS such as forget-me-nots (*Myosotis sylvatica*), foxgloves (*Digitalis*), rose campion (*Silene coronaria* syn. *Lychnis coronaria*), sweet Williams (*Dianthus barbatus*) and wallflowers (*Erysimum cheiri*). These will grow leaves after germinating and flower next spring and summer. Sow in the garden or in pots, and plant seedlings in their final positions in autumn or spring. ❷

PUDDLE IN NEW PLANTS in summer, to increase their chances of survival. Dig out a planting hole, then fill it with water. Refill several times after it has drained. Planting into this wet zone allows the roots to access the deep moist soil for many days, but continue to water regularly during dry spells.

PROVIDE WATER FOR BIRDS and other garden wildlife. A simple dish will do the trick if you don't have a pond – just remember to wash and rinse it regularly, to prevent diseases from building up. ❸

DEADHEAD LAVENDER by shearing lightly to remove the spent flowers, taking care not to cut into old wood lower down the stems. This will help to keep plants bushy and productive. ❹

In the fruit & veg patch

SOW PAK CHOI for a quick, nutritious crop of cut-and-come-again salad leaves within about six weeks or full-sized heads in eight to ten weeks. Like other brassicas, plants need protecting from cabbage root fly with insect-proof netting, which also retains the extra warmth this crop needs.

FEED TOMATOES AND PEPPERS now with a potassium-rich organic-based fertilizer, and cucumbers with a nitrogen-rich product. Cucumbers can flag in August, so also sow more seed now for replacements, which will crop until October. Remove any dead leaves and all the foliage below the point where you have harvested the fruits, to increase air circulation and prevent rot.

SOW SPRING CABBAGES in prepared beds, and cover your crops with insect-proof netting to protect them from cabbage white butterflies, root flies and moths. The leaves will then be ready to harvest from late winter as greens, and as full-headed cabbages next spring. ❺

SUMMER RASPBERRIES are coming to an end, and the fruited stems can be removed to leave vigorous young canes that will carry next year's crop. Thin the new growth by removing the weakest stems, to leave a strong cane every 15cm (6in). Also shear strawberries after cropping and remove unwanted runners, then apply a potassium-rich organic-based fertilizer fortnightly, to encourage next year's flower buds to form.

REMOVE STEM TIPS from outdoor cordon tomatoes once they have made four trusses of flowers, taking them back to one leaf beyond the top truss. This funnels the plant's energy into setting fruits. Bush and trailing tomatoes can be left unpruned. Keep watering as the tomatoes develop, to prevent blossom end rot and the fruits splitting.

Indoors

DEADHEAD FLOWERING PLANTS such as gardenias, begonias and *Streptocarpus* to encourage more blooms. Also remove old leaves and flowers from the top of the soil, to prevent fungal diseases.

WATERING HOUSEPLANTS while you are away can be a problem if neighbours and friends are not available. An alternative option is to fill a sink with water and set plants in plastic pots with drainage holes on a wet towel on the draining board. Place one end of the towel in the water, and it will then draw up moisture, which will pass through the drainage holes to irrigate the plants.

MONEY-SAVING IDEA
Freeze peas and beans
Make the most of a glut of beans by freezing them for use later. Top and tail the pods and cut into chunks, then blanch in a pan of boiling water for 3 minutes. Drain and plunge the beans into a bowl of icy water to stop the cooking process and to maintain their colour. Drain and pat them dry, then set the beans on a baking sheet lined with parchment and pop in the freezer until frozen. Once completely frozen, put them in a freezer bag and place back in the freezer. Use the same method for peas, but boil for just 1½ minutes.

Plants of the month

1. Phygelius (*Phygelius* CANDY DROPS CREAM pictured)
2. Agapanthus (*Agapanthus* 'Summer Days' pictured)
3. Yarrow (*Achillea* 'Petra' pictured)
4. Pot marigold (*Calendula officinalis* 'Candyman Orange' pictured)
5. Thalictrum (*Thalictrum delavayi* var. *mucronatum* pictured)
6. Cone flower (*Echinacea purpurea*)
7. Laceflower (*Orlaya grandiflora*)
8. Border phlox (*Phlox paniculata* 'Lavendelwolke' pictured)
9. Crocosmia (*Crocosmia* 'Emberglow' pictured)
10. Turk's cap lily (*Lilium martagon* var. *album* pictured)
11. Sunflower (*Helianthus annuus* 'Claret' pictured)

JULY / 127

Project: Make a potted seascape

Create a memory of happy holidays by the beach with this group of coastal plants in pots. Thrift (*Armeria maritima*), blue fescues (*Festuca glauca*), sea hollies (*Eryngium*), aloes and sedums are all good choices for a sunny patio. You can also pimp up your pots with seashells, acquired from a sustainable source, stuck on with silicon glue designed for outdoor use.

YOU WILL NEED
Selection of terracotta pots with drainage holes in the bottom
Seashells
Silicone glue for outdoor use
Peat-free John Innes No. 2 compost
Horticultural grit
Selection of coastal plants
Horticultural sand or pebbles

1 To decorate terracotta pots with shells, clean the surface with warm water and a mild detergent. Dry thoroughly, and then stick on the shells with the glue.

2 Add a 2:1 mix of peat-free John Innes compost and horticultural grit to each pot, filling them up to a few centimetres below the rim.

3 Plant your plants at the same depth as they were in their original containers and firm around the rootballs gently. Ensure plants have space to grow as, if hardy, they can remain in the pots for a few years.

4 Water, then add a layer of sand or pebbles over the compost to enhance the beach theme and to help lock in moisture. Keep plants watered from spring to autumn and place pots in a sheltered spot in winter.

Looking up

Sunrise and sunset

Long hours of sunlight and high temperatures this month mean soil is prone to drying out quickly. Also remember to protect your skin when working or relaxing outside.

	LONDON		EDINBURGH	
DAY	Sunrise	Sunset	Sunrise	Sunset
Tue, Jul 1	4:45:46 am	9:23:08 pm	4:29:18 am	10:04:10 pm
Wed, Jul 2	4:46:29 am	9:22:47 pm	4:30:12 am	10:03:39 pm
Thu, Jul 3	4:47:16 am	9:22:23 pm	4:31:09 am	10:03:04 pm
Fri, Jul 4	4:48:05 am	9:21:56 pm	4:32:09 am	10:02:25 pm
Sat, Jul 5	4:48:56 am	9:21:25 pm	4:33:12 am	10:01:43 pm
Sun, Jul 6	4:49:49 am	9:20:52 pm	4:34:18 am	10:00:57 pm
Mon, Jul 7	4:50:45 am	9:20:15 pm	4:35:28 am	10:00:07 pm
Tue, Jul 8	4:51:43 am	9:19:36 pm	4:36:40 am	9:59:13 pm
Wed, Jul 9	4:52:43 am	9:18:53 pm	4:37:55 am	9:58:16 pm
Thu, Jul 10	4:53:46 am	9:18:08 pm	4:39:12 am	9:57:15 pm
Fri, Jul 11	4:54:50 am	9:17:20 pm	4:40:32 am	9:56:11 pm
Sat, Jul 12	4:55:56 am	9:16:29 pm	4:41:55 am	9:55:04 pm
Sun, Jul 13	4:57:04 am	9:15:35 pm	4:43:20 am	9:53:53 pm
Mon, Jul 14	4:58:14 am	9:14:38 pm	4:44:47 am	9:52:39 pm
Tue, Jul 15	4:59:26 am	9:13:39 pm	4:46:17 am	9:51:22 pm
Wed, Jul 16	5:00:39 am	9:12:37 pm	4:47:48 am	9:50:02 pm
Thu, Jul 17	5:01:54 am	9:11:32 pm	4:49:21 am	9:48:38 pm
Fri, Jul 18	5:03:10 am	9:10:25 pm	4:50:57 am	9:47:12 pm
Sat, Jul 19	5:04:28 am	9:09:15 pm	4:52:34 am	9:45:43 pm
Sun, Jul 20	5:05:47 am	9:08:03 pm	4:54:13 am	9:44:11 pm
Mon, Jul 21	5:07:07 am	9:06:48 pm	4:55:53 am	9:42:36 pm
Tue, Jul 22	5:08:29 am	9:05:31 pm	4:57:35 am	9:40:59 pm
Wed, Jul 23	5:09:52 am	9:04:12 pm	4:59:19 am	9:39:19 pm
Thu, Jul 24	5:11:16 am	9:02:50 pm	5:01:03 am	9:37:36 pm
Fri, Jul 25	5:12:40 am	9:01:26 pm	5:02:49 am	9:35:51 pm
Sat, Jul 26	5:14:06 am	9:00:00 pm	5:04:36 am	9:34:04 pm
Sun, Jul 27	5:15:33 am	8:58:32 pm	5:06:25 am	9:32:15 pm
Mon, Jul 28	5:17:01 am	8:57:02 pm	5:08:14 am	9:30:23 pm
Tue, Jul 29	5:18:30 am	8:55:30 pm	5:10:04 am	9:28:29 pm
Wed, Jul 30	5:19:59 am	8:53:55 pm	5:11:55 am	9:26:33 pm
Thu, Jul 31	5:21:29 am	8:52:19 pm	5:13:47 am	9:24:35 pm

Moonrise and moonset

Moon phases

● **NEW MOON** 24 July
◐ **FIRST QUARTER** 2 July

○ **FULL MOON** 10 July
◑ **THIRD QUARTER** 18 July

DAY	LONDON Moonrise	LONDON Moonset	LONDON Moonrise	EDINBURGH Moonrise	EDINBURGH Moonset	EDINBURGH Moonrise
Jul 1		00:05	11:53		00:21	12:04
Jul 2		00:15	13:04		00:26	13:21
Jul 3		00:24	14:15		00:30	14:38
Jul 4		00:35	15:27		00:36	15:56
Jul 5		00:48	16:40		00:42	17:16
Jul 6		01:04	17:54		00:52	18:37
Jul 7		01:26	19:06		01:07	19:57
Jul 8		01:57	20:11		01:31	21:07
Jul 9		02:42	21:05		02:11	21:59
Jul 10		03:41	21:45		03:12	22:33
Jul 11		04:54	22:14		04:32	22:54
Jul 12		06:14	22:34		06:01	23:07
Jul 13		07:38	22:50		07:32	23:16
Jul 14		09:00	23:03		09:02	23:23
Jul 15		10:23	23:15		10:31	23:28
Jul 16		11:45	23:27		12:00	23:34
Jul 17		13:09	23:40		13:31	23:41
Jul 18		14:36	23:57		15:06	23:50
Jul 19		16:06			16:44	
Jul 20	00:19	17:36		00:05	18:23	
Jul 21	00:51	18:58		00:28	19:53	
Jul 22	01:39	20:04		01:09	20:59	
Jul 23	02:45	20:51		02:16	21:39	
Jul 24	04:06	21:22		03:44	22:01	
Jul 25	05:32	21:43		05:19	22:15	
Jul 26	06:57	21:59		06:52	22:23	
Jul 27	08:17	22:11		08:20	22:29	
Jul 28	09:33	22:21		09:42	22:34	
Jul 29	10:47	22:31		11:02	22:39	
Jul 30	11:59	22:42		12:19	22:44	
Jul 31	13:11	22:53		13:37	22:50	

Average rainfall

July is one of the driest months of the year, with an average UK rainfall of 94mm (3.7in). Use water resources wisely, and remember that most mature plants will withstand summer droughts and shouldn't need irrigating unless they're in a pot.

LOCATION	DAYS	MM	INCHES
Aberdeen	12	71	2.8
Aberystwyth	13	86	3.4
Belfast	13	74	2.9
Birmingham	10	66	2.6
Bournemouth	8	50	2.0
Bristol	10	59	2.3
Cambridge	8	48	1.9
Canterbury	7	43	1.7
Cardiff	11	84	3.3
Edinburgh	11	72	2.8
Exeter	9	74	2.9
Glasgow	13	83	3.3
Gloucester	11	71	2.8
Inverness	11	62	2.4
Ipswich	9	49	1.9
Leeds	11	75	3.0
Liverpool	11	65	2.6
London	8	50	2.0
Manchester	13	97	3.8
Newcastle upon Tyne	10	52	2.0
Norwich	9	57	2.2
Nottingham	9	65	2.6
Oxford	8	53	2.1
Sheffield	9	62	2.4
Truro	11	71	2.8

Food for thought

Applying fertilizers to ornamental plants and crops can promote healthy growth and heavier harvests, but the types you choose and how you apply them are important considerations if you want to garden sustainably.

Using natural methods is generally the best policy, but RHS research shows that, in many cases, you may not need to apply any additional fertilizers at all for optimum plant growth. Garden soils tested through the RHS Soil Analysis Service suggest that most have adequate supplies of the key plant nutrients potassium and magnesium, while phosphorus, responsible for healthy root growth, is often in excess. Poor plant growth is therefore more likely to stem from lack of water or nitrogen (the most important plant nutrient). Nitrogen is part of the chlorophyll molecule, which gives plants their green colour and helps to make the food they need.

Applying some fertilizer may have a beneficial effect, but giving too much can be detrimental, both to the plant and to the environment, since excess nutrients are washed down into the groundwater and, from there, go on to pollute rivers and oceans.

HOME-MADE SOLUTIONS
If your plants are performing poorly, an eco-friendly solution is to use home-made liquid fertilizers made from plants such as comfrey or nettles. While their nutrient content is very low, they should deliver a sufficient boost to plants when given frequently. Another benefit of using these natural fertilizers is that they rarely cause plant damage, unlike synthetic types, which must be carefully applied according to the manufacturer's guidance. To make them, simply cram the plants into a container with a lid, steep with a little water and, when well decomposed, dilute with water until the liquid is a straw colour. Apply this every few days until plants are growing well.

Collect comfrey and steep in water until decomposed, then dilute to a straw colour before applying to plants.

Products with a higher nutrient content may be needed for potted plants or fruit and vegetables. Here, seaweed fertilizer is a good choice, offering a good supply of nutrients, and some beneficial natural plant growth regulators. Alternatively, you can add extra well-rotted organic manures or composts – making your own compost in heaps or bins using garden plant and vegetable kitchen waste is the cheapest option. Like home-made fertilizers, these products have a low nutrient content, but when applied as a mulch over the soil in large quantities, typically a bucketful per square metre (square yard), they deliver extra nutrients, including nitrogen.

Compost and manure keep the soil in good condition, too, because both have a high carbon content, which feeds soil organisms that contribute to the health of plant roots by enhancing their ability to absorb nutrients. They also increase the soil's moisture-holding properties.

STRONGER STUFF
More concentrated organic fertilizers include dried poultry manures and fish, blood and bone. These release nutrients slowly over a prolonged period, aiding plant growth, but add little carbon and so contribute less to soil health. Organic potassium fertilizers, used to increase flowering and fruiting, are derived from the waste from sugar refining, but they are in short supply and quite expensive.

Dried poultry manure is a renewable, nitrogen-rich organic fertilizer.

Consequently, many fertilizers are sold as 'organic based', where the potassium content comes from potassium sulphate derived from mined minerals. However, reserves of mined minerals, particularly phosphorus, are limited and therefore less sustainable than organic sources.

Artificial nitrogen fertilizers produced from natural gas are a source of carbon dioxide, which causes climate change, and are not sustainable. However, renewable nitrogen made from wind or solar energy is now in development.

Edible garden

Bountiful harvests keep the fridge stocked, while sowing batches of hardy and tender vegetables regularly in beds outside will help to keep the produce coming as the months pass. July is also soft fruit season, and a time for jam-making to preserve any gluts.

Vegetables

SOW INDOORS Spring cabbages (to protect from slugs).

SOW OUTDOORS Beetroots ❶; carrots; chard; chicory and endive; Florence fennel; French beans; herbs including basil, coriander, parsley; kohlrabi; lettuce; mustard greens; pak choi; peas; perpetual spinach; runner beans; salad leaves ❷; spring cabbage; spring onions; turnips; winter and summer radishes.

PLANT OUT Plants sown in May, including sprouting broccoli.

HARVEST NOW Beetroots; broccoli; cabbage; calabrese; cauliflowers; chillies; courgettes; cucumbers; French and runner beans; garlic; herbs; lettuces; over-wintered onions ❸; peas; radishes; second early and salad potatoes; shallots; spinach; spring onions; small tomatoes.

Fruit

HARVEST Blueberries; cherries; currants; summer raspberries ❹; rhubarb; strawberries; gooseberries. ❺

HERB OF THE MONTH: FRENCH TARRAGON
French tarragon (*Artemisia dracunculus* French) is a tender perennial and not to be confused with the hardy Russian type (*A. dracunculus* Russian). Its sweet peppery flavour with aniseed overtones make it well worth growing. Buy a young plant and pot it up in peat-free compost or plant it in a sunny bed. Potted plants are easier to bring indoors in winter – a heated greenhouse, cool conservatory or a porch are ideal – when the top growth will die down. One plant will usually suffice for a family.

TOP TIP
Watering fruit trees and shrubs
The main task for gardeners during July is watering their crops, but it's important to use this precious resource wisely, especially when irrigating trees and shrubs. Healthy established fruit trees and bushes should survive fairly long periods of drought without additional irrigation, so prioritize those that have been planted within the last two or three years, watering them well every three days during periods of dry weather. Installing tree irrigation bays, available online and from tree specialists, help to keep fruit tree roots constantly moist and ease the burden of frequent watering, while minimizing wastage.

🍲 Ferment recipe

BEETROOT, CARROT AND CARAWAY PICKLE

Caraway seeds are an excellent herb to include in ferments. Traditionally used as an ingredient in sauerkraut, in this recipe the seeds' mildly peppery, aniseed flavour works as a subtle contrast to the sweet beetroot and carrot. The pickle makes a great accompaniment to smoked fish dishes.

INGREDIENTS
750g (1lb 10oz) beetroot
750g (1lb 10oz) carrots
2 tbsp salt
1 tbsp caraway seeds

1. Finely slice the beetroot and carrots, ideally using a mandolin to ensure the slices are very thin.

2. Rub the salt into the vegetables thoroughly, which will release the water in them to make a brine.

3. Stir in the caraway seeds.

4. Pack the ingredients tightly into a large kilner jar. Submerge the vegetables under the brine using glass weights, then seal them with an airlock (see p.58).

5. Leave to ferment at room temperature for 5–7 days or until it reaches your preferred degree of sourness.

6. Remove the airlock, and reseal the jar with a lid. This ferment should store in a fridge for at least three months.

Challenges this month

As well as protecting your crops from birds and flying insects, ensure plants are well hydrated and increase air circulation to protect them against fungal diseases. Red spider mite can also cause problems in greenhouses, where they thrive in the heat.

POWDERY MILDEW disease causes a white powdery fungal layer to develop on the upper leaf surfaces, stems and buds of a wide range of plants, including apples, broccoli, courgettes, peas, phlox, roses and squash. The spores are rich in fats and water, allowing them to infect plants even in dry weather – most other fungi require wet leaves. Drought-stressed plants are especially susceptible, and watering helps to reduce the incidence of this disease. Resistant cultivars are also available for many edible plants.

RUSTS are very common fungal diseases that affect many plants. Symptoms include pale leaf spots that eventually develop into raised orange, yellow, black, white or rusty brown pustules. In many cases, plants survive this disease, but, in some, it can reduce their vigour.

Increasing air circulation around plants helps to ward it off, while removing affected leaves as soon as symptoms appear can help, provided you take out only a small number. Over-using nitrogen fertilizers can also increase the incidence of rusts, as the resulting soft growth is more susceptible.

RED SPIDER MITE is a minute creature with eight legs and two dark spots on its back, but you are more likely to notice the mottled, pale foliage, with webbing on the underside, that this sap-sucking insect causes. If you look through a magnifying glass, you will also see immature 'nymphs' and dark red eggs. Frequent sprays of contact insecticides based on oils or soap can suppress numbers, after which, in greenhouse crops, predator mites can be introduced as a biological control.

EARWIGS prey on insects including greenfly, and while they may damage flower petals, they also keep other insects under control, so spare these nocturnal allies if possible. Where control is needed, trap them in flowerpots filled with straw and set upside down on canes near affected plants. The earwigs will shelter there by day, and can be released elsewhere.

Focus on wildlife

Elephant hawk-moth

The UK is host to 18 species of hawk-moth, half of which are annual migrants from Europe. Perhaps the most recognizable is the colourful elephant hawk-moth, which is resident here all year round. The moth's flamboyant good looks and large size – the wingspan can reach 60mm (2½in) – look tropical but, in fact, it is widespread in UK gardens, as well as woodland edges, rough grassland and sand dunes. It can sometimes be seen flying at dusk from May to early August, or snoozing during the day in sheltered areas such as greenhouses or among plants.

The adult elephant hawk-moth can be identified by the bright pink bars on its olive-green, furry body and wings. The vibrant colours help to disguise it among the flowers during the day and are also used to attract a mate.

The moth gets its name from its ability to hover like a 'hawk' when feeding, while the caterpillars of this species are said to look like elephants' trunks, with their mottled brown bodies and large eyespots, which help to scare off predators. They can also swell up to show off these spots, when threatened.

After mating, the female elephant hawk-moth lays her eggs on suitable plants such as fuchsia, rosebay willowherb (*Chamaenerion angustifolium*), lady's bedstraw (*Galium verum*) and purple loosestrife (*Lythrum salicaria*). The caterpillars then emerge to feed on the host plants, and pass through five stages of growth before moving to the ground to pupate. The adult emerges in spring and crawls away to complete the development of its wings before flying off.

Adult hawk-moths are sustained by the nectar of night-scented flowers such as honeysuckle and evening primrose (*Oenothera biennis*), so planting these will help lure them to your garden.

Spotlight on: Hardy perennial salvias (*Salvia*)

The *Salvia* genus includes a wide range of plants, from herbs such as culinary sage to shrubs and annuals, while the perennial types make an excellent addition to a herbaceous summer border. Their spikes of long-lasting, tubular flowers, with a distinctive upper and lower lip, appear over grey-green, aromatic foliage and come in many shades of blue, red, pink and white. The Balkan clary (*S. nemorosa*), *S.* × *sylvestris* and *S. microphylla* are among the most popular perennial species and hail from central and southern Europe, where summers are hot and dry, which means they enjoy a sunny spot and free-draining soil. In fact, all salvias are useful in drought-resistant planting schemes, while the nectar-rich flowers feed pollinators, including bees and butterflies.

SALVIA NEMOROSA 'CARADONNA'
Spikes of purple-black stems covered with rich violet-blue flowers appear from early summer to early autumn, the blooms emerging above a skirt of aromatic, grey-green foliage.
H x S: 50 x 30cm (20 x 12in)

SALVIA ULIGINOSA
The bog sage is a towering perennial with clear sky-blue summer flowers and slightly sticky, lance-shaped, yellow-green leaves. It is ideal for the back of a sunny border with reliably moist, but not waterlogged, soil.
H x S: 1.5 x 0.9m (5 x 3ft)

SALVIA 'HOT LIPS'
Masses of long-lasting, bicoloured, red and white flowers give rise to this salvia's name and appear from summer to the first frosts over small, grey-green leaves.
H x S: 90 x 75cm (36 x 30in)

SALVIA NEMOROSA SENSATION ROSE
A good choice for the front of a border, this sage produces spikes of dark purple buds that open to rose-pink flowers above aromatic grey-green leaves.
H x S: 30 x 30cm (12 x 12in)

SALVIA × SYLVESTRIS 'MAINACHT'
Tall stems of dark red buds open to reveal indigo-blue flowers from early to midsummer above grey-green foliage. It copes with light shade too.
H x S: 75 x 45cm (30 x 18in)

Seasonal planting ideas

STRIKING HUES

WHY IT WORKS
Combining the complementary colours of purple salvias and yellow euphorbia creates an exciting summer border. These hues are opposite each other on the colour wheel and really pop, while also visually balancing one another. The remaining plants help to soften the scheme. The *Veronica*, *Penstemon* and *Salvia* attract pollinators, too.

WHAT'S GROWING HERE
Salvia nemorosa 'Caradonna' is a perennial with upright spikes of violet-purple summer flowers above grey-green leaves. It grows to around 40cm (16in).

Euphorbia seguieriana is a semi-evergreen, clump-forming perennial, about 70cm (28in) tall. It features narrow, blue-green leaves on slender stems, topped with clusters of yellow to lime-green flowers in summer.

Veronica perfoliata is a perennial that reaches about 50cm (20in). It has round, grey-green, waxy leaves and spikes of small, drooping, blue-purple flowers in midsummer. Cut it back after flowering and it should bloom again in autumn.

Penstemon barbatus 'Coccineus' is an upright perennial, 1.5m (5ft) in height. From early summer to autumn, loose spires of hanging, tubular red flowers appear above semi-evergreen leaves.

Stipa tenuissima is a deciduous knee-high grass with thread-like leaves, and narrow, arching, feathery flowering panicles during the summer months.

WHEN TO PLANT
Plant in autumn or early spring, when conditions are not too hot or dry. These plants prefer a sunny aspect and well-drained soil.

WHERE TO SEE IT
Look out for this colourful combination during the summer in the Dry Garden at RHS Garden Hyde Hall.

Horticultural heroes

Constance Spry OBE · 1886–1960

Renowned for her spellbinding floral arrangements, which graced royal weddings and Queen Elizabeth II's coronation, Constance Spry revolutionized the floral arts with her use of wild and hedgerow plants, which she combined with ornamentals in humble containers such as jam jars. She was also a teacher, healthcare expert and celebrated author.

Born in Derby in 1886 to George and Henrietta Fletcher, the family later moved to Ireland, where Spry studied hygiene, physiology and district nursing. She then lectured on first aid and home care for the Irish Women's National Health Association. She married James Heppell Marr in 1910, but escaped the violent marriage and returned to England in 1916, becoming head of women's staff at the Ministry of Aircraft Production a year later.

She then went on to teach cookery, dressmaking and flower arranging to teenage factory workers at a school in East London, but gave it up while living with her lover, Henry Ernest Spry, whose name she adopted, to open her first shop, Flower Decoration, in 1929.

In 1934, Spry published her first book, *Flower Decoration*, and established the Constance Spry Flower School at her new shop in Mayfair. She created the flower arrangements for the Duke and Duchess of Windsor's wedding and those of both Princess Elizabeth and Princess Margaret. She also arranged the flowers at Westminster Abbey and along the processional route for the coronation of Queen Elizabeth II.

Spry continued to teach and lecture throughout the Second World War, and, in 1946, set up a domestic science school with her friend Rosemary Hume at Winkfield Place in Berkshire the two famously invented the new dish, Coronation Chicken. She was also appointed an OBE in the 1953 Coronation Honours.

At Winkfield Place, Spry cultivated many antique roses, and her name was given to David Austin's first rose introduction in 1961, a year after her death.

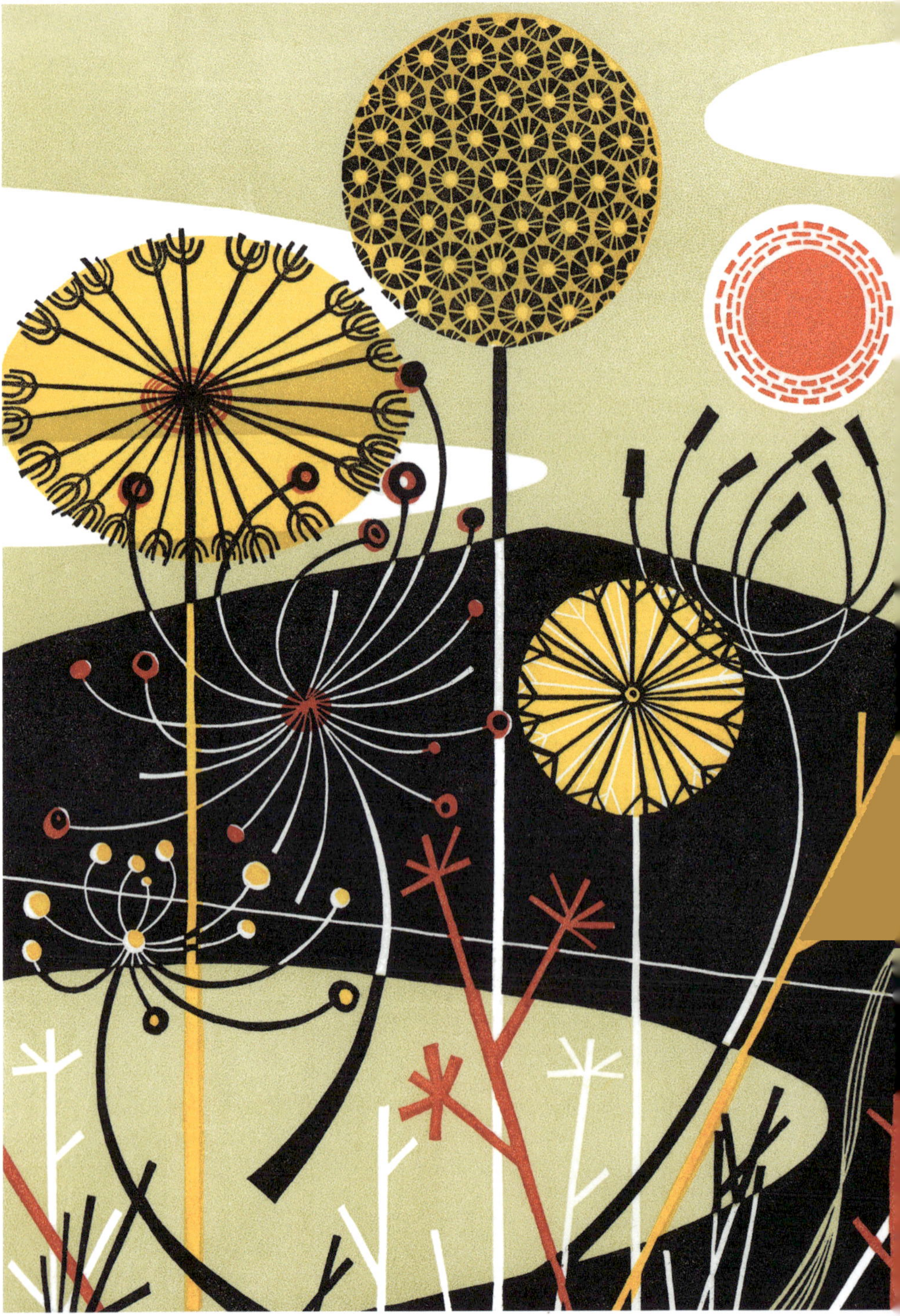

August

These precious last days of summer shimmer and glow under a blazing sun. Birds have flown their nests, and many flowers have dropped their petals to reveal ripe seed capsules, ready to burst open and generate new life. The heat may sap our energy, but the garden continues apace as dahlia, rudbeckia, aster and other late summer blooms remind us that the floral show is far from over.

KEY EVENTS
Bank Holiday (Scotland), 4 August
Janmashtami, 15–16 August
Summer Bank Holiday (England and Wales), 25 August

What to do in August

*While August allows time to rest before work begins again in earnest in autumn, there are still jobs to do, such as pruning trained apple and pears trees (see p.152) and, of course, watering crops, new plants and those in pots. Also sow hardy annuals where they are to flower next spring and early summer – crimson clover (*Trifolium incarnatum *subsp.* incarnatum*), linseed (*Linum grandiflorum*), Phacelia tanacetifolia and poached egg flower (*Limnanthes douglasii*) are good choices. You can also sow dwarf French beans now to deliver a crop later in autumn.*

In the garden

MAKE A SMALL POND for wildlife. Even a container such as an old washing-up bowl sunk into the ground and with a ramp on the inside edge, so wildlife can get in and out of the water easily, will sustain birds, amphibians and insects. In larger containers, such as a half barrel, you could add an aquatic plant or two: try the tiny waterlily *Nymphaea* 'Pygmaea Helvola', lesser spearwort (*Ranunculus flammula*) and flowering rush (*Butomus umbellatus*) (see also p.70). ❶

TRIM HEDGES after baby birds have fledged, but check for active nests before you start. Cut your hedge so that the base is slightly broader than the top, to allow light to reach the bottom – use taut strings as guides to achieve a level top and straight sides. Yew and deciduous hedges regrow from old wood, but only cut into new wood when trimming conifers (see also pp.152-3). ❷

TAKE SEMI-RIPE SHRUB CUTTINGS from *Choisya, Escallonia,* evergreen *Euonymus, Lonicera ligustrina* var. *yunnanensis* and conifers. Cut 10–15cm (4–6in) lengths of stem from the current season's growth. Remove the soft tips and all but the top four leaves. Plunge the stems into pots of gritty potting compost up to the first set of leaves, water and cover with a recycled plastic bag. They should root in a few weeks.

DEADHEAD DAHLIAS and other flowers, to prolong flowering. Dahlias bloom until the frosts, and plants should be bushy and well branched by now but, if not, pinch out the growing tips. Remove the cone-shaped, faded flowers and leave the new fat round buds. ❸

COLLECT SEEDS from ripe pods that have turned brown and you can hear seeds rattling inside, or wait until the plant sheds its first seeds. Cut stems of pods and pop them in paper bags or lay them in seed trays lined with newspaper. Once dry, extract the seeds and store in labelled containers for sowing next year. *Agapanthus*, *Nigella* and hardy geranium are easy to grow from collected seed – geranium pods explode and scatter seed, so leave them to ripen in paper bags. ❹

WATERING PARCHED LAWNS that have turned yellow or brown during prolonged dry periods is wasteful and unnecessary since the grass will soon green up again when rain returns. ❺

In the fruit & veg patch

PINCH OUT THE TOPS OF RUNNER BEANS, water plants regularly and dampen the foliage in the evenings in hot weather. Plants will then continue to produce pods, which are best picked when young and tender. Those left to overmature suppress further flowering, so pick the pods regularly to extend your harvest into early autumn.

AUGUST / 145

SOW SALAD ONIONS for crops in spring. 'White Lisbon' is a highly weatherproof choice. Sow 1cm (½in) deep in moist fertile soil in full sun, allowing a finger width between seeds and 30cm (12in) between rows. Cover with fleece, to exclude unwanted insects, until October. Apply a nitrogen-rich organic-based fertilizer around crops in late winter. ❻

TOPDRESS WINTER CROPS such as Brussels sprouts by applying a little all-purpose liquid organic-based fertilizer around plants, stimulating growth.

SOW MUSTARD AND ROCKET, to bio-fumigate the soil. These plants are rich in chemicals called glucosinolates, which will rid vegetable and fruit plots of many potentially harmful organisms and diseases. In October, run over the crops with a strimmer and fork the foliage into the soil. Cover with a plastic sheet for at least six weeks to help these plants do their work.

Indoors

REPOT OR DIVIDE CONGESTED PLANTS whose roots have filled their containers into pots one size larger, if you didn't do so earlier (see p.86).

CHECK HOUSEPLANTS regularly for unwelcome visitors. Wipe them off, remove affected areas or try soap-based products (see also pp.21, 39).

MONEY-SAVING IDEA
Buy bargain plants
Many garden centres have a table of reduced plants that are past their best, having flowered earlier in the season. Look out for hardy shrubs and perennials, which may be up to half the usual price, and select those that are free from unwanted insects and diseases, tipping them out of their pots and checking the roots as well. Most will start to put on new growth at this time of year when repotted in fresh compost or planted in the ground, before deciduous types lose their leaves in autumn. They should start back into growth in spring and bloom again.

Plants of the month

1. Japanese anemones (*Anemone × hybrida* pictured)
2. Helenium (*Helenium* MARDI GRAS pictured)
3. Caryopteris (*Caryopteris × clandonensis* pictured)
4. Chinese plumbago (*Ceratostigma willmottianum*)
5. Zinnia (*Zinnia elegans*)
6. Mexican sunflower (*Tithonia rotundifolia*)
7. Dahlia (*Dahlia* 'Diva US' pictured)
8. Globe thistle (*Echinops bannaticus* 'Taplow Blue' pictured)
9. Green cotton lavender (*Santolina rosmarinifolia*)
10. Alstroemeria (*Alstroemeria* INDIAN SUMMER pictured)
11. Korean feather reed grass (*Calamagrostis brachytricha*)

Project: Make space for wildlife

Nectar-rich plants support a range of pollinating insects, and you can double the benefits by planting them in a windowbox with bee nesting sites drilled into the sides. A windowsill around 1m (39in) above the ground, ideally in a sunny position that's not exposed to wind and driving rain, is a good spot to locate a bee hotel. This box is made from the end piece of a wooden pallet, which you can source online or from a garden centre.

YOU WILL NEED
Wooden pallet
Saw
Electric drill and drill bits
Sandpaper
Recycled plastic bag, optional
Peat-free John Innes No. 2
Horticultural grit
Selection of pollen-rich plants, such as *Sedum nussbaumerianum*, *Hylotelephium* 'Wildfire' (SunSparkler Series) and *Erigeron karvinskianus* (look for the RHS Plants for Pollinators logo)

1 Saw off the end of a pallet, including the solid chunks of wood that connect the front and back. This makes four sides of the box – depending on the design of the pallet you may need to screw on an extra plank to make the base.

2 Drill a few drainage holes in the base, then drill several holes at least 8cm (3in) deep into the wooden blocks from the front. Use a range of drill bit diameters from 2mm to 10mm (1/16–1/2in).

3 Sand all the surfaces, especially where the holes have been drilled. You can then line the insides of the planting space with plastic from a compost bag, to help preserve the wood.

4 Fill the box with drought-tolerant plants, using the planting method for coastal plants on p.128. Some plants will need to be replaced annually if they outgrow the box.

148 / AUGUST

Looking up

Sunrise and sunset

Temperatures often remain high in August, but the sun's intensity is waning, while the shorter days prompt late-summer flowers to bloom.

| | LONDON || EDINBURGH ||
DAY	Sunrise	Sunset	Sunrise	Sunset
Fri, Aug 1	5:23:00 am	8:50:41 pm	5:15:40 am	9:22:35 pm
Sat, Aug 2	5:24:31 am	8:49:01 pm	5:17:33 am	9:20:33 pm
Sun, Aug 3	5:26:03 am	8:47:20 pm	5:19:27 am	9:18:29 pm
Mon, Aug 4	5:27:35 am	8:45:37 pm	5:21:22 am	9:16:24 pm
Tue, Aug 5	5:29:08 am	8:43:52 pm	5:23:17 am	9:14:16 pm
Wed, Aug 6	5:30:41 am	8:42:05 pm	5:25:12 am	9:12:07 pm
Thu, Aug 7	5:32:14 am	8:40:17 pm	5:27:08 am	9:09:57 pm
Fri, Aug 8	5:33:48 am	8:38:27 pm	5:29:04 am	9:07:45 pm
Sat, Aug 9	5:35:23 am	8:36:36 pm	5:31:01 am	9:05:31 pm
Sun, Aug 10	5:36:57 am	8:34:43 pm	5:32:58 am	9:03:16 pm
Mon, Aug 11	5:38:32 am	8:32:49 pm	5:34:55 am	9:01:00 pm
Tue, Aug 12	5:40:07 am	8:30:54 pm	5:36:52 am	8:58:42 pm
Wed, Aug 13	5:41:42 am	8:28:57 pm	5:38:50 am	8:56:23 pm
Thu, Aug 14	5:43:18 am	8:26:59 pm	5:40:47 am	8:54:03 pm
Fri, Aug 15	5:44:53 am	8:25:00 pm	5:42:45 am	8:51:42 pm
Sat, Aug 16	5:46:29 am	8:23:00 pm	5:44:43 am	8:49:19 pm
Sun, Aug 17	5:48:04 am	8:20:59 pm	5:46:41 am	8:46:56 pm
Mon, Aug 18	5:49:40 am	8:18:56 pm	5:48:39 am	8:44:31 pm
Tue, Aug 19	5:51:16 am	8:16:52 pm	5:50:37 am	8:42:05 pm
Wed, Aug 20	5:52:52 am	8:14:48 pm	5:52:35 am	8:39:39 pm
Thu, Aug 21	5:54:28 am	8:12:42 pm	5:54:33 am	8:37:11 pm
Fri, Aug 22	5:56:04 am	8:10:36 pm	5:56:31 am	8:34:43 pm
Sat, Aug 23	5:57:40 am	8:08:29 pm	5:58:28 am	8:32:14 pm
Sun, Aug 24	5:59:16 am	8:06:20 pm	6:00:26 am	8:29:44 pm
Mon, Aug 25	6:00:52 am	8:04:11 pm	6:02:24 am	8:27:13 pm
Tue, Aug 26	6:02:28 am	8:02:01 pm	6:04:22 am	8:24:41 pm
Wed, Aug 27	6:04:03 am	7:59:51 pm	6:06:19 am	8:22:09 pm
Thu, Aug 28	6:05:39 am	7:57:40 pm	6:08:17 am	8:19:36 pm
Fri, Aug 29	6:07:15 am	7:55:28 pm	6:10:14 am	8:17:02 pm
Sat, Aug 30	6:08:51 am	7:53:15 pm	6:12:12 am	8:14:28 pm
Sun, Aug 31	6:10:27 am	7:51:02 pm	6:14:09 am	8:11:53 pm

Moonrise and moonset

Moon phases

- **NEW MOON** 23 August
- **FIRST QUARTER** 1 August / 31 August
- ○ **FULL MOON** 9 August
- ◐ **THIRD QUARTER** 16 August

DAY	LONDON Moonrise	Moonset	Moonrise	EDINBURGH Moonrise	Moonset	Moonrise
Aug 1	14:24	23:08		14:57	22:58	
Aug 2	15:37	23:27		16:18	23:11	
Aug 3	16:51	23:54		17:39	23:30	
Aug 4	17:59			18:54		
Aug 5		00:33	18:57		00:03	19:54
Aug 6		01:26	19:43		00:55	20:34
Aug 7		02:34	20:15		02:09	20:59
Aug 8		03:53	20:39		03:36	21:15
Aug 9		05:17	20:57		05:09	21:25
Aug 10		06:42	21:11		06:42	21:32
Aug 11		08:07	21:23		08:13	21:38
Aug 12		09:31	21:35		09:44	21:44
Aug 13		10:56	21:48		11:16	21:50
Aug 14		12:23	22:03		12:51	21:59
Aug 15		13:52	22:23		14:28	22:11
Aug 16		15:22	22:51		16:07	22:30
Aug 17		16:46	23:32		17:40	23:04
Aug 18		17:57			18:53	
Aug 19	00:31	18:48		00:00	19:40	
Aug 20	01:45	19:24		01:21	20:06	
Aug 21	03:09	19:48		02:53	20:22	
Aug 22	04:34	20:05		04:26	20:32	
Aug 23	05:55	20:18		05:55	20:39	
Aug 24	07:13	20:29		07:20	20:44	
Aug 25	08:28	20:39		08:41	20:49	
Aug 26	09:41	20:49		09:59	20:53	
Aug 27	10:54	21:00		11:18	20:59	
Aug 28	12:06	21:13		12:37	21:06	
Aug 29	13:20	21:30		13:58	21:16	
Aug 30	14:34	21:53		15:20	21:32	
Aug 31	15:44	22:26		16:37	21:58	

Average rainfall

The 20-year average rainfall for the UK in August is 117mm (4.6in), but in many areas this is often the driest month of the year, so ensure your pots and young plants and crops are well irrigated when the soil is parched.

LOCATION	DAYS	MM	INCHES
Aberdeen	11	68	2.7
Aberystwyth	13	86	3.4
Belfast	14	85	3.3
Birmingham	10	68	2.7
Bournemouth	8	60	2.4
Bristol	11	75	3.0
Cambridge	9	56	2.2
Canterbury	8	57	2.2
Cardiff	12	105	4.1
Edinburgh	10	72	2.8
Exeter	11	92	3.6
Glasgow	14	95	3.7
Gloucester	11	72	2.8
Inverness	12	65	2.6
Ipswich	8	48	1.9
Leeds	13	86	3.4
Liverpool	12	72	2.8
London	9	68	2.7
Manchester	15	100	3.9
Newcastle upon Tyne	10	64	2.5
Norwich	9	66	2.6
Nottingham	10	64	2.5
Oxford	9	62	2.4
Sheffield	10	65	2.5
Truro	12	71	2.8

Pruning masterclass: late summer

Although traditionally deciduous woody plants are pruned in winter (see pp.36–7), there is much to be said for late summer pruning when wounds heal much faster and the loss of green leafy material limits the vigour and extent of the regrowth. Birches, magnolias and walnuts, for example, are all best pruned in summer, although any tree can be tackled now, if they are not hosts to nesting birds, in which case, delay until September.

Reduce wisteria's long flexible shoots to 5–6 leaves in the summer to help boost flowering.

PLANTS TO CUT

Pruning the young growth of certain plants in summer not only reduces regrowth but can also promote flower bud formation by processes that remain unclear. Wisteria is a good example: it should be pruned now by shortening the long, whippy, new shoots to 5–6 leaves. Then the shoots should be pruned again in winter, to 2–3 buds, to keep the plant to a manageable size and encourage a better display of flowers.

Similarly, apples and pears grown as cordons and espaliers are pruned in late summer, once the bases of their new shoots have become woody and less flexible. Shorten lateral (side) shoots longer than 20cm (8in) to three leaves above the basal leaf cluster; ignore shorter shoots, as they often terminate in a flower bud. Cordon and espalier apples and pears need no further winter pruning, unlike other forms of fruit tree, which are cut when dormant after leaf fall (see pp. 226–7).

ANNUAL HEDGE TRIMMING

Hedges are ideally pruned just once a year in late summer, the resulting regrowth creating a smooth mossy finish for the winter in the case of evergreens, and neat, basket-like, twiggy growth in deciduous hedges. However, very vigorous hedges such as shrubby honeysuckle (*Lonicera ligustrina* var. *yunnanensis*) and privet (*Ligustrum*) usually need cutting more than once a year, because of their quick initial growth. Slower-growing hedges such as beech, hornbeam and yew require only one trim now and will not be injured if you cut into older leafless wood.

Reducing the shoots of trained apple trees in summer helps to boost fruit production.

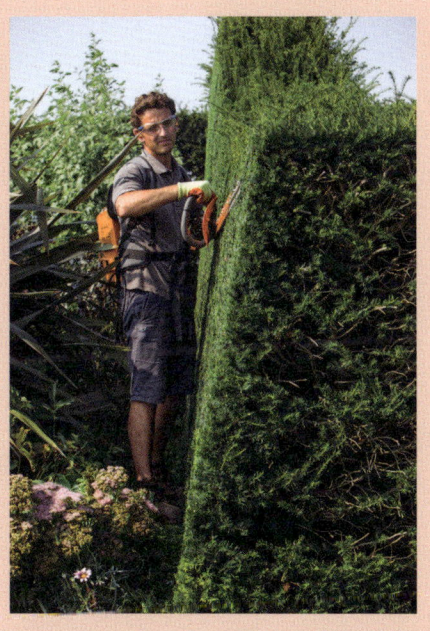

Trim your hedge into a wedge shape that will allow light to penetrate all the way to the bottom.

Conifer hedges also respond well to a single summer trim, but take care not to cut into older, bare, needle- or scale-less wood because, unlike yew, they usually fail to regrow. Even *Thuja*, often said to resprout from older wood, can be unreliable in this respect. Conifer hedges are prone to brown patches of dead shoots, too, and while the cause remains unclear, it appears to be related to stress from drought or waterlogging. However, RHS research found that pruning now causes the least harm, while pruning in early autumn is most damaging.

To prevent your hedge becoming thin or bare at the base due to insufficient light reaching the lower stems, make the bottom slightly wider than the top, to create a wedge shape, as shown above.

AUGUST / 153

Edible garden

There is an abundance of crops to harvest in August, and picking beans, courgettes and chillies regularly will help to prolong their productivity for a few more weeks. Also continue to sow small batches of fast-maturing vegetables for autumn crops.

Vegetables

SOW INDOORS Herbs for autumn crops.

SOW OUTDOORS Carrots; chard; chicory and endive; dwarf French beans; kohlrabi; lettuces and salad leaves; onions; pak choi; perpetual spinach; radishes; rocket; spring cabbages; turnips; winter-hardy spring onions.

PLANT OUT Plants sown in pots or trays earlier in the year, including autumn and winter cabbages, spring cauliflowers, kale.

HARVEST NOW Aubergines (in greenhouse); beetroots; broad beans; broccoli; calabrese; carrots; cauliflowers; chard; chicory and endive; chillies; courgettes ❶; cucumbers; French and runner beans; globe artichokes; herbs; lettuces; maincrop potatoes; marrows; onions; peas; peppers; radishes; spring onions; summer squash; sweetcorn; tomatoes.

HERB OF THE MONTH: OREGANO
One of the easiest herbs to grow, oregano (*Origanum vulgare*) is a drought-tolerant subshrub that thrives in pots or in the ground and delivers a spicy kick to many savoury dishes. Plant it in a sunny spot in a gravel or dry garden, and pick the leaves as needed from spring to early autumn. The summer flowers are also magnets for butterflies and bees. Oregano is sometimes confused with the sweeter-tasting sweet marjoram (*O. majorana*); the two herbs are from the same family and grow in similar conditions, so you could try both.

Fruit

HARVEST Early apples; blackberries; currants; blueberries; gooseberries; late-season strawberries; nectarines; early pears; peaches; plums.

Challenges this month

Stay vigilant for activity from flea beetles and vine weevils at this time of year. Blight can decimate tomato and potato crops now if early action is not taken, though sadly, because there is no remedy, some plants will inevitably be lost.

FLEA BEETLES are tiny, black-bodied insects with impressive rear legs that allow them to leap out of trouble. They puncture leaves (see right) causing pale brown areas and can reduce the vigour of affected plants, especially those in the cabbage family, such as radishes, turnips and wallflowers. They overwinter in leaf litter and are particularly damaging in late summer. The larvae feed on plant roots but rarely do any harm. Covering new sowings with fleece and watering crops well will help them to mature more quickly and minimize damage by flea beetles.

VINE WEEVIL are flightless black beetles that eat U-shaped notches from the edges of plant leaves but rarely cause much harm. However, they also lay hundreds of eggs that hatch into root-eating larvae in summer. Plants grown in the soil are much less vulnerable than those raised in containers, and strawberries and heucheras are particularly susceptible. The nematode biological control works well in warm weather and is approved for use in both borders and pots. If your plants are affected, try removing all the grubs from the chewed roots and place the plant with the leaves intact on a bed of compost, where it may re-root.

POTATO BLIGHT affects both potatoes and tomatoes, particularly in damp weather and on dewy nights when warm wet leaves and high humidity provide the perfect conditions for this fungal disease to spread. In tomatoes, symptoms include brown patches on the stems, leaves and fruits, which then rot. Although no garden fungicides or other treatments are available to control blight, prompt removal of infected material can slow the spread of the disease. The affected plant parts should be buried deeply, taken to your local council green waste collection site if permitted, or burned, rather than composted. Growing tomatoes in a greenhouse helps to keep the foliage dry and offers good protection, while disease-resistant varieties such as 'Crimson Crush' and 'Oh Happy Day' are also worth considering for future years.

Focus on wildlife

Swallow

The first sighting of swallows returning in April from their winter haunts to their nesting grounds in the UK ushers in the warmer months ahead.

Swooping and diving over farmland and fields, catching their insect prey on the wing, these small birds are constantly on the move, making it difficult to recognize them from their glossy, dark blue-black upper bodies, white below, and dark rusty red forehead and throat. However, their long-forked tails give them away, and distinguish them from swifts and house martins, whose tails are much shorter.

Despite their small size, these seasonal migrants undertake an epic journey across rainforests and the Sahara desert to reach our shores from their winter homes in South Africa. Travelling at an average 32km/h (20mph), the trip takes about six weeks. In autumn, they can be seen perching on wires and roosting in reedbeds, before heading south again to warmer climes.

Swallows are generally monogamous, and pairs stay together for the season, although males have been known to care for and feed chicks from a different male. In June and July, both sexes build a nest from mud and straw on ledges in farm buildings and outhouses, or under the eaves of houses close to their feeding grounds. Research shows that over 40 per cent of swallows return to the same nest each year, repairing it, as necessary, when they arrive.

The female lays between three and eight eggs, which both parents incubate. Once hatched, the young will leave the nest in 18–23 days. If conditions are good, the mating pair may then have a second brood later in the summer.

If you live in a rural area, consider installing swallow ledges and nesting boxes in outbuildings, to encourage these birds to take up residence.

Spotlight on: Hardy shrubby hydrangeas (*Hydrangea*)

Hydrangeas are among the few shrubs that flower from mid- to late summer and are prized for their showy blue, pink, red and white blooms. Some also sport contrasting dark leaves. They fall into three main groups: the mopheads (*H. macrophylla* and *H. arborescens*), with their large, dome-shaped flowerheads; lacecaps (*H. macrophylla, H. serrata* and *H. aspera*), which have flat lacy flowers; and those with cone-shaped blooms (*H. paniculata* and *H. quercifolia*). All need moist (not waterlogged) soil and the blue-flowered forms also demand acid soil to retain their colour. All will thrive in sun or part shade.

HYDRANGEA ARBORESCENS 'ANNABELLE'
Grown for its huge spherical heads of white sterile flowers, which form in summer on sturdy stems over broad, oval, green leaves.
H x S: 1.5 x 1.8m (5 x 6ft)

HYDRANGEA MACROPHYLLA 'LANARTH WHITE'
A compact lacecap hydrangea, 'Lanarth White' has flattened flowerheads comprising pink or blue central sterile florets surrounded by white petals, known as 'ray-florets'.
H x S: 1.2 x 1.2m (4 x 4ft)

HYDRANGEA ASPERA VILLOSA GROUP The lacecap flowers of this tall shrub comprise large white outer florets and small mauve inner florets. The large green leaves have a velvety texture.
H x S: 2.5 x 2.5m (8 x 8ft)

HYDRANGEA PANICULATA 'LIMELIGHT'
The conical heads of lime-green flowers turn cream and then become darker as they age, finally developing pinkish tints in autumn before the leaves fall.
H x S: 1.5 x 1.5m (5 x 5ft)

HYDRANGEA SERRATA 'BLUEBIRD'
Grow this lacecap form on acid soil to retain the flattened heads of blue-mauve flowers, which appear among pointed, mid-green leaves that turn dark red before falling.
H x S: 1.5 x 1.5m (5 x 5ft)

HYDRANGEA PANICULATA PINKY-WINKY
Red stems hold large, cone-shaped heads of fragrant white flowers that fade to dusky pink, with both colours often appearing on one spike to create a duo-tone effect.
H x S: 1.5 x 1.5m (5 x 5ft)

AUGUST

Seasonal planting ideas

SUMMER SPIKES

WHY IT WORKS
The individual plants in this colourful combination grow to different heights, taking the eye up in stages from the *Heuchera* in front to a middle layer of *Liatris* and then the taller *Coreopsis* at the back. The small airy foliage of both the *Liatris* and *Coreopsis* allows a view through the plants, creating a blend rather than distinct layers, while the larger *Heuchera* leaves help to give the scheme a feeling of weight and substance. All the flowers increase biodiversity by attracting pollinators.

WHAT'S GROWING HERE?
Liatris pycnostachya is an upright, clump-forming perennial that grows to 1.2m (4ft). It produces stems of narrowly lance-shaped, dark green leaves from which arise the tall feathery flower spikes in summer, comprising many small, purple-pink flowers. *Liatris spicata* is a similar but shorter species and more widely available.

Heuchera villosa 'Autumn Bride' is a mound-forming perennial with mid- to light green foliage and upright stems covered with dense panicles of white flowers, which appear in summer.

Coreopsis tripteris, commonly known as golden crown, is a tall, upright, clump-forming perennial that can reach 2m (6ft) in height. Slender stems of small, aromatic, lobed leaves are topped with bright yellow, daisy-like flowers with brown central discs, which appear from midsummer to autumn.

WHEN TO PLANT
Plant these perennials in autumn or early spring, avoiding summer, if possible, when warmer, drier conditions make establishment more difficult. These plants prefer a sunny aspect in a moisture-retentive yet well-drained soil.

WHERE TO SEE IT
This striking combination can be seen during summer in the Paradise Garden at RHS Garden Bridgewater.

Horticultural heroes

Sir Geoffrey Jellicoe · 1900–1996

The celebrated landscape architect Sir Geoffrey Jellicoe spent most of his professional life working as an architect and town planner. However, landscapes were his passion – he believed their design was 'the mother of all arts' – and his legacy includes many famous projects: for example, the Hemel Hempstead Water Gardens; Sandringham in Norfolk; Sutton Place near Guildford; the Jellicoe canal at RHS Garden Wisley; and the Kennedy Memorial at Runnymede.

Jellicoe was born in 1900 in London but grew up near the coast in Sussex. After qualifying as an architect, he visited the gardens of Italy, later writing a book together with his friend J.C. Shepherd on *Italian Gardens of the Renaissance*, which informed much of his later work.

A founding member of the Landscape Institute and its president from 1939 to 1949, he was also appointed founding President of the International Federation of Landscape Architects in 1948. Jellicoe qualified as a town planner after the war and produced a masterplan for Hemel Hempstead, which included the water gardens that can still be seen today.

He became interested in psychology, especially Carl Jung's theories on the conscious and subconscious mind, which he integrated into his designs.

The Kennedy Memorial in Surrey, completed in 1965, brought these ideas into focus. It represents a physical and metaphysical journey from darkness to light, with its winding paths, made of thousands of granite sets, threading through a wooded hillside and emerging at the memorial stone in a clearing flooded with sunlight.

In later life, Jellicoe wrote several books, including *The Landscape of Man* in 1975, co-authored with his wife Susan, in which he discusses how civilizations have shaped landscapes. This idea inspired his final project, the Moody Historical Gardens in Texas. His plans for the coastal marshes near Houston were to take the visitor on a botanical history of the world, and he worked on the project until his death in 1996. Sadly, his plans were never implemented.

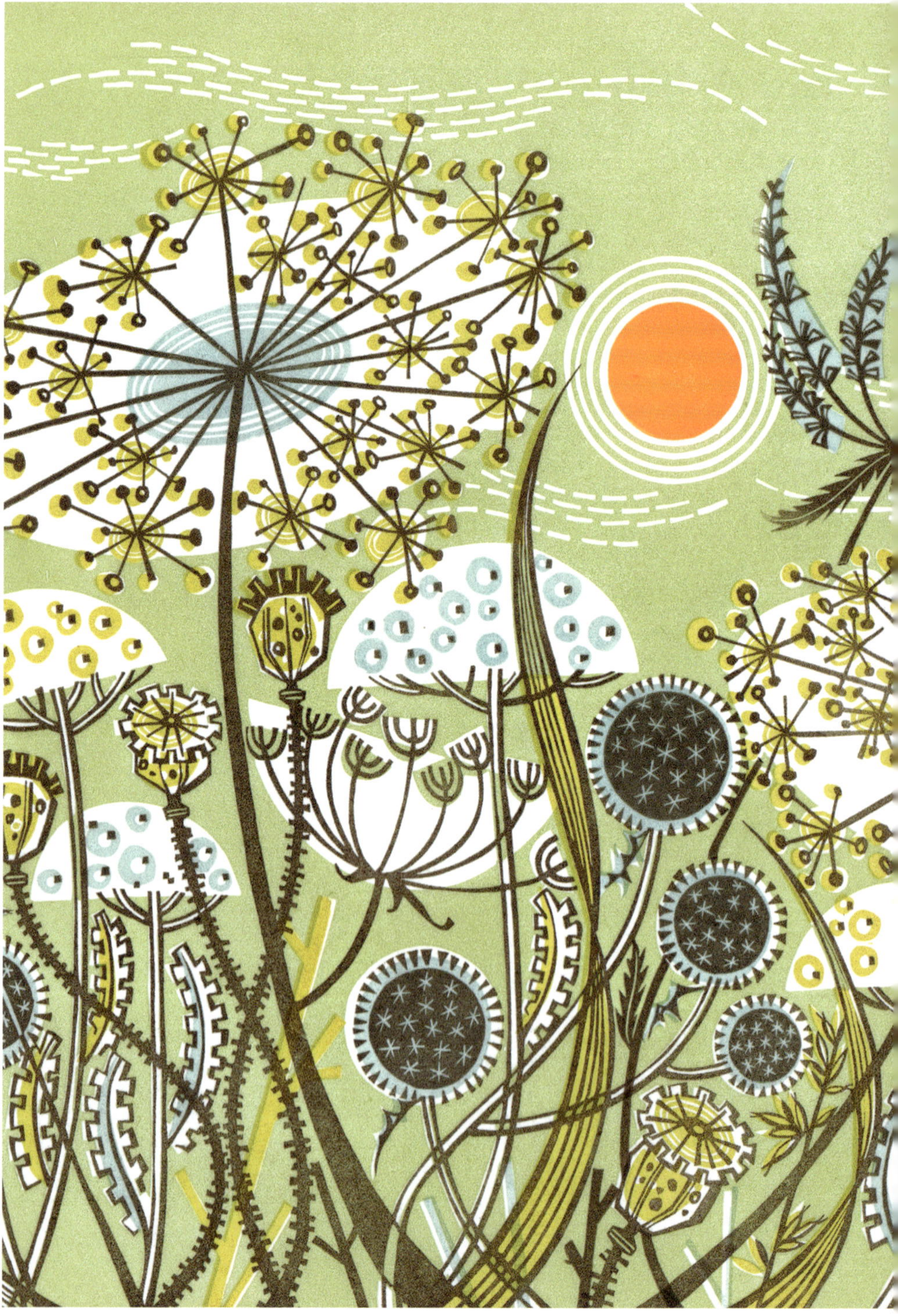

September

The dazzling summer light is mellowing now, with northerly breezes beckoning in a new season. As consolation, September delivers rich rewards, with apples glistening on trees and raspberries glowing like jewels. Pumpkins are beginning to swell, too, and early autumn crops are ready to harvest, while sedum, monk's hood and clematis sparkle among drifts of feathery grasses in the flower garden.

KEY EVENTS
International Day of Peace, 21 September
Autumn Equinox, 22 September
Michaelmas Day (last day of the harvest season), 29 September

What to do in September

September is the perfect month for planting hardy perennials, spring bulbs and pot-grown shrubs – the warm soil and showers creating ideal conditions for root growth. Sowing hardy crops for winter and early spring harvests is another task to complete, while continuing to sow hardy annuals for earlier blooms next year. It's also time to get busy in the kitchen, making jams, compotes and pickles with surplus crops that will bring the taste of summer to your table during the cold months ahead.

In the garden

TAKE RAMBLING ROSE CUTTINGS, many of which are closer to wild species and easier to propagate than bush roses. Using young shoots that have grown this year, take 25cm (10in) cuttings and remove the thorns and all but the top few sets of leaves. Place in deep pots filled with a 50:50 mix of peat-free potting compost and horticultural sand, or, in southern gardens, trenches outdoors. The cuttings should have rooted by spring. ❶

PLANT SPRING BULBS FOR WILDLIFE that will feed bees early in the year. For sunny spots, plant crocuses, or try grape hyacinths in sun or part shade. Later, bees relish alliums, especially honey garlic (*Allium siculum*). In large wildlife gardens, include native garlic and bluebells (*Hyacinthoides non-scripta*) sourced from a reliable nursery. ❷

AERATE LAWNS, if they are growing poorly, to introduce more oxygen to the root area. Hire a powered aerator or make a series of holes by plunging a garden fork into the lawn at regular intervals to a depth of about 10cm (4in). Then brush a lawn topdressing, made up of 3 parts sandy loam, 6 parts sharp sand and 1 part peat-free potting compost, over the surface. Also rake out some of the thatch (dead leaves and debris) from between the grass blades, and add it to the compost heap. ❸

PLANT AUTUMN CONTAINERS to bring colour to balconies and patios over the coming months. Plants grow little during winter, so choose bigger specimens of dwarf conifers, winter-flowering heathers, berried skimmia, euonymus and small-leaved ivies, with pops of colour from violas, pansies, bellis daisies and primulas, supplemented with spring bulbs, including aconites, crocuses, and dwarf narcissi and tulips. All thrive in shady spots, bar the crocuses and tulips. ❹

In the fruit & veg patch

SOW HARDY SPINACH such as 'Amazon' or 'Medania', to bridge the hungry gap next April, when little else is available. Sow in a sheltered sunny spot in good garden soil, allowing a finger width between the seeds, and 30cm (12in) in between rows. Thin to 15cm (6in) apart as soon as possible after germination. Feed next spring, to boost growth for an early crop.

LEAVE THE LAST PEPPERS to ripen on the plant, rather than harvesting when green, as you would earlier in the year to promote more flowers and fruits.

PLANT ELEPHANT GARLIC cloves now. This is technically a 'bulbous leek' rather than a true garlic, producing larger bulbs with a mild, sweet flavour, best appreciated when roasted. Plant the single cloves in full sun, 10cm (4in) apart, with 45cm (18in) between rows, and just cover them in fertile soil. The crops will be ready to harvest next summer once the foliage yellows and dies down.

SOW SALADS IN A COLD FRAME. Salad leaves such as chicory, endive, kale, lamb's lettuce, lettuce and mustard greens grow swiftly in mild autumns and can be thinned as they grow to form loose leafy heads to harvest before the frosts set in. In cold regions, sow the leafy crops in pots and raise plants in a bright conservatory or greenhouse, or on a windowsill.

TOMATOES CAN CROP for another month in a greenhouse, when given a weekly dose of potassium-rich organic-based fertilizer as the fruit ripens. Outdoor tomatoes usually find what they need in the soil, but, if ripening is slow, an additional feed now will help. ❺

MONEY-SAVING IDEA
Split new perennials to make more plants
September is a great time to plant hardy perennials, and one easy way to stretch your money is to divide your new purchases into two or three plants. Look for pots of clump-forming plants such as asters, crocosmia, houseleeks (*Sempervivum*) and hardy geraniums. When you get them home, tip them out and prise apart the rootball into two or three pieces using your hands or a sharp knife, ensuring each has stems of healthy leaves attached to some roots. Pot up into individual containers of peat-free potting compost or plant directly in the ground.

Indoors

PLANT BULBS indoors for flowers in December. Plant prepared hyacinths or daffodil bulbs in a bowl of bulb fibre, with their tips just showing above the surface, and moisten the compost. Leave in a dark cupboard to root. When shoots are 2.5cm (1in) high, place in a bright area, keeping the fibre moist but never soggy until the bulbs flower.

AFRICAN VIOLETS (*Saintpaulia*) bloom for months if plants receive 12 hours of sunlight per day (avoid direct summer sun). Keep them at 18–24°C (64–75°F) by day, 16°C (61°F) at night. Water only when the top of the soil feels dry.

Plants of the month

1. Crimson flag lily (*Hesperantha coccinea*)
2. Autumn crocus (*Colchicum autumnale*)
3. Abelia (*Abelia × grandiflora*)
4. Pineapple flower (*Eucomis*: pink-flowered variety pictured)
5. Ice plant (*Hylotelephium* syn. *Sedum*) (*H. spectabile* 'Stardust' pictured)
6. Monk's hood (*Aconitum carmichaelii* (Wilsonii Group) 'Kelmscott' pictured)
7. Blue passion flower (*Passiflora caerulea*)
8. Aster (*Symphyotrichum* 'Prairie Purple' pictured)
9. Black bugbane (*Actaea racemosa*)
10. Toad lily (*Tricyrtis* 'Shinalins' pictured)
11. Strawberry tree (*Arbutus unedo*)

Project: Make your own bug hotel

It's easy to create habitats and nesting sites for insects and other invertebrates with a few bug hotels for different species. Several hotels distributed around the garden are more effective than just one, and these three simple ideas are easy to make from found and recycled materials. Mid-autumn is also the perfect time to get started, since insects such as lacewings are looking for places to shelter over winter. A sunny spot, away from the worst of the wind and rain, is best for bees and insects, but woodlice and centipedes prefer shadier, cooler conditions close to the ground.

YOU WILL NEED
2 wire hanging baskets
Chicken wire
Sturdy wire
Old bricks
Old drainpipe
To fill the hotels: pine cones (shown), terracotta crocks, seedheads, hollow bamboo canes, compost, ivy, moss

PROJECT 1 This hanging hotel can be suspended from a hook on a balcony or patio wall. Simply line two metal hanging baskets with chicken wire and fill with found materials such as pine cones, broken pots and seedheads. You can also add some compost and plant small ivies. Attach the baskets together with wire to make a ball and hang in a sunny, sheltered spot.

PROJECT 2 Pile up old bricks, leaving spaces between them for dried hollow stems, twigs and seedheads. Spiders may create webs across the airbricks, while other invertebrates will find their way into the stems and seedheads.

PROJECT 3 A section of old drainpipe stuffed with cut bamboo canes will provide a nesting site for solitary bees such as leafcutters, which lay their eggs in the hollow centres, and cap off the pipe ends with sections of foliage.

Looking up

Sunrise and sunset

As we move into autumn, the angle of the sun and reduced daylight hours slow down growth, and many perennials that flowered earlier in the year will start to die down.

DAY	LONDON Sunrise	LONDON Sunset	EDINBURGH Sunrise	EDINBURGH Sunset
Mon, Sep 1	6:12:02 am	7:48:48 pm	6:16:06 am	8:09:18 pm
Tue, Sep 2	6:13:38 am	7:46:34 pm	6:18:03 am	8:06:42 pm
Wed, Sep 3	6:15:14 am	7:44:19 pm	6:20:00 am	8:04:06 pm
Thu, Sep 4	6:16:49 am	7:42:04 pm	6:21:57 am	8:01:30 pm
Fri, Sep 5	6:18:25 am	7:39:48 pm	6:23:54 am	7:58:53 pm
Sat, Sep 6	6:20:01 am	7:37:32 pm	6:25:51 am	7:56:15 pm
Sun, Sep 7	6:21:36 am	7:35:15 pm	6:27:47 am	7:53:38 pm
Mon, Sep 8	6:23:12 am	7:32:58 pm	6:29:44 am	7:50:59 pm
Tue, Sep 9	6:24:47 am	7:30:41 pm	6:31:41 am	7:48:21 pm
Wed, Sep 10	6:26:23 am	7:28:23 pm	6:33:37 am	7:45:43 pm
Thu, Sep 11	6:27:58 am	7:26:06 pm	6:35:34 am	7:43:04 pm
Fri, Sep 12	6:29:34 am	7:23:48 pm	6:37:30 am	7:40:25 pm
Sat, Sep 13	6:31:09 am	7:21:30 pm	6:39:27 am	7:37:46 pm
Sun, Sep 14	6:32:45 am	7:19:11 pm	6:41:23 am	7:35:06 pm
Mon, Sep 15	6:34:21 am	7:16:53 pm	6:43:20 am	7:32:27 pm
Tue, Sep 16	6:35:56 am	7:14:34 pm	6:45:17 am	7:29:47 pm
Wed, Sep 17	6:37:32 am	7:12:15 pm	6:47:13 am	7:27:08 pm
Thu, Sep 18	6:39:08 am	7:09:57 pm	6:49:10 am	7:24:28 pm
Fri, Sep 19	6:40:44 am	7:07:38 pm	6:51:07 am	7:21:49 pm
Sat, Sep 20	6:42:20 am	7:05:19 pm	6:53:04 am	7:19:09 pm
Sun, Sep 21	6:43:56 am	7:03:00 pm	6:55:01 am	7:16:30 pm
Mon, Sep 22	6:45:33 am	7:00:42 pm	6:56:58 am	7:13:50 pm
Tue, Sep 23	6:47:09 am	6:58:23 pm	6:58:55 am	7:11:11 pm
Wed, Sep 24	6:48:46 am	6:56:05 pm	7:00:52 am	7:08:32 pm
Thu, Sep 25	6:50:22 am	6:53:46 pm	7:02:50 am	7:05:53 pm
Fri, Sep 26	6:51:59 am	6:51:28 pm	7:04:47 am	7:03:14 pm
Sat, Sep 27	6:53:36 am	6:49:11 pm	7:06:45 am	7:00:35 pm
Sun, Sep 28	6:55:13 am	6:46:53 pm	7:08:43 am	6:57:57 pm
Mon, Sep 29	6:56:51 am	6:44:36 pm	7:10:41 am	6:55:19 pm
Tue, Sep 30	6:58:28 am	6:42:19 pm	7:12:40 am	6:52:41 pm

Moonrise and moonset

Moon phases

● **NEW MOON** 21 September
◐ **FIRST QUARTER** 30 September

○ **FULL MOON** 7 September
◑ **THIRD QUARTER** 14 September

DAY	LONDON Moonrise	LONDON Moonset	LONDON Moonrise	EDINBURGH Moonrise	EDINBURGH Moonset	EDINBURGH Moonrise
Sep 1	16:47	23:12		17:43	22:41	
Sep 2	17:37			18:31	23:45	
Sep 3		00:14	18:15			19:02
Sep 4		01:28	18:42		01:07	19:21
Sep 5		02:50	19:01		02:38	19:33
Sep 6		04:15	19:17		04:11	19:41
Sep 7		05:41	19:30		05:45	19:48
Sep 8		07:07	19:42		07:18	19:54
Sep 9		08:34	19:55		08:52	20:00
Sep 10		10:03	20:09		10:28	20:08
Sep 11		11:35	20:28		12:08	20:18
Sep 12		13:07	20:53		13:49	20:35
Sep 13		14:35	21:30		15:26	21:04
Sep 14		15:51	22:23		16:47	21:53
Sep 15		16:48	23:33		17:41	23:06
Sep 16		17:27			18:12	
Sep 17	00:54	17:53		00:35	18:31	
Sep 18	02:17	18:12		02:07	18:42	
Sep 19	03:39	18:26		03:36	18:49	
Sep 20	04:57	18:37		05:01	18:55	
Sep 21	06:12	18:47		06:22	18:59	
Sep 22	07:25	18:57		07:41	19:04	
Sep 23	08:37	19:08		08:59	19:09	
Sep 24	09:50	19:20		10:18	19:15	
Sep 25	11:04	19:35		11:39	19:24	
Sep 26	12:18	19:56		13:00	19:37	
Sep 27	13:29	20:24		14:20	19:59	
Sep 28	14:35	21:04		15:30	20:34	
Sep 29	15:29	21:5		16:25	21:28	
Sep 30	16:11	23:06		17:02	22:41	

Average rainfall

The 20-year average rainfall for the UK in September is 116mm (4.6in), almost the same as for August. Temperatures early in the month are often as high as those in summer, too, so continue to water new and potted plants and crops in dry spells.

LOCATION	DAYS	MM	INCHES
Aberdeen	10	61	2.4
Aberystwyth	13	97	3.8
Belfast	12	70	2.8
Birmingham	10	68	2.7
Bournemouth	9	69	2.7
Bristol	10	64	2.5
Cambridge	8	48	1.9
Canterbury	8	55	2.2
Cardiff	12	86	3.4
Edinburgh	10	55	2.2
Exeter	10	94	3.7
Glasgow	14	98	3.9
Gloucester	10	69	2.7
Inverness	12	63	2.5
Ipswich	8	49	1.9
Leeds	12	82	3.2
Liverpool	12	77	3.0
London	9	59	2.3
Manchester	13	90	3.9
Newcastle upon Tyne	9	45	1.8
Norwich	9	60	2.4
Nottingham	10	57	2.2
Oxford	9	62	2.4
Sheffield	9	63	2.5
Truro	12	77	3.0

Edible garden

Tender crops such as tomatoes, peppers, aubergines, courgettes and cucumbers will continue to provide a good harvest in September, particularly if they are being grown in a greenhouse. You can also sow crops indoors to overwinter under cover.

Vegetables

SOW INDOORS OR UNDER CLOCHES
Herbs; pak choi; spring cabbages.

SOW OUTDOORS Salad leaves; spinach; turnips; winter-hardy spring onions; winter lettuce.

PLANT OUT Onion sets; spring cabbage sown in summer.

HARVEST NOW Aubergines; beetroots; broccoli; calabrese ❶; carrots; cauliflowers; celery; chicory and endive; Chinese cabbage, chillies; courgettes; cucumbers; French and runner beans; globe artichokes; herbs; lettuces; maincrop potatoes; marrows, pumpkins; parsnips ❷; peas; peppers ❸; radishes; spring onions; summer squash; sweetcorn; tomatoes; winter squash.

Fruit

PLANT NOW Strawberry plants at beginning of month.

HARVEST Apples ❹; autumn raspberries; blackberries; blueberries; late-season strawberries; medlars; pears; quinces.

TOP TIP
Plant a green manure or cover crop
September is a good time to sow cover crops such as crimson clover (above) and Italian ryegrass, where plants have been harvested, leaving bare patches of soil. By smothering the soil with their dense leaves, these green manures reduce weed growth over winter. Just before they flower in spring, dig the plants into the ground, where they will release nutrients and improve the soil structure.

HERB OF THE MONTH: MINT
An easy-to-grow perennial herb, mint (*Mentha*) is best raised in large pots of peat-free compost, since its spreading roots can become invasive in a garden border. It is also one of the few herbs that tolerates some shade. There are many flavours to choose from, including spearmint, apple mint and chocolate mint. Keep plants watered during dry spells and harvest the leaves from late spring to early autumn, before the plant becomes dormant in winter. Repot plants in fresh compost in spring.

Ferment recipe

TRADITIONAL SAUERKRAUT

Crunchy cabbage, sweet carrot and a hint of bitter lemony aniseed from dill – this classic pickle is resoundingly popular and with good reason. It can be made using traditional white cabbage, or try a red variety instead for a colourful alternative. Winter cabbages and carrots are in season now, so you can use your home-grown ingredients for this tangy pickle, which tastes delicious and helps to maintain good gut health.

INGREDIENTS
800g–1kg (1lb 12oz–2lb 3oz) cabbage
2–3 carrots
1½ tbsp salt
Handful of chopped dill
1 tbsp caraway seeds (these are optional, and make a delicious addition)

1. Slice the cabbage and carrots to the desired thickness – try using a mandolin for thin slices. Then rub the salt into the vegetables thoroughly. The proportion of salt should be 2 per cent of the total weight of the vegetables, so check and adapt the levels as necessary.

2. Stir in the chopped dill and caraway seeds, if using, and pack all the ingredients tightly into kilner jars using a tamper or the bottom of a glass. Place glass weights on top to help submerge the sauerkraut under the brine.

3. Seal with an airlock (see p.58) and leave for 5–7 days at room temperature, or longer if you want a sourer taste. Remove the airlock, seal the jars with their lids and store in the fridge. The sauerkraut will keep for about three months.

Challenges this month

Fungal diseases are on the rise as cool, damp weather arrives, providing ideal conditions for them to spread – look out for mildews and take action to avert serious harm. Also check apples and pears for signs of codling moth, before storing them.

DOWNY MILDEW (shown) is a fungal disease that thrives in mild early autumn weather and can infect many plants, causing mould growth on the undersides of the leaves. Resistant cultivars are available for many flowers and crops, including busy Lizzies, hebes, onions and spinach. No chemical remedies are available but allowing space between plants and removing unwanted plants will limit damage. Bag up or burn all affected plant material, as resistant spores can persist for several years.

HORSETAIL or mare's tail (*Equisetum arvense*) is a persistent perennial that produces fine, ferny foliage on tall straight stems and spreads via deep roots (rhizomes). In spring, fertile, light brown stems, up to 50cm (20in) tall, with cone-like structures at the tips appear, which also allow it to spread. It can form dense masses of plants in borders and between paving, especially in damp areas. Repeated hoeing and winter digging suppresses horsetail, but complete eradication is seldom possible due to the very deep roots. In lawns, frequent mowing helps keep it at bay.

CODLING MOTH is the cause of 'maggoty apples' and can also affect pears. The caterpillars bore into the fruits from mid- to late summer and cause them to ripen and drop early. You will see the larvae's exit holes on the side of the ripe fruit or at the 'eye' end, opposite the stalk. The damage and excrement pellets (frass) are revealed when the fruit is cut open.

Since only a small number of fruits are usually affected, codling moth is often best tolerated. Encourage birds, hedgehogs and ground beetles that prey on the larvae into the garden. Pheromone traps can be used in spring to lure the males, thereby reducing mating, which may help keep numbers in check on isolated trees, but this rarely works in areas with a few trees. Alternatively, try a biological control by spraying pathogenic nematodes on the trunk, branches and soil under the tree, where the caterpillars overwinter.

Focus on wildlife

Red admiral butterfly

One of the UK's best-known and most widely distributed butterflies, the red admiral makes a colourful contribution to our gardens in summer and autumn. Some are residents here all year, but most fly in during May and June from central Europe and North Africa.

These large butterflies' velvety black wings, adorned with striking orange-red and white bands, make them easy to spot. As well as feeding on nectar-rich plants, they can be seen in late summer and autumn feasting on fallen fruit, such as plums and apples, which offer them a boost of energy before they fly back to their winter grounds or overwinter here in the UK.

The females usually lay their eggs between April and September on nettles (*Urtica dioica* and *U. urens*) or, occasionally, on hops (*Humulus lupulus*). The caterpillars that emerge are black, spiny and covered with fine hairs, with a pale yellow stripe on either side of their bodies. They feast on the nettles, eventually turning into chrysalises, which are attached to leaves with a special kind of silk. The adults then emerge between August and October, which is when they are often seen feeding and sunning themselves in our gardens. You may also find them overwintering in houses, log piles, greenhouses, sheds and other sheltered places around the garden.

To encourage these beautiful butterflies into your patch include nectar-rich plants – look out for the RHS Plants for Pollinators logo on labels. Favourites include blue-flowered *Veronicastrum*, scabious, ivy, sedum (*Hylotelephium spectabile*), asters and *Buddleja*. If you have space, also nurture a large clump of nettles in a quiet area to provide caterpillar food, and avoid pesticides.

Spotlight on: Rudbeckia (*Rudbeckia*)

Known as coneflowers, this dazzling group of perennials and annuals is guaranteed to light up the garden from midsummer to the frosts in autumn. The most commonly available perennials are hardy and produce their yellow flowers with brown central cones from late summer, while the annuals include some more tender types and come in shades of yellow, orange, dark red and brown – some varieties also have flatter faces like common daisies. The blooms appear above green or grey-green foliage. These plants are rich in pollen and their seedheads provide food for birds and overwintering insects. Grow rudbeckias in full sun and moisture-retentive soil that drains easily.

RUDBECKIA AMPLEXICAULIS
This hardy annual is grown from seed in spring and produces tall stems of yellow flowers with prominent brown central discs from late summer to early autumn. The distinctive blooms are said to look like Mexican hats.
H x S: 90 x 50cm (36 x 20in)

RUDBECKIA FULGIDA VAR. SULLIVANTII 'GOLDSTURM'
This popular perennial produces an abundance of large, bright golden-yellow, daisy flowers with rich brown central cones from August to October, above narrow green leaves.
H x S: 60 x 45cm (24 x 18in)

RUDBECKIA SUBTOMENTOSA 'HENRY EILERS'
This unusual perennial coneflower produces tall stems of eye-catching flowers with slim, quilled, yellow petals and round orange-brown central discs from late summer.
H x S: 1.2 x 0.6m (4 x 2ft)

RUDBECKIA LACINIATA 'HERBSTSONNE'
A tall perennial, 'Herbstsonne' produces branched stems of golden-yellow flowers with a greenish-yellow central disc. It is ideal for the back of a sunny border and the sturdy stems rarely need staking.
H x S: 2 x 1m (6 x 3ft)

RUDBECKIA HIRTA 'CHERRY BRANDY'
The colourful flowers of this short-lived perennial, often grown as an annual, comprise dark brown-black central discs surrounded by cherry red petals. The blooms are good for cutting and appear from midsummer to mid-autumn. **H x S:** 60 x 30cm (24 x 12in)

Seasonal planting ideas

DYNAMIC DUO

WHY IT WORKS
Using just one focal plant, the eastern redbud (*Cercis canadensis*), with a carpet of the groundcovering *Bistorta* beneath, this simple yet effective combination draws the eye in autumn. Hints of the pink *Bistorta* flowers are picked up in the leaves of the redbud, which change from deep purple to orange and bronze through September and October, before falling. Creating a graphic picture from late summer to autumn, the mat of *Bistorta* also helps to prevent weed seeds from germinating and reduces soil moisture loss, while the flowers attract pollinators to the garden.

WHAT'S GROWING HERE?
Cercis canadensis 'Forest Pansy' is a small, often multi-stemmed, deciduous tree that grows to around 6m (20ft) in height. Small, bright-pink flowers appear in clusters on bare stems before the deep purple leaves unfurl in spring. The broadly heart-shaped foliage then turns to shades of orange, bronze and red-purple in autumn.

Bistorta amplexicaulis 'Ample Pink', formerly known as *Persicaria*, is a clump-forming perennial with slim, oval, green leaves and upright spikes of rose-pink flowers that reach up to 70cm (28in) in height and appear from July through to October. There are many other pink forms of *B. amplexicaulis* to choose from, which would achieve a similar effect, including *B.a.* 'Rosea' and *B.a.* 'Rubie's Pink'.

WHEN TO PLANT
Plant the tree and perennials in autumn or early spring, in sun or part shade and moisture-retentive yet well-drained soil.

WHERE TO SEE IT
Visit RHS Garden Harlow Carr from summer to autumn to see this eye-catching combination.

Horticultural heroes

Beth Chatto OBE · 1923–2018

Renowned gardener and plantswoman Beth Chatto rose to fame when she converted an overgrown wasteland at Elmstead Market in Essex into one of the most famous gardens in the world. During her long life, she also won ten Gold Medals at the RHS Chelsea Flower Show, the RHS Victoria Medal of Honour and RHS Lawrence Medal, as well as two honorary doctorates from Essex University and Anglia Ruskin University.

Chatto was born in 1923 in Essex and initially trained to be a teacher, but after marrying fruit farmer Andrew Chatto in 1943, she took up flower arranging while bringing up her two daughters. Her interest in plants grew further after meeting artist and plantsman Sir Cedric Morris, who bred irises and ran an art school at Benton End in Suffolk.

In the late 1950s, Chatto moved to a new house she and Andrew had built on his fruit farm in Elmstead Market where, in 1967, she opened her nursery. She also created a garden on the plot's dry gravelly soil, stream-fed ditches and shady woodlands, basing her designs on Andrew's research into plant ecology and selecting species naturally adapted to thrive in the different conditions.

In 1975, Chatto entered some plants into an RHS show in London and won a Flora Silver medal, which gave her confidence to enter an exhibit at the RHS Chelsea Flower Show a year later. She secured a Flora Silver Gilt medal on that occasion, but it was the ten successive gold medals she won after that which put her garden and nursery firmly on the map. Visitors flocked to see the displays of drought-tolerant plants on the site of an old car park, while her theories about plant selection reached an even wider audience when, in 1978, she wrote her first book, *The Dry Garden*, followed in 1982 by *The Damp Garden*. These and her later books cemented her reputation as one of the world's most accomplished horticulturists.

Chatto's sustainable and ecological approach is more relevant now than ever, and her garden continues to inspire visitors under the direction of her granddaughter, Julia Boulton.

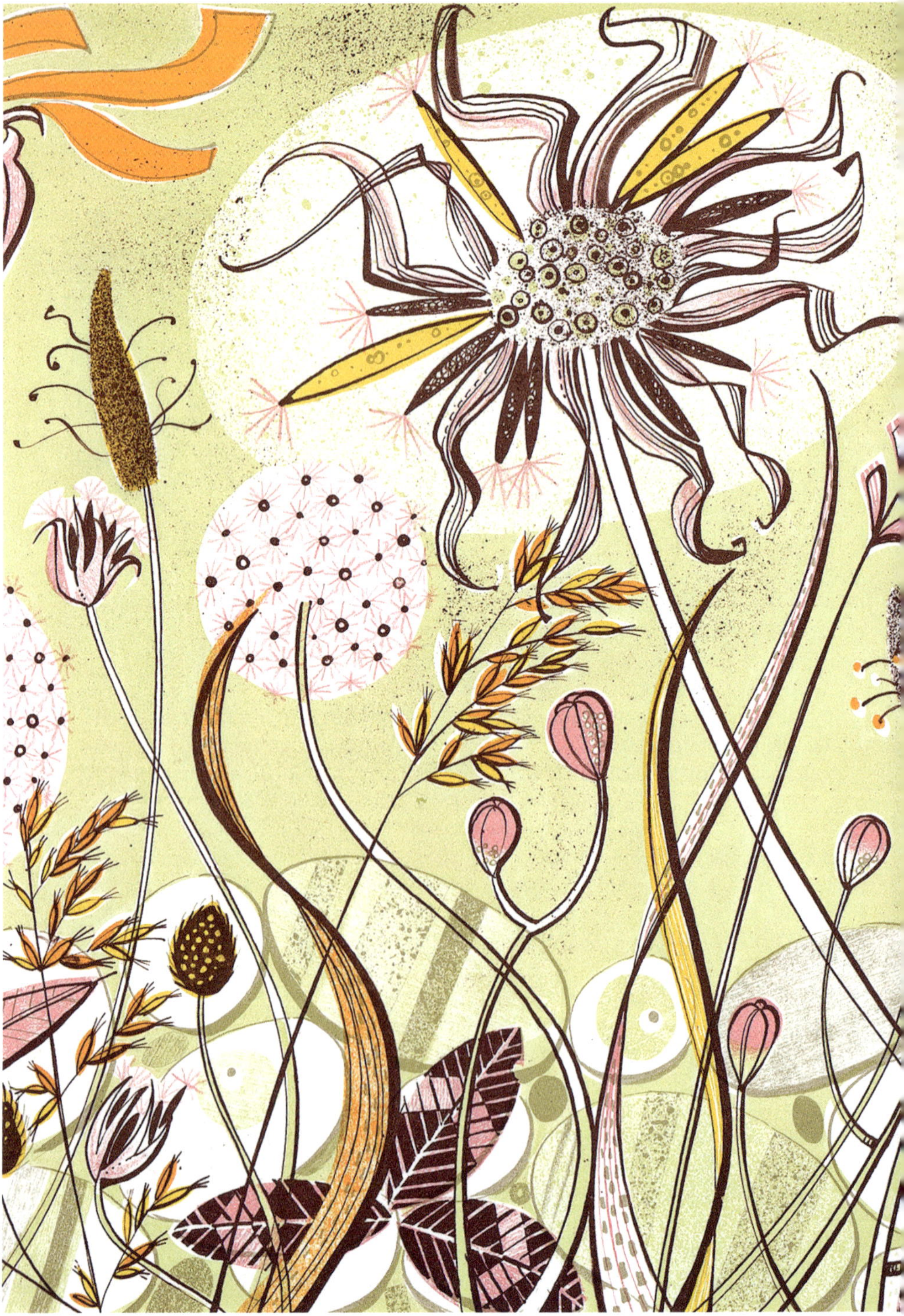

October

As colder days arrive and the nights draw in, many plants are preparing to rest, weary after putting on their dazzling shows of vibrant flowers. Others take this quiet moment to shine, as deciduous trees and shrubs don their gold and crimson cloaks, fizzing like fireworks before shedding their leafy loads. In the vegetable plot, there's still plenty to harvest, while ripe fruits glisten under a slanting sun.

KEY EVENTS
Yom Kippur, 1–2 October
National Apple Day (celebration of British apples), 21 October
Diwali/Deepavali, 21 October
British Summer Time ends, 26 October
Halloween, 31 October

What to do in October

Continue planting perennials, evergreen shrubs and spring bulbs this month, and move any large plants that are in the wrong place. You can also dig up and divide perennials that are flagging or have outgrown their space (see p.46), and give away any spare clumps to friends and neighbours. Make use of this month's bounty by piling up raked leaves in a mesh container or bin in a quiet corner, where they can be left to rot down to form a rich soil conditioner (see p.189).

In the garden

KEEP BEDDING PLANTS, rather than composting them, to save money next year. *Diascia*, fuchsias, salvias, marguerites, osteospermum (shown), penstemons and verbena will survive a few degrees of frost in mild areas or you can overwinter them in an unheated greenhouse, porch, conservatory or a cold frame. ❶

MOVE HARDY EVERGREEN SHRUBS and perennials that are in the wrong position, digging around the rootballs carefully. Place them in their new spots, taking care to plant them at the same depth as they were originally. ❷

LIFT AND STORE tender summer bulbs such as begonias and gladioli before the frosts arrive. Remove the excess soil clinging to them and leave them to dry off before storing over winter in a cool, dry, frost-free place with good air circulation to prevent them rotting. Dahlias can be left *in situ* in milder areas of the country, with a thick mulch placed over the roots. ❸ ❹

SOW SWEET PEAS to give plants a head start next year, when they will flower earlier and for longer than spring-sown plants. Chip the hard coating on the seeds with a knife or sandpaper to speed up germination and sow in pots of peat-free seed compost. Place in a propagator or an unheated greenhouse or cold frame. The sweet peas should have developed a good root system and be ready to plant outside in April. ❺

CLEAN PONDS now, when required. Ideally drain most of the water (pumps can be hired) and remove the plants and pond life, setting them aside in containers. Remove debris and algae, leaving it around the pond overnight to allow wildlife to return to the water, before composting. Once cleaned, refill the pond with water, ideally from water butts, then return the plants. You can also place netting over the water to collect autumn leaves, making sure there is space for creatures to get in and out, and that it won't trap birds. ❻

In the fruit & veg patch

PLANT ONION SETS as soon as possible in October, followed by shallots and garlic before December. There is also still time to plant spring cabbages and lettuces – the latter may need some protection on cold nights to deliver a crop later in the season.

ORDER STRAWBERRIES, which will be available next month as 'runners', or plantlets, that are formed where the wandering strawberry stems take root. They will be sent out when they have become dormant in November, and should then be planted as soon as possible after receipt, when the ground is dry and not frozen. Early ordering is recommended as there is usually a limited supply.

HARVEST POTATOES once the skins are firm enough to resist light rubbing, digging them up when no rain is forecast and leaving the tubers to dry for a couple of hours on the soil surface. Do not leave them any longer or they may turn green and become inedible. Healthy crops can then be stored in a dark, frost-free place for use over winter and should keep until April.

SOW BROAD BEANS from now until mid-November in milder regions of the country, for early summer crops the following year. Buy winter-hardy cultivars such as 'Aquadulce'. In smaller gardens or cold regions where the beans will need protection under cloches, try the robust dwarf 'The Sutton'. ❼

Indoors

BRING HOUSEPLANTS INDOORS at the beginning of the month, if they have been enjoying the summer on your patio, as many will suffer when night-time temperatures start to plunge.

WINTER CACTUS such as *Schlumbergera truncata* and *S. × buckleyi* inject sparkling flowers over the Christmas period. Keep them in a cool room, but as soon as you see buds appearing in autumn, bring plants into a warmer area. They should start to flower in November. Continue to water these cacti lightly while they are in bloom.

MONEY-SAVING IDEA
Order bare-root plants
Bare-root trees, shrubs and perennials are generally better value than pot-grown specimens because they are cheaper to grow. Raised in a nursery field and dug up when dormant from November to early spring, they are dispatched with hessian or a similar material protecting their roots. Bare-root plants often establish more quickly than those grown in pots, too, because a larger surface area of the root system is in direct contact with the soil. The only downside is that they will need to be planted very soon after you receive them, as long as the soil is not waterlogged or frozen.

Plants of the month

1. Harlequin glorybower (*Clerodendrum trichotomum* var. *fargesii*)
2. Big blue lilyturf (*Liriope muscari*)
3. Pyracantha (*Pyracantha* 'Fiery Cascade' pictured)
4. Yew (*Taxus baccata* 'Standishii')
5. Chinese Virginia creeper (*Parthenocissus henryana*)
6. Fortune saxifrage (*Saxifraga fortunei*)
7. Nerine (*Nerine* 'Jaunty' pictured)
8. Heuchera (*Heuchera* 'Sugar Berry' pictured)
9. Autumn-flowering camellia (*Camellia sasanqua* 'Mignonne' pictured)
10. Ivy-leaved cyclamen (*Cyclamen hederifolium*)
11. Japanese maple (*Acer palmatum* 'Orange Dream' pictured)

OCTOBER / 183

Project: Make an autumn wreath

Many of us make wreaths at Christmas, but you can decorate your door or garden earlier in the year with this beautiful feature that celebrates autumn's bounty. To create your wreath, collect plants from your garden, such as skimmia berries, ivy leaves, dried hydrangea flowerheads, sedums and crab apples. When the plants have faded, add them to the compost heap and reuse the frame and moss for a winter wreath.

YOU WILL NEED
Florist wire
Moss
Flat wire wreath frame
Seeds, berries, dried flowerheads, leaves
Sturdy wire
Secateurs

1 Using the florist wire, fix the moss to the wreath frame. If you don't have a lawn from which to collect moss, you can buy sustainably sourced moss in bags from the garden centre.

2 Group together a small bunch of stems, and lay them over the moss, at a slight angle so the berries, seedheads or flowers extend over the outer edge of the frame. Fix the stems to the ring with florist's wire, but do not cut it at this stage.

3 Repeat with a new bunch of stems, laying them over the first bunch to cover its stems, and secure with wire.

4 Continue to cover the wreath with bunches of stems until you cannot see any moss and the frame is completely covered. Then cut the wire. You can fill gaps by pushing extra stems under the wires used to secure the small bunches.

5 Make a loop of wire at the top. Hang the wreath on your front door or from a tree.

Looking up

Sunrise and sunset

The nights start to close in during October, and the days seem to contract further after the clocks go back by one hour on the last weekend of the month.

	LONDON		EDINBURGH	
DAY	Sunrise	Sunset	Sunrise	Sunset
Wed, Oct 1	7:00:06 am	6:40:02 pm	7:14:39 am	6:50:03 pm
Thu, Oct 2	7:01:44 am	6:37:46 pm	7:16:38 am	6:47:26 pm
Fri, Oct 3	7:03:23 am	6:35:30 pm	7:18:37 am	6:44:49 pm
Sat, Oct 4	7:05:01 am	6:33:14 pm	7:20:36 am	6:42:13 pm
Sun, Oct 5	7:06:40 am	6:30:59 pm	7:22:36 am	6:39:37 pm
Mon, Oct 6	7:08:19 am	6:28:45 pm	7:24:36 am	6:37:02 pm
Tue, Oct 7	7:09:59 am	6:26:31 pm	7:26:36 am	6:34:27 pm
Wed, Oct 8	7:11:38 am	6:24:17 pm	7:28:37 am	6:31:52 pm
Thu, Oct 9	7:13:18 am	6:22:04 pm	7:30:37 am	6:29:19 pm
Fri, Oct 10	7:14:58 am	6:19:52 pm	7:32:39 am	6:26:46 pm
Sat, Oct 11	7:16:39 am	6:17:41 pm	7:34:40 am	6:24:13 pm
Sun, Oct 12	7:18:20 am	6:15:30 pm	7:36:42 am	6:21:41 pm
Mon, Oct 13	7:20:01 am	6:13:20 pm	7:38:44 am	6:19:10 pm
Tue, Oct 14	7:21:42 am	6:11:10 pm	7:40:46 am	6:16:40 pm
Wed, Oct 15	7:23:24 am	6:09:02 pm	7:42:49 am	6:14:10 pm
Thu, Oct 16	7:25:06 am	6:06:54 pm	7:44:52 am	6:11:41 pm
Fri, Oct 17	7:26:48 am	6:04:47 pm	7:46:56 am	6:09:13 pm
Sat, Oct 18	7:28:31 am	6:02:41 pm	7:48:59 am	6:06:46 pm
Sun, Oct 19	7:30:13 am	6:00:36 pm	7:51:03 am	6:04:20 pm
Mon, Oct 20	7:31:56 am	5:58:32 pm	7:53:08 am	6:01:55 pm
Tue, Oct 21	7:33:40 am	5:56:29 pm	7:55:12 am	5:59:31 pm
Wed, Oct 22	7:35:23 am	5:54:28 pm	7:57:17 am	5:57:07 pm
Thu, Oct 23	7:37:07 am	5:52:27 pm	7:59:23 am	5:54:45 pm
Fri, Oct 24	7:38:51 am	5:50:27 pm	8:01:28 am	5:52:25 pm
Sat, Oct 25	7:40:36 am	5:48:29 pm	8:03:34 am	5:50:05 pm
Sun, Oct 26*	6:42:20 am	4:46:32 pm	7:05:40 am	4:47:46 pm
Mon, Oct 27	6:44:05 am	4:44:36 pm	7:07:46 am	4:45:29 pm
Tue, Oct 28	6:45:50 am	4:42:42 pm	7:09:52 am	4:43:13 pm
Wed, Oct 29	6:47:35 am	4:40:48 pm	7:11:58 am	4:40:59 pm
Thu, Oct 30	6:49:20 am	4:38:57 pm	7:14:05 am	4:38:46 pm
Fri, Oct 31	6:51:05 am	4:37:07 pm	7:16:11 am	4:36:34 pm

*Note: hours shift because clocks change backward 1 hour.

Moonrise and moonset

Moon phases

- **NEW MOON** 21 October
- **FIRST QUARTER** 29 October
- **FULL MOON** 7 October
- **THIRD QUARTER** 13 October

DAY	LONDON Moonrise	Moonset	Moonrise	Moonset	EDINBURGH Moonrise	Moonset	Moonrise
Oct 1		16:42			17:25		
Oct 2			00:23	17:04		00:07	17:39
Oct 3			01:46	17:21		01:38	17:49
Oct 4			03:10	17:35		03:10	17:56
Oct 5			04:36	17:48		04:43	18:03
Oct 6			06:03	18:00		06:17	18:09
Oct 7			07:32	18:14		07:53	18:16
Oct 8			09:05	18:31		09:34	18:26
Oct 9			10:40	18:55		11:19	18:40
Oct 10			12:14	19:28		13:02	19:05
Oct 11			13:38	20:17		14:33	19:47
Oct 12			14:43	21:23		15:38	20:54
Oct 13			15:28	22:42		16:16	22:20
Oct 14			15:58			16:38	23:52
Oct 15	00:05		16:19			16:51	
Oct 16	01:27		16:34		01:22	16:59	
Oct 17	02:45		16:46		02:47	17:05	
Oct 18	04:00		16:56		04:08	17:10	
Oct 19	05:13		17:06		05:27	17:15	
Oct 20	06:25		17:16		06:44	17:20	
Oct 21	07:37		17:28		08:03	17:26	
Oct 22	08:50		17:42		09:22	17:34	
Oct 23	10:04		18:01		10:43	17:45	
Oct 24	11:16		18:26		12:03	18:04	
Oct 25	12:24		19:02		13:18	18:33	
Oct 26*	12:22		18:50		13:18	18:20	
Oct 27	13:08		19:52		14:01	19:26	
Oct 28	13:42		21:05		14:27	20:45	
Oct 29	14:06		22:23		14:44	22:12	
Oct 30	14:25		23:44		14:56	23:40	
Oct 31	14:40				15:04		

*Note: hours shift because clocks change backward 1 hour.

Average rainfall

The second wettest month of the year, the 20-year average rainfall for the UK in October is 159mm (6.3in). While this limits the time you can spend outside, it provides much-needed irrigation for newly planted hardy shrubs, climbers and perennials.

LOCATION	DAYS	MM	INCHES
Aberdeen	14	100	3.9
Aberystwyth	16	123	4.8
Belfast	14	96	3.8
Birmingham	12	81	3.2
Bournemouth	13	101	4.0
Bristol	13	86	3.4
Cambridge	10	59	2.3
Canterbury	11	80	3.1
Cardiff	15	129	5.0
Edinburgh	12	76	3.0
Exeter	15	159	6.3
Glasgow	16	132	5.2
Gloucester	13	80	3.1
Inverness	14	78	3.0
Ipswich	10	60	2.4
Leeds	14	98	3.9
Liverpool	14	90	3.5
London	11	79	3.1
Manchester	15	117	4.6
Newcastle upon Tyne	11	55	2.2
Norwich	11	70	2.8
Nottingham	11	72	2.8
Oxford	11	73	2.9
Sheffield	13	79	3.1
Truro	15	108	4.3

Recycling your garden waste

Composting waste from your garden and kitchen, such as prunings, peelings, eggshells and fallen leaves in autumn, couldn't be easier, and the resulting products offer a sustainable way to improve the performance of both your plants and the soil.

Autumn is a good time to start a compost heap or bin, and to recycle the leafy bounty falling from the trees. Most gardeners have an abundance of old flower stems and spent crops now, cleared from beds, borders and the fruit and vegetable patch, which can then be recycled. These straw-like stems are rich in carbon and, while they will rot in time, the quickest results and best compost come from mixing in soft, green, nitrogen-rich leafy material and kitchen scraps at twice the volume of the strawy matter.

You will probably accumulate more soft material than strawy throughout the year, so, when the latter is in short supply, include scrunched or shredded paper or torn-up cardboard pieces to balance the mix. Where strawy material predominates, add a sprinkle of dried poultry manure or lucerne (alfalfa) pellets, both rich in nitrogen, to speed things up. The best way to achieve thorough decomposition is to 'turn' the heap at least once, removing all the contents, mixing them up and

Running the mower over autumn leaves will help speed up the composting process.

then returning them, but you can miss out this step if you are prepared to wait a bit longer for your compost.

A compost heap that heats up will produce results quickly, but it requires large volumes of materials, all added at the same time. When filling a bin little by little, expect it to remain cool, and the process to take longer. However, if you can use your autumn abundance to fill a bin of at least 1 x 1 x 1m (3 x 3 x 3ft) in one go, and then turn the contents

Top Leave large logs to decompose in a quiet corner.
Bottom Filling a large bin quickly will make it heat up and produce compost within a few months.

after the initial heat subsides, you should have usable, sweet-smelling dark compost by spring.

LEAFY GOLD
By the end of October, most deciduous trees will be shedding their leaves, which you can add to your compost bin, perhaps running the lawnmower over them first to shred them and incorporate some nitrogen-rich grass clippings into the mix. Alternatively, place them in a wire mesh enclosure or hessian bag on their own to rot down. After two years, your leaf pile will turn into crumbly leafmould, which is an invaluable substitute for peat. Peat should be left in bogs and mires where it supports biodiversity and counters climate change, rather than used in gardens.

Another simple idea is to rake the leaves under shrubs and trees in places where they won't suffocate other garden plants. Natural processes then incorporate them into the ground as nature intended, where they will boost desirable biological activity and improve the health of the soil.

COMPOSTING PRUNINGS
Woody prunings are slow to rot and are traditionally consigned to the bonfire, where this is not prohibited by bye-laws and won't inconvenience neighbours.

While this is a very effective way to destroy diseased matter, healthy woody waste can be shredded for use as a mulch or simply stacked up in neat heaps to decompose naturally over a year or two. Creating a woody waste pile has the added benefit of providing a home to sustain insects, spiders, amphibians and larger garden wildlife, including hedgehogs and birds.

OCTOBER / 189

Edible garden

Many root crops are ready to harvest, but some, including parsnips and carrots, taste sweeter after being exposed to frost, so leave them in the ground, as long as it is not waterlogged. Gluts of tree fruits can be cooked and stored in airtight jars for use later.

Vegetables

SOW INDOORS OR UNDER CLOCHES
Herbs; pak choi; spring onions; winter lettuce; winter salad leaves.

SOW OUTDOORS Broad beans (see p.182); overwintering peas (in mild areas)

PLANT OUT Garlic sets; onion sets; spring cabbages and pak choi sown in summer.

HARVEST NOW Pumpkins ❶; beetroots ❷; cabbages, including storing and red cabbage, and savoys ❸; calabrese; carrots; cauliflowers; celery; celeriac; chicory and endive; Florence fennel; French beans; greenhouse-grown chillies; herbs; kohlrabi; lettuces; maincrop potatoes; pak choi, parsnips peppers; winter radishes, winter squash; tomatoes; turnips.

Fruit

PLANT NOW Pot-grown fruit trees and bushes; rhubarb crowns

HARVEST Apples; autumn raspberries; medlars; pears ❹; quinces.

TOP TIP
Storing autumn fruits
Enjoy apples and pears throughout the winter months by storing them in slatted containers that offer good ventilation. Arrange the fruits in a single layer, and store mid-season and late-season varieties in separate containers. Keep in a cool, frost-free place, free of rats, such as a shed or garage. Check the fruits regularly, removing any that show signs of rot. Bring pears into a warm room to soften when they change colour but are still hard.

HERB OF THE MONTH: FENNEL
The aniseed flavour of common fennel (*Foeniculum vulgare*) makes a tangy addition to many savoury dishes and aromatic teas, while the seeds are also flavoursome. This tall hardy perennial is very easy to grow in a sunny spot and free-draining soil. Although it reaches about 1.8m (6ft) in height, its airy stems and leaves can be squeezed between other plants in an ornamental or productive bed. The flat-topped, yellow flowers will also attract pollinators.

Ferment recipe

KOHLRABI WITH LOVAGE AND CELERY SEED

The crunchy texture of kohlrabi is retained during fermentation, and its mild taste offers an excellent foundation to layer with other ingredients. Lovage and celery are strong flavours but, when used in moderation, they give a wonderful savoury complexity to this ferment – the rich tangy flavour making it an excellent companion to any sort of cheese dish.

INGREDIENTS

1kg (2lb 3oz) kohlrabi
1½ tbsp salt
1 tbsp celery seeds
1 handful of chopped lovage leaves
Small lemon (zest and juice)

1 Slice the kohlrabi thinly using a mandolin, then chop it into strips.

2 Rub the salt into the vegetable slices thoroughly. The salt causes moisture to be released, which creates a brine.

3 Mix in the celery seeds, chopped lovage leaves and the zest and juice of the lemon.

4 Pack the kohlrabi mixture into jars – wide-mouthed kilner jars are ideal. Weigh down your mixture with a glass weight to ensure the ingredients remain submerged under the brine.

5 Seal the ferment with an airlock (see p.58) and leave for 5–7 days at room temperature, or until the ferments have achieved the level of sourness you desire.

6 Remove the airlock and reseal with the jar lids. This ferment should store in a fridge for a minimum of three months.

Challenges this month

With autumn in full swing, take time to check trees and shrubs for honey fungus, a fatal plant disease that will need prompt attention if found. Other fungal diseases are also on the rise this month, so keep your eyes peeled for infections.

HONEY FUNGUS is the single most destructive garden plant disease and produces clumps of honey-coloured toadstools, with a 'frill' around the stalk below the cap, which often arise from infected stumps, roots and the base of trees in autumn. However, the toadstools are easily confused with other fungi, and are not always present on the ailing tree itself, so check for other signs, too. These include the white fungal material with a distinctive mushroom smell between the bark and the wood at the base of plants, and bootlace-like, fungal threads that, unlike roots, lack an internal core. Known as 'rhizomorphs', you will find these threads under the bark and in the soil around the roots. Infected trees and shrubs must be removed, and all the root and stump material burned or buried in landfill to destroy the rhizomorphs. To prevent it spreading, install a physical barrier such as a strip of pond liner or heavy-duty plastic sheet buried vertically 45cm (18in) deep in the soil, with 2.5cm (1in) above the ground.

FAIRY RINGS are caused by a fungus (*Marasmius oreades*) that spreads to produce circular colonies in lawns, initially making the grass greener but then killing it. Toadstools occasionally appear, too. Other fungi that don't harm the grass also produce fairy rings and may even help it grow, so wait to see which you have before taking any action. There are no remedies bar replacing the turf and soil.

LEATHERJACKETS are the larvae of craneflies or daddy longlegs, which you will see flying around the garden from late summer, when each lays up to 300 eggs before winter. Most cranefly species feed on rotting organic matter and do no harm, but six species eat plant roots, particularly those of lawn grasses. The larvae are greyish-brown, caterpillar-like creatures, about 3cm (1¼in) in length, and the damage will be evident in early summer. Nematodes are the only control, and can be used in autumn, while soil temperatures are 12°C (54°F) or higher.

Focus on wildlife

Bank vole

Many gardens in the UK provide a home to a family of bank voles. Similar in appearance to a mouse, this small, chestnut-brown native rodent can be identified by its stout little body, small eyes, short furry tail and rounded snout. The bank vole also has relatively large ears, but not as large as those of a mouse, which distinguishes it from other vole species.

These little creatures live in woodlands, hedgerows, parks and gardens, where they spend their time searching for fruit and nuts, and occasionally worms, snails and small insects. Their favourite fare includes hazelnuts and blackberries, but they also enjoy fungi and plant roots, as well as seeds, seedlings and other fruit. They may be seen on bird feeders, too, looking for an easy meal.

Bank voles help to bolster the biodiversity in our gardens and do no real harm to crops or other plants. They are agile but shy, always wary of their many predators, which include owls, kestrals, weasels and foxes. They do not hibernate, and you may hear them rustling through the undergrowth at any time of the year, or become aware of their chattering squeaks. Some may even emit a low growl or sob, when they are stressed.

These small mammals breed between March and October in shallow burrows or on the ground, if there is sufficient plant cover to hide their brood. They produce three or four litters of three to five young per year, and the offspring are weaned after about 25 days.

Female voles reach sexual maturity after six weeks and the males after eight, and while they can live for up to two years, many fall victim to predators long before that.

Spotlight on: Euonymus (*Euonymus*)

This group of hardy shrubs includes dwarf evergreens, ideal for edging beds and borders, deciduous plants, known as spindles, that offer great autumn colour, and tree-like species, which also lend height and structure. Grow euonymus on moist but free-draining soil in full sun or part shade – the evergreens will also need a sheltered site to retain their leaves in winter. Deciduous plants can be cut back in late winter or early spring to keep them in shape, while the evergreens are best pruned in mid- or late spring to encourage bushy growth. The leaves and fruit of native spindles are also beneficial to wildlife.

EUONYMUS EUROPAEUS 'RED CASCADE'
This large deciduous UK native produces small, dark green leaves that in autumn turn bright scarlet, while the insignificant summer flowers go on to produce decorative orange-pink, winged fruits at the same time.
H x S: 3 x 2.5m (10 x 8ft)

EUONYMUS ALATUS 'COMPACTUS'
The winged spindle or burning bush is a deciduous shrub, grown for its eye-catching, pinky red, autumn leaves and similarly coloured fruit cases that open to reveal orange berries.
H x S: 1.5 x 1.5m (5 x 5ft)

EUONYMUS PHELLOMANUS
The winged spindle tree is a large deciduous shrub that produces simple green leaves that turn bright red in autumn, when the long-lasting pink fruits that split to reveal bright orange seeds also appear.
H x S: 4 x 2.5m (13 x 8ft)

EUONYMUS FORTUNEI 'EMERALD 'N' GOLD'
This compact evergreen is grown primarily for its bright gold-edged green leaves that take on reddish tints in winter. Clusters of insignificant green flowers appear in May and June.
H x S: 60 x 90cm (24 x 36in)

EUONYMUS FORTUNEI 'SILVER QUEEN'
This decorative evergreen has dark green leaves with cream-coloured margins that become tinted with pink as they age. In summer, tiny green flowers appear, followed by round white fruits.
H x S: 2 x 1.5m (6 x 5ft)

Seasonal planting ideas

FIERY FOCUS

WHY IT WORKS
An arresting contrast of red autumn foliage on the winged spindle (*Euonymus alatus*) and the green grassy leaves and beige autumn flowers of the *Miscanthus* creates a dazzling combination. The see-through *Miscanthus* flower stems help to connect the grass with the colourful shrub behind, and this pairing provides interest for many months before peaking in autumn. In addition, the *Euonymus* has a wonderfully tactile, corky bark, while the *Miscanthus* sways and rustles in the wind, adding movement and gentle sound.

WHAT'S GROWING HERE?
Euonymus alatus 'Compactus' is a compact, spreading, deciduous shrub that grows to 1m (3ft) in height. It develops prominent corky ridges on the branches, and the small green flowers in spring are followed by red-purple fruits containing orange seeds in autumn, when the small oval leaves also turn from green to scarlet.

Miscanthus sinensis 'Kleine Silberspinne' is a tall deciduous grass that reaches about 1.2m (4ft) in height. It forms a compact clump of arching narrow leaves with white midribs, while feathery reddish flowerheads appear in late summer, and turn pale brown to grey in autumn and winter.

WHEN TO PLANT
Plant in autumn or early spring, avoiding summer, if possible, when the warmer, drier conditions can make establishment more difficult. These plants prefer a sunny aspect and moisture-retentive yet well-drained soil.

WHERE TO SEE IT
View this joyous mix at RHS Garden Harlow Carr in October.

Horticultural heroes

Piet Oudolf · b.1944

Dutch nurseryman and garden designer Piet Oudolf is a pioneer of the New Perennial Movement, a style that weaves together bold drifts of structural perennials and grasses to create year-round colour and form, with minimal maintenance. His work includes the walled garden at Scampston Hall, North Yorkshire; the Millennium Garden, Pensthorpe, Norfolk; the garden at Hauser & Wirth sculpture park and gallery in Somerset; RHS Garden Wisley's Oudolf Landscape; and the planting design for the High Line in New York, a 2.5km- (1½-mile-) long park built on an elevated disused railway line. Oudolf is also a prolific author, many of his books co-written with Noel Kingsbury.

Born in 1944 in Haarlem in the Netherlands, one of his first jobs was in a garden centre, after which he returned to formal education to hone his plant knowledge and horticultural skills. He married his wife Anja in 1970, and the pair started a design consultancy in Haarlem, before moving to a farmhouse with a large plot of land in Hummelo, where they set up their nursery in 1982. Specializing in unusual perennials and grasses, chosen for their enduring structural qualities such as their foliage and seedpods, rather than flowers, the Oudolfs' plants soon caught the public's attention. The couple also created a garden around their home, which provided a testbed for plants and design ideas. People flocked to visit the nursery and garden, while design commissions also came in from forward-thinking clients who embraced Oudolf's new planting style, inspired by natural landscapes such as the American prairies, meadows and woodlands.

During the 1990s, an increasing number of designers began emulating Oudolf's planting, leading to what has become known as the New Perennial Movement. His work continues to resonate today, the ecological principles at the heart of his designs informing many contemporary gardens and paving the way for the new trend for native plantings. However, designers still seek out Oudolf's garden-worthy species for projects where structure and form, and low maintenance, are required.

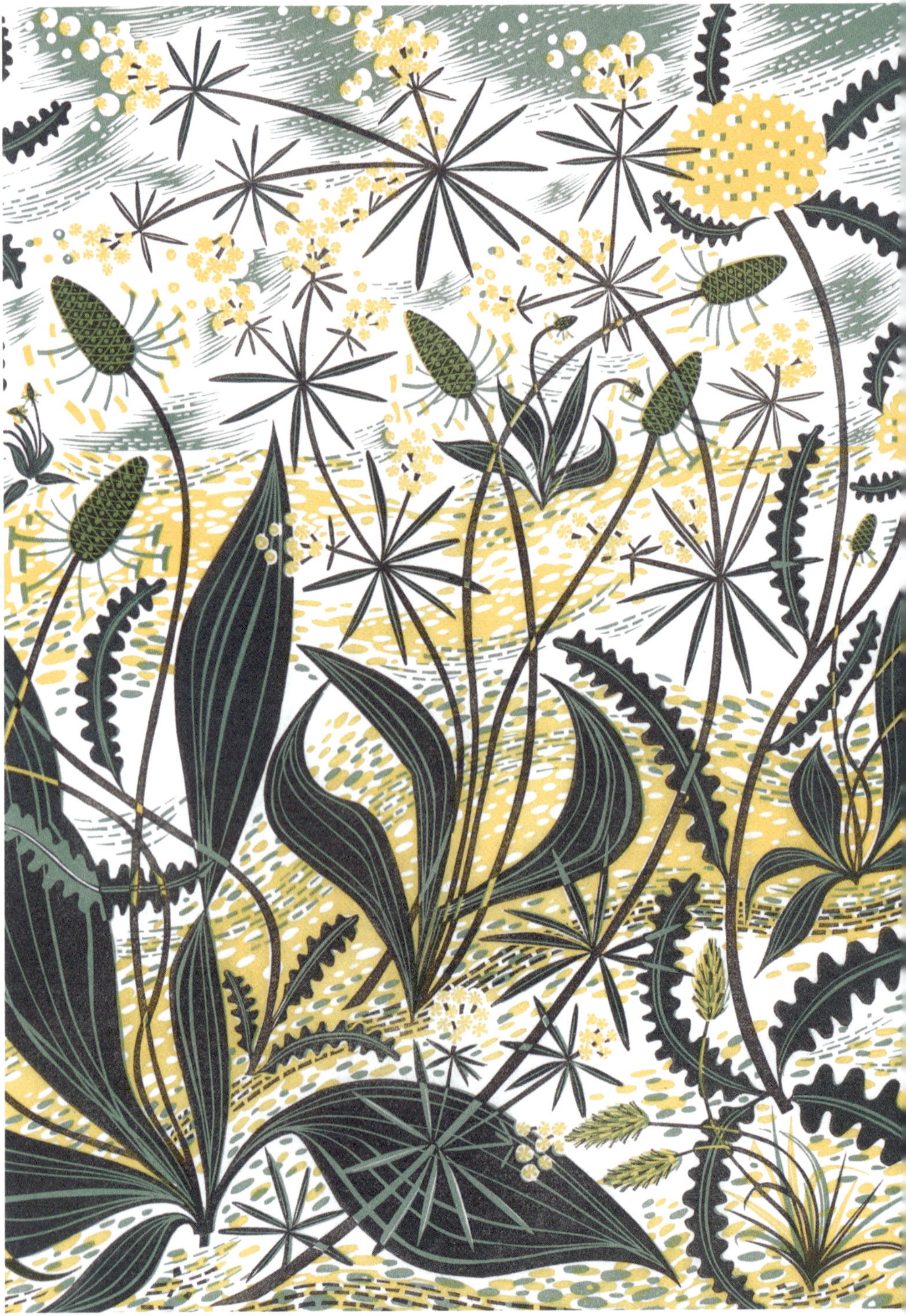

November

During late autumn, the garden lies in wait for the long dark winter ahead. While many perennials have retreated beneath the soil, grasses continue to wave a feathery greeting to those braving the cold, and beaded stems of phlomis stand strong among the evergreens challenging the sepia landscape with their emerald gaze. Sunny mornings bring cheer, too, accompanied by dustings of sparkling frost.

KEY EVENTS
Guy Fawkes Night, 5 November
Remembrance Sunday, 9 November
St Andrew's Day, 30 November
National Tree Week, 29 November–7 December

What to do in November

Short days limit our time in the garden but there are some key jobs that are best completed now. Bare-root trees and shrubs are available now, while bulbs are often on special offer and can be planted until the first couple of weeks in December, to flower next spring. You can also use this quiet time to mulch beds and borders, especially in areas with clay soil, and to make chutneys and ferments with autumn crops such apples, beetroots and onions.

In the garden

TULIP BULBS are traditionally planted from September to November. Discard any bulbs showing signs of disease, and plant at a depth of two to three times the height of the bulb in well-drained soil and a sunny or lightly shaded area. Also consider the little species tulips that reliably repeat-flower year after year. The bright red *Tulipa linifolia* (Batalinii Group) 'Red Hunter', and pink *T. humilis* 'Eastern Star' are good choices. ❶

TAKE HARDWOOD SHRUB CUTTINGS after leaf fall, cutting bare shoots about 25cm (10ins) long below a bud. Insert your cuttings in pots of gritty potting compost and keep in a greenhouse or a cold frame over winter until roots form next spring, when they can be planted outside. ❷

APPLY A 5CM (2IN) LAYER (mulch) of wood chips or bark around slightly tender plants, such as hardy fuchsias, *Melianthus*, *Phygelius* and *Zantedeschia*, to protect the roots from the cold. The tops may die back, but the plants will regrow in spring, when the mulch will also benefit the soil.

PLANT BARE-ROOT TREES AND SHRUBS, making sure you set them at the same depth they were growing at in their nursery beds, indicated by a darker soil mark on their stems. In wet soils, prevent rot by planting them on 30cm (12in) mounds, so that the roots are never waterlogged for long. ❸

PUT UP NESTING BOXES to provide roosting places for birds in cold winter weather. The boxes will also become familiar to them when they begin to breed next spring. Remember to put out water for the birds during freezing weather, using clean containers and replenishing them with fresh water every few days to prevent diseases. ❹

PLANT A HEDGE using inexpensive bare-root plants. Consider a wildlife feature with berried plants such as spindle (*Euonymus*), hawthorn (*Crataegus*), yew (*Taxus*), *Rosa rugosa* and crab apple (*Malus*), which provide flowers for pollinators in spring and fruit for birds and mammals during the autumn months (see also pp.18–19). ❺

NOVEMBER / 201

In the fruit & veg patch

PLANT HONEYBERRIES (*Lonicera caerulea*), which produce small blue fruits, similar to blueberries, for preserving, cooking or eating fresh. This fast-growing, undemanding bushy honeysuckle reaches 1.8m (6ft), and will grow in any fertile soil in full sun. It flowers in late winter, and the berries, rich in vitamin C and antioxidants, ripen in summer. Ideally, include at least two plants, since honeyberries are not self-fertile and more than one is needed for cross-pollination. ❻

PLANT BARE-ROOT PERENNIAL and shrubby fruit crops at the same depth as they were in their nursery beds.

MONEY-SAVING IDEA
Make cloches from plastic bottles
Think ahead and start collecting bottles to make little cloches for young plants that will need some frost or slug protection next spring. You can also use them to cover late-sown salad leaves and parsley that may continue to crop for a few more weeks under a cloche. Simply make a hole about 2cm (¾in) above the base of a clear plastic bottle that will allow you to insert a pair of sharp scissors. Cut off the base and remove the cap, then pop the bottle over your young crops or seedlings.

TAKE CURRANT AND GOOSEBERRY CUTTINGS, removing pencil-thick stems 20–30cm (10–12in) long for currants, or 10–15cm (4–6in) long for gooseberries, after leaf fall. Bury two-thirds of each stem in garden soil; the cuttings should root by late spring.

STORE LEEKS and parsnips when the ground is frozen outside in a bucket against a wall or in a shed to keep them dry. Frost-prone roots, such as beetroots and carrots, can be stored in boxes of old potting compost or sand in a cool shed, while cabbages also last well when kept in a cool dark shed.

Indoors

REDUCE WATERING and stop feeding houseplants, now that they are growing slowly or dormant.

INDOOR AZALEA (*Rhododendron simsii*) from India are in flower now. Keep them on a cool windowsill, and water when the top of the soil feels dry, ideally using rainwater. You can place them outside in summer in part shade.

Plants of the month

1. Chinese red birch (*Betula utilis* subsp. *albosinensis*)
2. Bergenia for the leaves (*Bergenia* 'Wintermärchen' pictured)
3. Heavenly bamboo (*Nandina domestica*)
4. Mountain witch alder (*Fothergilla major* Monticola Group pictured)
5. Smoke bush (*Cotinus coggygria* 'Grace' pictured)
6. Ghost bramble (*Rubus thibetanus*)
7. Coral bark willow (*Salix alba* var. *vitellina* 'Britzensis' pictured)
8. Korean mountain ash (*Sorbus alnifolia*)
9. Chinese fountain grass (*Pennisetum alopecuroides*)
10. Pansy (*Viola*)
11. Golden clematis (*Clematis* 'Bill MacKenzie' pictured)

NOVEMBER / 203

Project: Combine bright winter pots

After summer flowers fade, patios can look a little drab, but you can bring them back to life with containers filled with sparkling autumn berries. Shrubs such as *Pyracantha* and prickly heath (*Gaultheria mucronata*) put on a wonderful show from now until late winter and, while the others may fade a little earlier, they all have evergreen foliage to sustain the show. Buying plants now also allows you to match up the berry colours to create an attractive display. The larger shrubs, including the *Pyracantha* and *Hypericum*, will grow well for a few years in a pot, but then need to be planted in the ground.

YOU WILL NEED
Selection of large and smaller pots with drainage holes
Peat-free multipurpose compost
Cane support
Plant ties
Peat-free ericaceous compost
Selection of berried shrubs: those used here include *Pyracantha* 'Soleil d'Or'; *Gaultheria procumbens* VERY BERRY; *Gaultheria mucronata* pink- and white-berried forms; and *Hypericum* MIRACLE BLOSSOM

1 Half-fill a large pot with John Innes No. 2 compost and add a cane support at the back. Plant the *Pyracantha*, ensuring it is at the same depth as it was in its original container, and that there is a 2.5cm (1in) gap between the top of the compost and the pot rim. Fix the stems to the support with plant ties.

2 Plant the other shrubs in the same way (without a support), using the ericaceous compost, since the *Gaultheria* prefer acid conditions. The *Hypericum* will cope with acid, neutral or more alkaline conditions and could be planted in John Innes No. 2, if growing in a pot of its own.

3 Place in a partly shaded area. Water during prolonged dry periods, especially after the plants start to grow again in spring.

Looking up

Sunrise and sunset

With winter just around the corner, the sun is dipping below the horizon at teatime, leaving precious few hours to complete the jobs to be done in the autumn garden.

	LONDON		EDINBURGH	
DAY	Sunrise	Sunset	Sunrise	Sunset
Sat, Nov 1	6:52:50 am	4:35:18 pm	7:18:18 am	4:34:24 pm
Sun, Nov 2	6:54:36 am	4:33:31 pm	7:20:25 am	4:32:16 pm
Mon, Nov 3	6:56:21 am	4:31:45 pm	7:22:32 am	4:30:09 pm
Tue, Nov 4	6:58:06 am	4:30:01 pm	7:24:38 am	4:28:04 pm
Wed, Nov 5	6:59:52 am	4:28:19 pm	7:26:45 am	4:26:00 pm
Thu, Nov 6	7:01:37 am	4:26:39 pm	7:28:51 am	4:23:59 pm
Fri, Nov 7	7:03:22 am	4:25:00 pm	7:30:57 am	4:21:59 pm
Sat, Nov 8	7:05:07 am	4:23:24 pm	7:33:03 am	4:20:01 pm
Sun, Nov 9	7:06:51 am	4:21:49 pm	7:35:09 am	4:18:05 pm
Mon, Nov 10	7:08:36 am	4:20:16 pm	7:37:14 am	4:16:12 pm
Tue, Nov 11	7:10:19 am	4:18:45 pm	7:39:19 am	4:14:20 pm
Wed, Nov 12	7:12:03 am	4:17:17 pm	7:41:23 am	4:12:31 pm
Thu, Nov 13	7:13:46 am	4:15:50 pm	7:43:27 am	4:10:44 pm
Fri, Nov 14	7:15:29 am	4:14:26 pm	7:45:30 am	4:08:59 pm
Sat, Nov 15	7:17:11 am	4:13:04 pm	7:47:33 am	4:07:16 pm
Sun, Nov 16	7:18:52 am	4:11:44 pm	7:49:34 am	4:05:37 pm
Mon, Nov 17	7:20:33 am	4:10:27 pm	7:51:35 am	4:03:59 pm
Tue, Nov 18	7:22:13 am	4:09:12 pm	7:53:35 am	4:02:24 pm
Wed, Nov 19	7:23:52 am	4:07:59 pm	7:55:33 am	4:00:52 pm
Thu, Nov 20	7:25:30 am	4:06:50 pm	7:57:31 am	3:59:23 pm
Fri, Nov 21	7:27:08 am	4:05:42 pm	7:59:27 am	3:57:57 pm
Sat, Nov 22	7:28:44 am	4:04:37 pm	8:01:22 am	3:56:33 pm
Sun, Nov 23	7:30:19 am	4:03:35 pm	8:03:16 am	3:55:13 pm
Mon, Nov 24	7:31:53 am	4:02:36 pm	8:05:08 am	3:53:55 pm
Tue, Nov 25	7:33:26 am	4:01:40 pm	8:06:59 am	3:52:41 pm
Wed, Nov 26	7:34:57 am	4:00:46 pm	8:08:47 am	3:51:30 pm
Thu, Nov 27	7:36:27 am	3:59:55 pm	8:10:34 am	3:50:22 pm
Fri, Nov 28	7:37:55 am	3:59:07 pm	8:12:19 am	3:49:18 pm
Sat, Nov 29	7:39:22 am	3:58:23 pm	8:14:02 am	3:48:17 pm
Sun, Nov 30	7:40:47 am	3:57:41 pm	8:15:43 am	3:47:19 pm

Moonrise and moonset

Moon phases

- **NEW MOON** 20 November
- **FIRST QUARTER** 28 November
- **FULL MOON** 5 November
- **THIRD QUARTER** 12 November

DAY	LONDON Moonrise	LONDON Moonset	LONDON Moonrise	EDINBURGH Moonrise	EDINBURGH Moonset	EDINBURGH Moonrise
Nov 1		01:06	14:53		01:10	15:10
Nov 2		02:30	15:05		02:40	15:17
Nov 3		03:56	15:18		04:13	15:23
Nov 4		05:26	15:33		05:51	15:32
Nov 5		07:01	15:54		07:35	15:44
Nov 6		08:39	16:23		09:22	16:04
Nov 7		10:11	17:05		11:03	16:38
Nov 8		11:28	18:07		12:23	17:37
Nov 9		12:23	19:24		13:14	19:00
Nov 10		12:59	20:50		13:42	20:34
Nov 11		13:24	22:14		13:58	22:07
Nov 12		13:41	23:35		14:08	23:35
Nov 13		13:54			14:15	
Nov 14	00:51	14:05		00:57	14:20	
Nov 15	02:04	14:15		02:16	14:25	
Nov 16	03:15	14:25		03:33	14:30	
Nov 17	04:26	14:36		04:50	14:36	
Nov 18	05:38	14:50		06:09	14:43	
Nov 19	06:52	15:07		07:29	14:54	
Nov 20	08:05	15:30		08:49	15:10	
Nov 21	09:14	16:03		10:06	15:36	
Nov 22	10:16	16:47		11:11	16:17	
Nov 23	11:05	17:45		11:59	17:17	
Nov 24	11:42	18:54x		12:30	18:33	
Nov 25	12:09	20:10		12:50	19:56	
Nov 26	12:29	21:28		13:02	21:22	
Nov 27	12:45	22:47		13:11	22:48	
Nov 28	12:58			13:18		
Nov 29		00:06	13:10		00:14	13:24
Nov 30		01:28	13:22		01:42	13:30

Average rainfall

One of the wettest months of the year, the 20-year average rainfall for the UK in November is 166mm (6½in). Since most plants are growing slowly or dormant, few will need extra irrigation now, but check those in pots don't dry out.

LOCATION	DAYS	MM	INCHES
Aberdeen	15	93	3.7
Aberystwyth	18	123	4.8
Belfast	16	102	4.0
Birmingham	13	79	3.1
Bournemouth	14	108	4.3
Bristol	15	90	3.5
Cambridge	10	53	2.0
Canterbury	11	75	3.0
Cardiff	16	131	5.2
Edinburgh	12	65	2.6
Exeter	16	155	6.1
Glasgow	17	132	5.2
Gloucester	14	89	3.5
Inverness	13	67	2.6
Ipswich	11	55	2.2
Leeds	16	109	4.3
Liverpool	15	82	3.2
London	12	76	3.0
Manchester	17	124	4.9
Newcastle upon Tyne	12	70	2.8
Norwich	13	71	2.8
Nottingham	13	69	2.7
Oxford	12	71	2.8
Sheffield	13	85	3.3
Truro	18	128	5.0

Garden eco-warriors

Millions of trees are being planted throughout the UK to capture carbon dioxide, the most significant greenhouse gas, and thereby mitigate the effects of climate change. While few of us can plant a forest, even a small garden tree will make a contribution. These majestic plants offer many other benefits besides: their bark, flowers and fruits inject colour and interest, while their architectural forms offer privacy, shade and shelter. In addition, trees' huge value to wildlife is rivalled only by garden ponds.

Gardeners are spoilt for choice when it comes to trees, but bear in mind that even smaller garden trees will attain about 8m (26ft) in height when mature. Attempting to restrict the size of a tree by regular pruning is generally not recommended, as it can result in unsightly and unhealthy specimens, but coppicing and pollarding are options. Coppicing involves cutting the stems down to near ground level, while those of a pollard are cut at the top of a permanent trunk to create a vase-like shape above (see p.10). The sticks and stakes that are removed make useful sustainable garden timber, and can be woven into screens or plant supports.

Top Coppicing a *Catalpa* reduces its size and prompts larger leaves to develop.
Bottom An apple tree offers benefits to the environment, as well as fruits in autumn.

Beech (*Fagus sylvatica*), foxglove tree (*Paulownia tomentosa*), cider gum (*Eucalyptus gunnii*), hazel (*Corylus*) and hornbeam (*Carpinus*) are good choices for coppicing, while lime (*Tilia × europaea*), hornbeam, London plane (*Platanus × hispanica*) and oak (*Quercus*) can be pollarded. Visit rhs.org.uk for more examples.

Fruit trees are good choices for small gardens and offer many wildlife benefits, as well as yielding fruits. Suppliers will now be offering them as bare-root specimens, and you can choose from apples, pears, cherries, medlars and quinces grown on a variety of rootstocks that limit their size.

Underplanting a tree with shade-tolerant plants such as *Mahonia aquifolium* and periwinkle (*Vinca minor*) will add to the carbon capture and other environmental and wildlife benefits, while offering a colourful layer beneath the boughs.

SQUEEZE IN A SHRUB
Where space is limited, consider a large shrub instead of a tree. Examples include *Amelanchier*, smoke bush (*Cotinus*) and arrowwood (*Viburnum* × *bodnantense*), which are highly ornamental and offer similar benefits. More compact shrubs, and climbers, are also worth including in the mix.

Hedges offer another possibility, providing many attributes that trees deliver, but without casting as much shade. When used instead of timber fences they also help to preserve forests. See pp.18–19 for hedge planting advice.

> **MATURE CARBON STORES**
> As well as planting new trees, retaining older specimens is even more beneficial, since they are already storing large volumes of carbon. If you have a large tree that is a little too big for your space, rather than removing it, consider coppicing or pollarding it – a qualified aborist will advise you and can raise, lower or shrink the canopy of even large trees, although this work will need to be repeated every few years.

Viburnum × *bodnantense* is a large, decorative shrub that absorbs carbon and flowers in winter and early spring.

Edible garden

The autumn feast continues, with plenty of hardy vegetables to harvest and tree fruits to pick early in the month. Take time to sow a few herbs and leafy crops to grow under cover and supply fresh greens for your plate during the winter months.

Vegetables

SOW INDOORS OR UNDER CLOCHES Herbs such as basil, chives, dill and parsley for overwintering indoors; pak choi; pea shoots; spring onions; winter salad leaves.

SOW OUTDOORS Broad beans.

PLANT OUT Asparagus crowns; garlic sets; shallots; spring cabbages (at the beginning of the month) and pak choi sown in summer. ❶

HARVEST NOW Beetroots; Brussels sprouts; carrots; cauliflowers; celeriac; chicory and endive; Chinese artichokes; Florence fennel; hardy salad leaves; kale; leeks; pak choi; parsnips; perpetual spinach; spring-sown cabbages; swedes; turnips.

Fruit

PLANT NOW Bare-root fruit trees and bushes such as gooseberries, currants, blackberries; potted blueberry plants; potted patio fruits; raspberry canes; rhubarb; strawberry runners.

HARVEST Apples; medlars; pears; quinces.

HERB OF THE MONTH: BAY
An attractive, Mediterranean, evergreen shrub, bay (*Laurus nobilis*) leaves can be harvested year-round for use in soups, stews and many other slow-cooked dishes. Bay is an undemanding plant and will thrive in free-draining soil in sun or part shade – surprisingly, it can even tolerate quite deep shade. In colder areas, plant it in a pot and keep in a sheltered area overwinter or bring into a cool conservatory or unheated greenhouse.

Challenges this month

Fungal diseases continue to plague woody plants in November, some more serious than others, so check your plants regularly for telltale signs and act quickly if you find them. Also keep on top of plants that might get out of hand, and remove them quickly.

BRACKET FUNGI can be seen more easily in autumn after the leaves have fallen. The horizontal fruiting bodies of fungi living inside trees and shrubs look like a series of stacked saucers jutting out from the trunks and stems. These fungi grow slowly, so plants with brackets are not necessarily doomed immediately and can often last for years, but usually decline over time and branches eventually die off. An arborist can advise on the safety of tall, bracket-bearing trees that might cause harm, should they topple.

CORAL SPOT is a fungus that usually affects only dead wood, but can also damage weak living shoots, particularly of maples (*Acer*) and soft fruit, although most deciduous shrubs and trees are susceptible. Coral-pink pustules (pictured), seen more easily after leaf fall, form on the shoots, which then die back. The only remedy is to prune out affected parts and other weak shoots and take steps to improve the plant's growing conditions, which will make it more resilient. Also, when pruning, ensure you make clean cuts and do not leave behind large stubs.

ANNUAL AND PERENNIALS such as cleavers, speedwell, hairy bittercress, red deadnettle, willowherbs, meadow grass, chickweed and shepherd's purse germinate on bare soil, even in late autumn. As seeds will not be set until spring, consider leaving them *in situ* to protect the soil and benefit wildlife – they provide food and pollen. However, be ready to dig them in or smother with black sheeting or a thick cover of mulch in February, after which, if left untreated, they will become amazingly vigorous and harder to control. Other competitive plants such as brambles and bindweed can be seen more easily now that many ornamental perennials have died down, allowing you to dig them out or smother the growth with black sheets – both will grow through a mulch.

Focus on wildlife

Fieldfare

The fieldfare is a beautiful thrush that can be seen in gardens bordering farmland and woodlands from October to April, when it flies in from its summer haunts in Scandinavia and western parts of Russia. Similar in size and shape to a mistle thrush, the fieldfare has a slate-grey head, rich chestnut-red back and wings, and a black tail, with a reddish-brown and black speckled chest and yellow beak.

This beautiful bird migrates to our shores in winter to look for food, when its main diet of grubs and worms are buried beneath the snow and ice in its homeland. Once here, fieldfares consume windfall apples and berries, and sometimes grain, together with invertebrates when they are available.

More birds can be seen in particularly harsh winters when they can arrive in large numbers. Despite this, fieldfares are in decline and are currently on the red list, which means populations here are under threat, while numbers in Scandinavia and Russia are more stable.

Fieldfares return to their homelands in spring to breed, often forming loose colonies in woodlands or hedgerows, where the female builds a cup-shaped nest. She lays a clutch of 5–6 eggs and both parents feed the chicks, which fledge after 14–16 days.

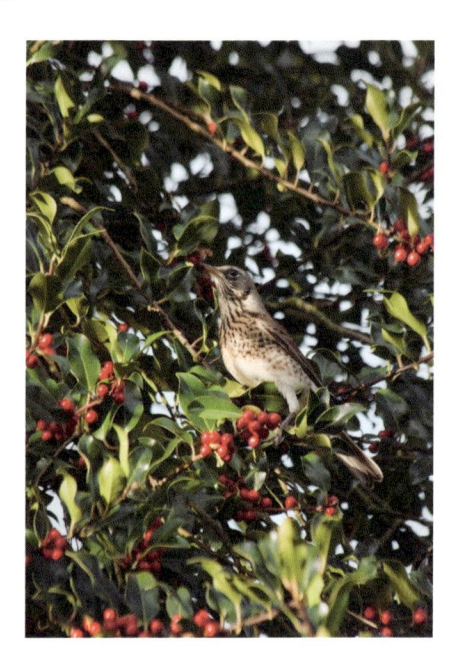

If you live near open countryside, you can encourage fieldfares to your garden by planting hawthorn, holly, rowan, yew, juniper, dog rose, cotoneaster, pyracantha and berberis, the fruits of which will sustain them through winter. Tall trees and hedges also provide secure roosting sites.

Spotlight on: Roses (*Rosa*) for hips

While roses' big, blowsy blooms catch the eye in summer, some put on an equally colourful show of hips in autumn and winter. Most roses produce hips, their bright colours designed to attract birds, which eat them and distribute the seeds inside. The most ornamental with hips are those of species such as *Rosa rugosa* and *R. moyesii* and their hybrids and cultivars. Old shrub roses such as *R. pimpinellifolia,* which produces black hips, also put on a good display, while some ramblers are covered in masses of small hips from late summer. Roses like moist but well-drained soil and a spot in full sun or part shade. For autumn hips, remember not to deadhead the flowers.

ROSA 'GERANIUM'
A *moyesii* hybrid, this large shrub produces scented, single, cherry-red flowers in early summer among dark green leaves, but it is grown more for its flagon-shaped, orange-red autumn hips.
H x S: 2 x 1.5m (6 x 5ft)

ROSA 'FRU DAGMAR HASTRUP'
This *rugosa* hybrid produce prickly stems covered with glossy foliage and pale rose-pink, scented blooms in summer, followed by large, orange-red hips.
H x S: 90 x 1.2m (3 x 4ft)

ROSA NITIDA
A compact species rose, ideal for a small garden, it produces an abundance of small, pink, single flowers, followed in autumn by red hips held on dark red stems.
H x S: 90 x 90cm (36 x 36in)

ROSA 'SCHARLACHGLUT'
A cultivar of an old *gallica* rose, this beauty produces scarlet single flowers in summer, followed by large, urn-shaped hips in autumn.
H x S: 3 x 1.8m (10 x 6ft)

ROSA FILIPES 'KIFTSGATE'
This vigorous rambler bears large sprays of small, fragrant, single white flowers from mid- to late summer, followed by masses of small orange-red hips.
H x S: 10 x 10m (30 x 30ft)

Seasonal planting ideas

FROSTED FUSION

WHY IT WORKS
The West Himalayan birch (*Betula utilis* subsp. *jacquemontii*), with its startling white bark, and the dogwood's (*Cornus*) crimson stems are a classic winter combination. A Mexican orange blossom (*Choisya ternata*) injects more foliage colour and structure here, while the hellebores below offer the promise of late winter and early spring flowers that attract pollinators.

WHAT'S GROWING HERE?
Betula utilis subsp. *jacquemontii* reaches around 16m (52ft), and provides vertical interest, while the white bark on the trunk and branches creates a striking focal point in winter. Yellow-brown male catkins, 12cm (5in) in length, appear in early spring, and the green leaves turn buttery yellow in autumn.

Cornus alba 'Sibirica' is a deciduous shrub that grows to 2m (6ft). Its thickets of red stems turn bright crimson in winter, while small cream flowerheads appear in spring and early summer, followed by bluish-white berries. The green foliage also turns red in autumn.

Choisya ternata SUNDANCE is a rounded evergreen shrub, to 2m (6ft) high and wide, with glossy, aromatic, bright yellow leaves and small clusters of fragrant white flowers in spring, sometimes followed by a second flush in autumn.

Helleborus × *hybridus* is a semi-evergreen perennial that grows to around 40cm (16in). It produces dark green leaves and bowl-shaped flowers in a range of colours, including white, pink, green, yellow and purple, some spotted within.

WHEN TO PLANT
Plant in autumn or early spring. These plants prefer full sun or part shade and a moist but well-drained soil.

WHERE TO SEE IT
Visit the Winter Walk at RHS Garden Harlow Carr to see this grouping.

Horticultural heroes

Margaret Bentinck, Duchess of Portland · 1715–1785

The British aristocrat Margaret Cavendish Bentinck, Duchess of Portland, was the richest woman in eighteenth-century Britain. She used her incredible wealth to accumulate the largest natural history collection in the country, with the aim of amassing and describing every living species and advancing botanical knowledge.

Born in 1715 to the 2nd Earl of Oxford and Lady Henrietta Holles, her mother was the sole heir of the 1st Duke of Newcastle and Lady Margaret Cavendish. Aged 19, she married William, 2nd Duke of Portland, and began her collection at Bulstrode, her country home in Buckinghamshire. Bentinck had a special interest in seashells, and also collected plants, fossils, birds, fungi, beetles, butterflies, porcelain and pottery. She created many gardens at Bulstrode, as well as an aviary and a zoo to house her animals.

The Duchess was held in high esteem by the scientific community for her botanical knowledge and research. She employed the Swedish botanist Daniel Solander to catalogue her botanical collections using Linnaeus' classification, and helped to fund Sir Joseph Banks' plant-hunting trips to North America (see p.63). The Reverend John Lightfoot, a respected botanist, was her librarian and personal chaplain, while the famous philosopher Jean-Jacques Rousseau appointed himself as her 'herborist'.

The Duchess' collections gained national attention when she opened The Portland Museum at Bulstrode to visitors, along with the zoo, aviary and botanic gardens. Her home was referred to as 'the hive', referencing the scientific and artistic activities that took place there, and she was also a prominent member of The Bluestockings, a group of aristocratic women who championed intellectual opportunities for 'the fairer sex'.

After she died, her collections were dissolved and sold at auction to pay debts and for her son's political career, but the knowledge she and her team accrued helped to progress our understanding of plants and animals.

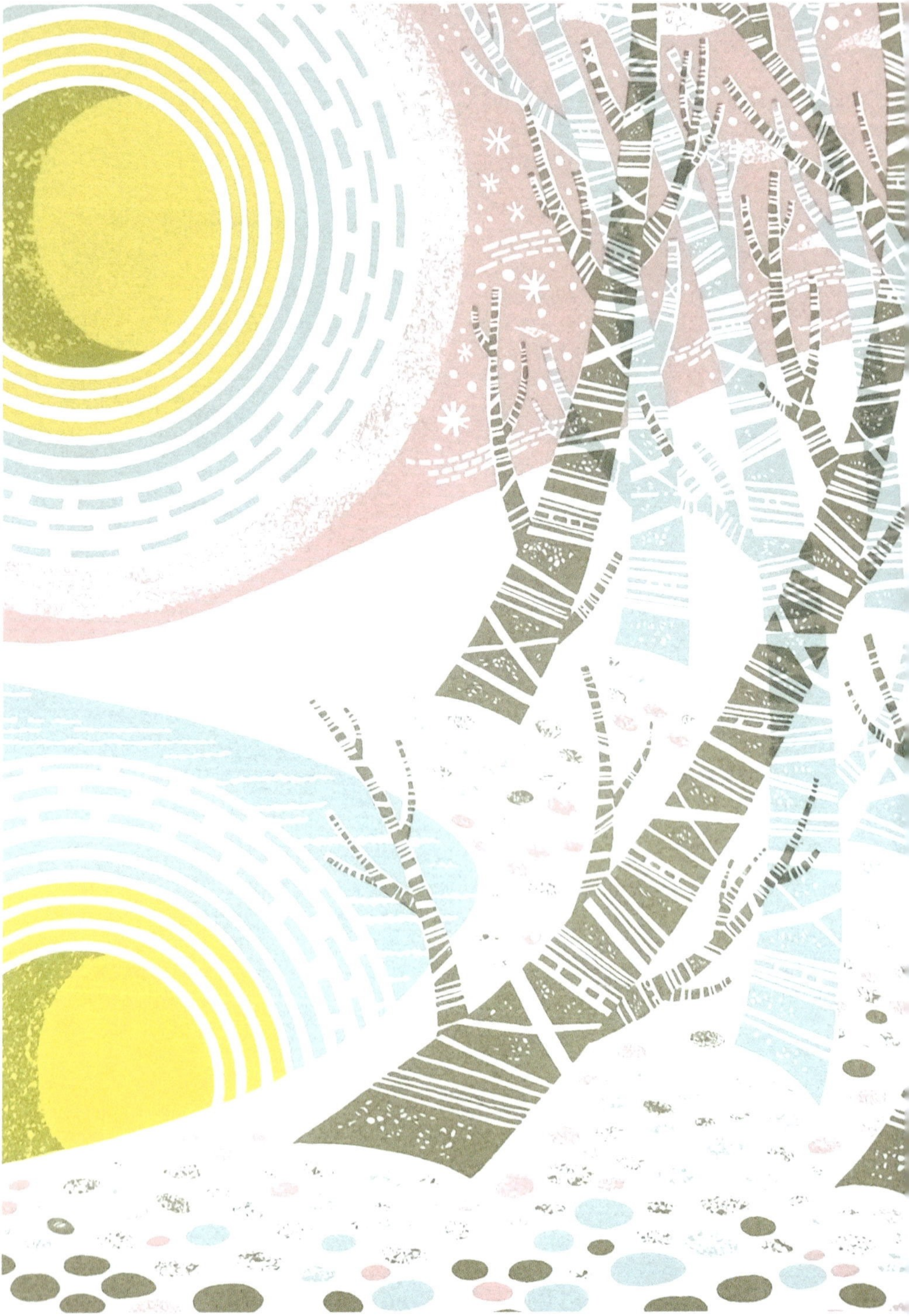

December

The year is coming to a close and there's excitement in the air as midwinter festivities get underway. In the garden, a hush falls over the iced landscape, broken only by the whir of pigeon wings and a robin's trill song, begging gardeners to dig up some worms for his supper. Skeletal trees arch overhead, while wreaths of glossy green holly and red berries welcome guests with sparkling colours.

KEY EVENTS
Hanukkah, 14–22 December
Winter Solstice (shortest day of the year), 21 December
Christmas Day, 25 December
New Year's Eve, 31 December

What to do in December

With midwinter in sight, the work in the garden slows down as light levels dim, offering us a moment to plan for the coming seasons and order seeds and plants. There's still time to plant bare-root trees, shrubs and roses, which will be available for another couple of months. You can also prune fruit trees now (see pp.226–7) and clean out the shed and greenhouse while it's relatively empty. Keep birds thriving, too, with fresh water and high-calorie foods (see below) and continue putting up nesting boxes to keep them warm and dry during periods of harsh weather (see p.201).

In the garden

RESTORE BEECH AND HORNBEAM HEDGING that has become overgrown. These plants respond well to hard pruning and can be renovated in two stages: in winter, cut one side and the top to the required dimensions, then leave the hedge to recover in summer and cut the remaining side the following winter. This regime works equally well for all deciduous hedges. ❶

FEED THE BIRDS now that natural food sources are in short supply. Offer high-calorie, nutritious foods such as fat blocks (never in nets), peanuts and sunflower seeds, or 'hearts' in feeders, and, for smaller birds, place finely grated cheese on tables. ❷

PLANT HOLLY to bring winter cheer to the garden. Hedging specialists will be offering bare-root plants now or, for a focal point, select a larger potted specimen. Male and female flowers are found on separate plants, and both are needed for berries, although if you live near woodland you will probably already have males in the vicinity. Good varieties to try include *Ilex aquifolium* 'Handsworth New Silver' (female), with its spiky, green and white variegated leaves, and *I. aquifolium* 'Pyramidalis' (female), prized for its glossy rounded leaves and clusters of red berries. ❸

MEND OR RENEW TRELLIS and supports for climbers while plants are not growing vigorously. Detach and fold down plants (pruning, if required), and replace wires and any nails or vine eyes. Vertical wires look particularly smart and tend to sag less than horizontal ones. Rotted trellis is best replaced with new. Reattach plants with coated wires or tubing ties.

TAKE ROOT CUTTINGS when plants are dormant in December. Remove a couple of healthy roots of pencil thickness or thicker from perennials such as Oriental poppies (*Papaver orientale*), Japanese anemones (*Anemone* × *hybrida*), phlox and verbascum. Cut the root into 5–10cm (2–4in) segments, using a sloping cut to indicate the lower end, which was deepest in the ground. Pot up the cuttings into gritty potting compost, with the pointed end at the bottom. Keep in an unheated greenhouse or cold frame until spring, when roots and shoots should have formed.

BRUSH SNOW FROM HEDGES and shrubs that may break under the weight.

In the fruit & veg patch

DIVIDE RHUBARB PLANTS, using a sharp knife or spade to cut the rootball into sections, each with a bud or two, and replant. Divide plants only when cropping declines, usually after about five years.

WASH OUT POTS AND SEED TRAYS ready for spring. With just over month until the sowing season begins again, it's useful to have plenty of pots and trays ready to go. Most items scrub up well with a stiff brush, hot water, detergent or garden disinfectant. When buying new, select the heavy-duty types that have long lives when reused. ❹

PLANT BARE-ROOT FRUIT TREES. Try red-fleshed apples for extra nutrient value. Research shows that these may contain up to 40 per cent more health-promoting phytochemicals, which reduce inflammation and can help protect the immune system. The pink-fleshed TICKLED PINK ('Baya Marisa') and 'Red Devil', and red 'Rosette' and REDLOVE ERA apples are good choices.

PLANT UP FRUIT IN PATIO POTS with mini versions of popular fruits, such as raspberry 'Ruby Beauty'; mulberry 'Charlotte Russe' (*Morus rotundiloba* 'Matsunaga') from Japan; and the little quince 'Leskovac', whose beautiful, downy yellow fruits are preceded by attractive, green-pink spring flowers.

ERECT BIRD CAGES to protect soft fruit from being eaten. Choose a cage with an aluminium frame that allows you to remove the net roof so birds can access insects in winter, and bees can enter to pollinate your plants.

Indoors

COLOURFUL POINSETTIAS are synonymous with Christmas and last for weeks, given plenty of light, a warm room above 13°C (55°F) and careful watering to prevent wet compost. Avoid buying them in outdoor markets, since chilling inflicts serious damage, from which plants may never recover.

MONEY-SAVING IDEA
Keep tools in good working order
Buying good-quality tools pays dividends since they will last many years if maintained regularly. Brush off the dirt from spades and forks, and use wire wool to clean secateur and pruning tool blades. Then clean off the rest of the dirt with water, dry thoroughly using an old towel and apply an alcohol-based disinfectant to kill off any diseases. If blades are made from stainless steel, that's all you need to do, but, for others, rub the blades with a few drops of camellia oil, applied with rag. Sharpen any blunt blades with a sharpening stone.

Plants of the month

1. Holly (*Ilex aquifolium* 'Argentea Marginata' pictured)
2. Hart's tongue fern (*Asplenium scolopendrium* 'Golden Queen' pictured)
3. Dwarf juniper (*Juniperus squamata* 'Blue Star' pictured)
4. Paperbark maple (*Acer griseum*)
5. Christmas rose (*Helleborus niger*)
6. Darwin's barberry (*Berberis darwinii*)
7. Honesty (*Lunaria annua*)
8. Carex (*Carex* 'Feather Falls' pictured)
9. Coronilla (*Coronilla valentina* subsp. *glauca*)
10. Japanese spurge (*Pachysandra terminalis* 'Variegata' pictured)
11. Oleaster (*Elaeagnus* × *submacrophylla* 'Viveleg' pictured)

Project: Planet-friendly bird feeders

Birds can suffer during winter when food is scarce, so the British Trust for Ornithology (BTO) suggests supplementing their diets with a range of seeds, nuts, fruit and fat-rich foods such as mild cheese. These easy feeders allow you to offer birds small quantities at regular intervals, to prevent the food from spoiling. You can also compost the feeders (bar the wire, which can be reused) when they start to deteriorate. Hang them from a branch that offers birds good all-round visibility, and also provide fresh water in a shallow dish, cleaning it and replacing the water regularly to prevent diseases.

YOU WILL NEED
Teasel seedheads
Suet, mixed bird seed, apples, sunflower seeds, raisins, cheese
Garden twine
Scissors
Twigs
Garden wire
Orange
Knife

PROJECT 1 To make the teasel feeders, spread some of the suet over the prickly seedheads, then dip them into mixed bird seed. Warming the suet in a pan to soften it makes it easier. Add twine to hang it up.

PROJECT 2 Make an apple feeder by removing the core from the fruit, and pushing sunflower seeds into the flesh. Create a perch for birds to access the feeder by tying together two twigs with twine. Then thread the twine through the middle of the apple to hang it up.

PROJECT 3 Thread a selection of fruits and mild cheese or suet onto a piece of garden wire and twist the ends together into a circle.

PROJECT 4 Cut an orange in half and scoop out the flesh. Use a sharp knife to make holes in the side and thread twine through, to create two loops to hang up the cut orange. Finally, fill it with bird seed.

Looking up

Sunrise and sunset

With the sun is at its lowest angle in December, perhaps not even reaching areas that are flooded with light in summer, most deciduous plants become dormant.

	LONDON		EDINBURGH	
DAY	Sunrise	Sunset	Sunrise	Sunset
Mon, Dec 1	7:42:11 am	3:57:02 pm	8:17:22 am	3:46:26 pm
Tue, Dec 2	7:43:32 am	3:56:27 pm	8:18:58 am	3:45:35 pm
Wed, Dec 3	7:44:51 am	3:55:54 pm	8:20:31 am	3:44:49 pm
Thu, Dec 4	7:46:09 am	3:55:25 pm	8:22:02 am	3:44:06 pm
Fri, Dec 5	7:47:24 am	3:54:59 pm	8:23:31 am	3:43:27 pm
Sat, Dec 6	7:48:38 am	3:54:36 pm	8:24:56 am	3:42:52 pm
Sun, Dec 7	7:49:48 am	3:54:17 pm	8:26:19 am	3:42:21 pm
Mon, Dec 8	7:50:57 am	3:54:01 pm	8:27:38 am	3:41:54 pm
Tue, Dec 9	7:52:03 am	3:53:48 pm	8:28:55 am	3:41:31 pm
Wed, Dec 10	7:53:07 am	3:53:39 pm	8:30:08 am	3:41:12 pm
Thu, Dec 11	7:54:08 am	3:53:33 pm	8:31:18 am	3:40:58 pm
Fri, Dec 12	7:55:06 am	3:53:30 pm	8:32:24 am	3:40:47 pm
Sat, Dec 13	7:56:02 am	3:53:31 pm	8:33:27 am	3:40:40 pm
Sun, Dec 14	7:56:55 am	3:53:35 pm	8:34:27 am	3:40:38 pm
Mon, Dec 15	7:57:45 am	3:53:43 pm	8:35:22 am	3:40:40 pm
Tue, Dec 16	7:58:32 am	3:53:54 pm	8:36:14 am	3:40:46 pm
Wed, Dec 17	7:59:16 am	3:54:08 pm	8:37:02 am	3:40:57 pm
Thu, Dec 18	7:59:58 am	3:54:26 pm	8:37:47 am	3:41:12 pm
Fri, Dec 19	8:00:36 am	3:54:47 pm	8:38:27 am	3:41:30 pm
Sat, Dec 20	8:01:11 am	3:55:12 pm	8:39:03 am	3:41:54 pm
Sun, Dec 21	8:01:42 am	3:55:40 pm	8:39:36 am	3:42:21 pm
Mon, Dec 22	8:02:11 am	3:56:11 pm	8:40:04 am	3:42:52 pm
Tue, Dec 23	8:02:36 am	3:56:45 pm	8:40:28 am	3:43:28 pm
Wed, Dec 24	8:02:58 am	3:57:23 pm	8:40:48 am	3:44:07 pm
Thu, Dec 25	8:03:17 am	3:58:03 pm	8:41:04 am	3:44:51 pm
Fri, Dec 26	8:03:33 am	3:58:47 pm	8:41:16 am	3:45:39 pm
Sat, Dec 27	8:03:45 am	3:59:34 pm	8:41:23 am	3:46:30 pm
Sun, Dec 28	8:03:54 am	4:00:24 pm	8:41:26 am	3:47:26 pm
Mon, Dec 29	8:03:59 am	4:01:17 pm	8:41:25 am	3:48:25 pm
Tue, Dec 30	8:04:01 am	4:02:12 pm	8:41:20 am	3:49:28 pm
Wed, Dec 31	8:04:00 am	4:03:11 pm	8:41:11 am	3:50:34 pm

Moonrise and moonset

Moon phases

● **NEW MOON** 20 December
◐ **FIRST QUARTER** 27 December
○ **FULL MOON** 4 December
◐ **THIRD QUARTER** 11 December

MONTH	LONDON Moonrise	LONDON Moonset	LONDON Moonrise	EDINBURGH Moonrise	EDINBURGH Moonset	EDINBURGH Moonrise
Dec 1		02:53	13:36		03:14	13:38
Dec 2		04:22	13:53		04:51	13:48
Dec 3		05:57	14:17		06:35	14:03
Dec 4		07:33	14:52		08:20	14:29
Dec 5		09:00	15:44		09:54	15:16
Dec 6		10:08	16:57		11:01	16:30
Dec 7		10:54	18:23		11:40	18:04
Dec 8		11:24	19:51		12:01	19:41
Dec 9		11:45	21:17		12:14	21:14
Dec 10		12:00	22:36		12:23	22:41
Dec 11		12:12	23:52		12:29	
Dec 12		12:22		00:02	12:34	
Dec 13	01:04	12:33		01:21	12:39	
Dec 14	02:16	12:43		02:38	12:45	
Dec 15	03:28	12:56		03:56	12:52	
Dec 16	04:41	13:12		05:16	13:01	
Dec 17	05:54	13:34		06:36	13:16	
Dec 18	07:04	14:03		07:54	13:38	
Dec 19	08:09	14:44		09:03	14:15	
Dec 20	09:02	15:39		09:57	15:10	
Dec 21	09:43	16:45		10:33	16:22	
Dec 22	10:13	18:00		10:55	17:44	
Dec 23	10:35	19:17		11:10	19:10	
Dec 24	10:51	20:36		11:19	20:35	
Dec 25	11:05	21:54		11:27	21:59	
Dec 26	11:17	23:12		11:33	23:24	
Dec 27	11:28			11:38		
Dec 28		00:33	11:41		00:51	11:45
Dec 29		01:57	11:55		02:22	11:53
Dec 30		03:26	12:15		03:59	12:05
Dec 31		04:58	12:43		05:41	12.24

Average rainfall

The 20-year average rainfall for the UK in December is 166m (6½in), making it the wettest month of the year, alongside January. The high rainfall helps to replenish groundwater supplies but also increases the risk of flooding in low-lying areas.

LOCATION	DAYS	MM	INCHES
Aberdeen	13	78	3.0
Aberystwyth	17	127	5.0
Belfast	15	93	3.7
Birmingham	13	84	3.3
Bournemouth	13	104	4.1
Bristol	13	90	3.5
Cambridge	10	49	1.9
Canterbury	12	72	2.8
Cardiff	15	140	5.5
Edinburgh	12	67	2.6
Exeter	17	186	7.3
Glasgow	17	161	6.3
Gloucester	13	85	3.3
Inverness	14	73	2.9
Ipswich	11	57	2.2
Leeds	16	121	4.8
Liverpool	15	92	3.6
London	12	68	2.7
Manchester	18	139	5.5
Newcastle upon Tyne	11	55	2.2
Norwich	13	64	2.5
Nottingham	12	70	2.7
Oxford	12	66	2.6
Sheffield	14	87	3.4
Truro	17	116	4.6

Pruning masterclass: winter time

Many deciduous plants with woody stems, including fruit and other trees, respond well to pruning in winter, after their leaves have fallen and they are dormant. Not only can you see the stem structure more clearly once the trees are bare, but also cutting them back now avoids sap bleeding from the wounds, which can occur in spring.

HOW TO PRUNE A FRUIT TREE
Apple and pear trees are usually pruned in winter, although restricted forms such as cordons and espaliers are best pruned in summer to limit their growth (see pp. 112–13). Your aim is to create and maintain a goblet-shaped tree with an open centre that allows light to penetrate to the leaves and fruits when they appear, while maximizing airflow through the branches, which will help to suppress diseases.

Typically, you should remove 10–20 per cent of the tree canopy each year. Cutting out more stems can result in the growth of unproductive water shoots (see opposite). Start by taking out dead, diseased, rubbing and dead material, and thin very congested growth. Then remove stronger shoots growing into the centre of the tree and leave the short weaker growth. Downward-growing branches tend to be a drain on the tree and are best

Prune apple trees to create an open centre that will allow light to penetrate to the leaves and fruits.

removed, too, while strong vertical shoots can dominate, making the tree too tall, so shorten all of them to a sideshoot.

The next step is to shorten the new stems on each of the main branches by one third, cutting to just above an outward-facing bud, to promote fruitful growth. When thinning congested growth, aim for a fruiting 'spur' (short stem that produces fruit) every 10–15cm

(4–6in) on each branch. Some trees, including 'Bramley's Seedling' apples, fruit at the tips of their shoots and are commonly referred to as 'tip bearers'. Avoid shortening all the shoots on these trees, as it will limit fruiting; instead, cut back the older branches by one quarter to a strong young shoot. The effect will be to limit the size of the tree while maintaining a good crop each year.

DEALING WITH WATER SHOOTS
If you are confronted by a tree that has been drastically pruned, thereby promoting a thick regrowth of vigorous vertical but unfruitful water shoots, you can encourage it to bear fruit again by retaining about half of them and removing the others.

Cut out all of the shoots growing directly from the trunk or lower parts of the main branches, removing them at the base, without leaving a stub (see left). Then prune out about half of the shoots on the other branches, ensuring those you retain are spaced 45cm (18in) or more apart at the base of the stem from which they are growing. These shoots will, in time, resume cropping; regular pruning can then be reinstated.

Top Reduce congested growth so the plant can put more energy into the fruiting stems that remain.
Bottom Thin watershoots to avoid congested, unproductive, disease-prone growth.

DECEMBER / 227

Edible garden

Growth slows down as winter takes hold, the low light conditions minimizing photosynthesis, while cold temperatures limit germination. However, a few crops can be sown successfully this month in a heated greenhouse or on warm windowsill.

Vegetables

SOW INDOORS OR UNDER CLOCHES
Broad beans; herbs such as basil, chives, dill and parsley for growing overwinter indoors; pea shoots; winter salad leaves.

HARVEST NOW Brussels sprouts; cabbages including savoys; carrots; celeriac ❶; hardy salad leaves; Jerusalem artichokes; kale; leeks; parsnips; perpetual spinach; swedes; turnips.

Fruit

PLANT NOW Bare-root fruit trees (see p.220) and bushes such as gooseberries, currants and blackberries; potted blueberry plants; raspberry and hybrid berry canes; rhubarb crowns; strawberry runners.

HARVEST Citrus grown indoors. ❷

HERB OF THE MONTH: SAGE
This Mediterranean aromatic shrub makes a beautiful border plant in a sunny sheltered spot with free-draining soil, and the leaves add flavour to many savoury dishes. Common sage (*Salvia officinalis*) is hardy, but plants go dormant in winter, so to guarantee a small crop now, and to protect plants from wet soils, pot them up and place them in a sunny area close to the house or bring them indoors into a cool but bright conservatory or porch.

Challenges this month

While most insects have died or are sitting out the winter in a sheltered spot, a few are on the move now and may cause problems later in spring or summer. Rots and fungal diseases are still prevalent this month, too.

WINTER MOTH caterpillars make holes in the leaves, blossom and fruitlets of a wide range of trees in early spring and pupate later in the summer and autumn. In winter, the adults emerge and the flightless females crawl up trees to lay their eggs after fertilization by the free-flying males. While they do harm some fruit and flowers, they are an important food for birds and other wildlife, so in most cases they should be tolerated, since the damage is limited and short-lived. Grease bands are sometimes used to intercept the females on apple trees, which can limit winter moth populations. Stakes should also be greased.

PHYTOPHTHORA ROOT ROT (shown) is fungus-like disease that affects trees and many other plants, especially if growing in waterlogged soils, and can result in the death of affected plants. The problem is not always evident above the ground until the rot has seriously undermined the plant, when the fine feeder roots have rotted away and larger roots are also decaying. At this point, the plant will show signs of wilting, yellow or sparse foliage and branch dieback. To prevent root rot, plant on mounds to keep the base dry, or install drains to ensure waterlogging does not occur, and always plant in pots with drainage holes at the bottom. Affected plants should be destroyed and the soil from the root-run replaced with fresh topsoil.

OAK GALLS cause growths on trees and are induced by about 70 different gall wasps to accommodate their larvae. In some years, particularly when acorns are galled, it may seem like these beautiful trees will not survive, but, in fact, oaks support numerous galls with no discernible ill effects. Common galls include the acorn or knopper gall wasp, which turns acorns into knobbly, red or brown woody structures; the common spangle gall wasp, which produces brown discs below the leaves; and the oak artichoke gall wasp, which induces a little globe artichoke-like structure on leaf buds. As they do no harm, just enjoy these quirks of nature.

Focus on wildlife

Blackbird

One of the UK's favourite birds, the blackbird is resident here all year round and can be seen eating berries and worms during the cold winter months. The male has black plumage, with orange rings around the eyes and a bright orange-yellow beak, while the females are dark brown with pale brown streaks on their chests, and have a duller yellow-brown beak.

Blackbirds live in a wide range of habitats, from woodlands and grasslands to parks and gardens. Often heard before they are seen, the male blackbird has a distinctive, melodious, whistling call – or high-pitched chatter when threatened – while the female rarely sings but produces a high-pitched call when trying to attract a mate. The birds' diet consists primarily of worms, which they can hear under the soil by cocking their heads to one side. Other favourite foods include caterpillars, fallen fruits and berries.

Blackbirds breed from March to late July, depending on the weather, and they are monogamous, with pairs often mating for life. The female builds a round nest close to the ground beneath a bush or small tree, using twigs, grass and other plant materials to create the structure. She will have two or three broods per year, with an average clutch of three to five eggs each time.

The female also incubates the eggs, and the chicks fledge about 14 days after hatching. They are then fully independent about three weeks later.

Planting berried shrubs and trees will help to sustain blackbirds during the winter months, while providing mealworms, uncooked oats, fat balls (remove netting) and flaked maize on a table or scattering it on the ground will also nourish them when natural resources are low.

Spotlight on: Ivy (Hedera)

Ivy has long been associated with Christmas and other winter festivals – its long flexible stems of triangular evergreen leaves ideal for decorating homes at this time of the year. Ivy's autumn flowers are also rich in nectar and offer a late-season feast for pollinators, including bees. When used to cover a building, this climber can help to keep homes cool in summer and less damp in winter, but it needs regular pruning to prevent it blocking drains and covering windows. Alternatively, grow it up a fence or wall, if the masonry is sound. Ivy thrives in most soils and in part or full shade, as well as sun.

HEDERA COLCHICA 'SULPHUR HEART'
A good choice for groundcover or to cover buildings, this vigorous climber produces large, ovate, dark green leaves with a yellow splash.
H x S: 8 x 4m (26 x 13ft)

HEDERA HELIX 'MIDAS TOUCH'
Well-behaved and compact, this ivy has triangular to heart-shaped, green leaves with golden-yellow splashes, held on red stems. It is ideal as a houseplant or for a patio container.
H x S: 90 x 50cm (36 x 20in)

HEDERA HIBERNICA 'RONA'
This form of Irish ivy produces cream-coloured new foliage, speckled with green, which becomes greener as it matures, creating a vibrant two-tone effect in deep shade.
H x S: 2.5 x 2.5 (8 x 8ft)

HEDERA HELIX 'BUTTERCUP'
The bright yellow lobed leaves of this decorative ivy need a little sun to maintain their colour and will turn paler or greenish-yellow in shady situations.
H x S: 2.5 x 1.5 (8 x 5ft)

HEDERA HELIX 'GLACIER'
A popular cultivar, loved for its three- to five-lobed, grey-green leaves with cream edges, this medium-sized climber will soon cover a wall or fence.
H x S: 2 x 2m (6 x 6ft)

Seasonal planting ideas

BUFF BEAUTIES

WHY IT WORKS
In winter, this group of flowers and grasses develops beautiful seedheads, adding form and structure to the garden. Flat-topped sedums (*Hylotelephium*) contrast with tiny *Rudbeckia* seedheads and the soft swaying foliage of the feather reed grass (*Calamagrostis*). While the flowers of these plants have passed their peak, their stems and seedheads continue to offer a wonderful winter treat, especially with a light touch of frost adding some sparkle.

WHAT'S GROWING HERE?
Hylotelephium 'Matrona' (formerly *Sedum* 'Matrona') is an upright deciduous perennial that grows to 60cm (2ft) tall. It produces large, fleshy, grey-green leaves tinged purple near the margins, and dense, flat-topped clusters of pale pink flowers in late summer and early autumn. The dried flowerheads and stems create great winter interest.

Calamagrostis is a clump-forming perennial grass, up to 1.8m (6ft) in height, with arching green leaves and bronze flowering panicles that fade to pale brown in autumn. The open structure allows views through the grass stems, making a scheme feel more open and airy. Most *Calamagrostis* like an open sunny site, but *C.* × *acutiflora* 'Overdam' and *C.* × *a* 'Avalanche' will tolerate a position in part shade.

Rudbeckia fulgida var. *deamii* is a hardy perennial growing to 60cm (2ft), with golden-yellow, daisy-like flowers from late summer to autumn, followed by chocolate-brown seedheads that persist for most of the winter.

WHEN TO PLANT
Plant in autumn or early spring. These plants prefer a position in full sun in well-drained soil, although the *Rudbeckia* likes a little more moisture than the others in summer.

WHERE TO SEE IT
Discover this wintry scene at the Clover Hill borders at RHS Garden Hyde Hall.

Horticultural heroes

Vita Sackville-West · 1892–1962

Garden designer, journalist, poet and novelist Vita Sackville-West is today most famous for creating the gardens at Sissinghurst Castle in Kent. However, during her lifetime, she was equally renowned for her books and articles, and she was the inspiration for *Orlando: A Biography*, the novel by her lover and friend, Virginia Woolf.

Born in Kent in 1892 to cousins Victoria Sackville-West and Lionel Sackville-West, Vita split her time between London, Knole in Kent and Paris, after her parents' marriage broke down. In 1913, she married diplomat Sir Harold Nicolson, and the couple moved to Long Barn in Kent, where she created her first garden. In 1930, they bought Sissinghurst Castle, near Cranbrook, which had once been owned by Sackville-West's ancestors.

Sissinghurst was an Elizabethan ruin with 180 hectares (450 acres) of land that had been badly neglected when the couple arrived, and they worked for the next 30 years to create a home and garden there. Together, they carved out a series of enclosures or garden 'rooms', each with its own character, with Nicolson designing the architectural structure and Vita in charge of the planting. Considered innovative at the time, when the garden opened to the public in 1938 it created much interest, with its single colour-themed White Garden and informal planting in the Orchard, Cottage Garden and Nuttery.

Visitor numbers grew after Vita began writing a weekly column in *The Observer* newspaper, sharing her plant knowledge and experiences of creating the gardens. Her writing fees, together with sales from her garden books and novels, helped to pay for Sissinghurst's upkeep, and she continued to write the column until a year before her death. In 1948, she became a founder member of the National Trust's Garden committee, and she was awarded the Veitch Memorial Medal from the Royal Horticultural Society in 1955.

Sissinghurst's Grade I listed garden is owned and run by the National Trust, and open to the public all year round.

RHS Gardens to Visit

The RHS has five beautiful gardens to visit, which are open all year round and free to enter for RHS members and a family guest or two children (four children for joint memberships). There are also over 220 RHS partner gardens in the UK and abroad that offer free entry to RHS members, the details of which can be found at rhs.org.uk/gardens/partner-gardens/.

For opening times, visit the garden websites listed.

BRIDGEWATER
The RHS's newest garden, Bridgewater opened in 2021 and has been dazzling visitors with its stunning garden displays ever since. A tour begins in the Worsley Welcome Garden, its ribbons of colourful planting setting the tone for your visit. The jewel in Bridgewater's crown is the Weston Walled Garden, which houses the stunning Paradise Garden, based on the layout of ancient Islamic gardens, and a contemporary Kitchen Garden that showcases a range of innovative productive growing ideas. The wider woodland, meadows and lakes add to the visitor experience, while the sparkling water and Asian-inspired planting in the Chinese Streamside Garden are not to be missed.

To plan your visit and for more details about the garden, head to rhs.org.uk/gardens/bridgewater/.

RHS Garden Bridgewater
Occupation Road
Off Leigh Road
Worsley, Salford
Greater Manchester
M28 2LJ

HARLOW CARR
Set deep in the Yorkshire countryside, Harlow Carr offers a variety of beautiful gardens to enjoy, from lush lakeside walks to woodland and wildflower meadows. Highlights include the Main Borders, bursting with colourful, prairie-style planting; the stunning Winter Garden, with its inspiring, cold-season planting; a Kitchen Garden packed with ideas for home growers; and a Subtropical Garden that takes its inspiration from the colourful planting at Great Dixter in Sussex.

To plan your visit and for more details about the garden, head to rhs.org.uk/gardens/harlow-carr/.

RHS Garden Harlow Carr
Crag Lane
Beckwithshaw
Harrogate
North Yorkshire
HG3 1QB

HYDE HALL

A jewel in the heart of rural Essex, Hyde Hall offers an eclectic mix of traditional and modern gardens, the most famous of which is the Dry Garden, showcasing colourful, drought-tolerant plants. Other highlights include the Hilltop Garden, with its roses and herbaceous borders; the Global Growth Vegetable Garden; ponds and meadows buzzing with wildlife; and an adventure playground where the children can let off steam.

To plan your visit and for more details about the garden, head to rhs.org.uk/gardens/hyde-hall/.

RHS Garden Hyde Hall
Creephedge Lane
Rettendon, Chelmsford
Essex
CM3 8ET

ROSEMOOR

Surrounded by woodland and rolling hills, Rosemoor sits in heart of the Torridge Valley in north Devon and offers a range of dazzling gardens to enjoy all year round. The Cherry Garden and orchards are decked with blossom in spring, while the romantic Rose Garden and Hot Garden are the stars of summer. The woods and Lady Anne's Arboretum blaze with fiery colours in autumn, and the Winter Garden is a must for cold-season inspiration.

To plan your visit and for more details about the garden, head to rhs.org.uk/gardens/rosemoor/.

RHS Garden Rosemoor
Great Torrington
Devon
EX38 8PH

WISLEY

The RHS's flagship garden in Surrey, Wisley houses one of the largest plant collections in the world and offers 24 hectares (60 acres) to explore. From gardens showcasing prairie-style plants, roses and Mediterranean species to those designed for wildlife and wellbeing, Wisley offers something for everyone. The famous Glasshouse sits at the heart of the garden, its huge cathedral-like structure housing a world-class tender plant collection, while RHS Hilltop is the home of Gardening Science, where you can discover fascinating facts about plants and take part in a range of ongoing horticultural research studies.

To plan your visit and for more details about the garden, head to rhs.org.uk/gardens/wisley/.

RHS Garden Wisley
Wisley Lane
Surrey
GU23 6QB

Index

A
African violets 164
airplant mobile 14
algae 97
anemones 79
annuals 29, 46, 66, 211
aphids 77
apple blossom 68
apple sawflies 117
April 64–81
artichokes 68
asparagus: fennel, asparagus and orange pickle 96
asters 143
August 142–59
autumn bedding 105
azaleas 202

B
bank vole 194
Banks, Sir Joseph 63
bare-root plants 10, 182
barley straw 47
basil, Greek 95
bath bog garden 70
bay 210
beans 68, 126
bedding plants 30, 84–5, 105, 180
beech 218
bees 66, 103
beetles 97
beetroot 106
  beetroot, carrot and caraway pickle 136
Bentinck, Margaret 215
biennials 124

birds 217, 220
  feeding 218, 222
  nesting boxes 201
  water for 125
  see also individual species
blackbirds 230
blight, potato 155
blueberries 68
bluetits 40
bog garden, bath 70
bracken 59
bracket fungi 211
broad beans 182
Brown, Lancelot 'Capability' 25
bug hotels 166
bulbs 66, 162, 164, 180
butterflies 174
butternut squash 86

C
cabbage 126
  kimchi with chive flowers 116
cactus, winter 182
capsid bugs 117
caraway seeds: beetroot, carrot and caraway pickle 136
carbon capture 208–9
carrots 106
  beetroot, carrot and caraway pickle 136
catkins 42
celery seeds, kohlrabi with lovage and 192
Chatto, Beth 177
Chelsea chop 85

chives 115
  kimchi with chive flowers 116
clematis 61, 161
cloches 202
clubroot 77
codling moth 173
colour, seasonal planting ideas 140
composting prunings 189
congested plants, dividing 68, 146
coral spot 211
coriander 106
cornfield annuals 55
cover crops 170
currants 202
cuttings, root 219

D
daffodils 27, 46
dahlias 48, 143, 145
damping-off diseases 39
damselflies 118
deadheading 126
December 216–33
deer 21
dill 57
diseases 39, 77, 137, 155, 173, 193, 211, 229
dividing plants 68, 146, 164
downy mildew 173
dwarf iris 41

E
earwigs 137
elephant hawk-moth 138

236 / INDEX

euonymus 195
evergreens 9, 66, 112, 180

F
fairy rings 193
February 26–43
fennel 191
    fennel, asparagus and
        orange pickle 96
ferments 58
    beetroot, carrot and caraway
        pickle 136
    fennel, asparagus and
        orange pickle 96
    kimchi with chive flowers
        116
    kohlrabi with lovage and
        celery seed 192
    rhubarb kombucha 76
    traditional sauerkraut 172
fertilizers 132–3
fieldfare 212
flea beetles 155
flies, houseplant 21
flowers: deadheading 126
    flower meadows 54–5
    wild flowers 84
French tarragon 134
frost 97
fruit 95, 190
    what to grow and when 20,
        38, 56, 74, 115, 134, 154,
        170, 190, 210, 228
    see also individual types
        of fruit
fruit trees 29, 135, 209, 220
    pruning 226–7

G
garlic 12, 164
glasshouse mealybugs 39
gooseberries 202
grasses, ornamental 28
great spotted woodpecker 60
Greek basil 95
green manure 170

H
half-hardy annuals 46
hardy annuals 29
hedgehog hideouts 108
hedges 218, 219
    planting 18–19, 201
    trimming 144, 152–3
herbs 20, 88
    see also individual types
        of herb
holly 218
honey fungus 193
honeyberries 202
hornbeam 218
horsetail 173
houseplants 106, 182
    cuttings 106
    dusting 48
    feeding 12, 86
    pests 21, 146
    repotting 86
    watering 30, 68, 126, 202
hunger gap 74
hydrangeas 124, 157

I
insulation box 32
intercropping 85

irises, dwarf 41
ivy 231

J
January 8–25
Japanese knotweed 77
Jekyll, Gertrude 43
Jellicoe, Sir Geoffrey 159
July 122–41
June 102–21

K
kimchi with chive flowers 116
kohlrabi with lovage and celery
    seed 192
kombucha, rhubarb 76

L
ladybirds 98
lavender, deadheading 125
lawns 54–5, 105
    aerating 162–3
    lawn moss 47
    watering 145
leatherjackets 193
leeks 202
light levels 12
lilies, planting 28
little owl 22
lovage: kohlrabi with lovage
    and celery seed 192

M
Maathai, Wangari Muta 81
magnolia 65
March 44–63
May 82–101

INDEX / **237**

meadows, flower 54–5
mealybugs 39
Mediterranean feasts 94
microgreens, sowing 12
mildew 137, 173
mint 30, 171
moles 39
the Moon: moonrise and moonset 16, 34, 52, 72, 90, 110, 130, 150, 168, 186, 206, 224
  phases of 7
moss, lawn 47
moths 138, 173, 229
mulches 29, 86, 200
mustard 146

N
nectar plants 11
nesting boxes 201
newts 78
November 198–215

O
oak galls 229
October 178–97
onion sets, planting 181
oranges: fennel, asparagus and orange pickle 96
oregano 154
organisms, beneficial 92–3
ornamental grasses, cutting back 28
Oudolf, Piet 197
owl, little 22

P
pak choi 125
parsley 20
pear midges 117
peas, freezing 126
peonies 119
peppers 125, 163
perennials 30, 59, 104, 211
  dividing 46, 164
  planting bare-root 10, 202
pests 21, 39, 59, 92–3, 97, 117, 155, 193, 229
phlomis 199
phytophthora root rot 229
pickles: beetroot, carrot and caraway 136
  fennel, asparagus and orange 96
pinching out 104
pineapple lily 47
planting schemes 62
plants: buying bargain plants 146
  natural plant protection 92–3
  plants of the month 13, 31, 49, 69, 87, 107, 127, 147, 165, 183, 203, 221
  puddling in new 124–5
  seasonal planting ideas 24, 42, 62, 80, 100, 120, 140, 158, 176, 196, 214, 232
poinsettias 220
polianthes, planting tubers 48
pollarding trees 10–11
pollinators, biennials for 124

pollution 18
pomegranates 68
ponds 47, 144, 181
potatoes: blight 155
  chitting 12
  earthing up 105
  harvesting 182
  planting 47–8, 67
pots 86, 104, 128, 163, 204, 220
powdery mildew 137
predators 92–3
pruning: Chelsea chop 85
  composting prunings 189
  pollarding 10–11
  summer 112–13, 152–3
  tender perennials and shrubs 30
  when to prune 36–7
  winter 226–7
Prunus, pruning 113
puddling 124–5

R
rabbits 59
radishes 106
rainfall 17, 35, 53, 73, 91, 111, 131, 151, 169, 187, 207, 225
  capturing rainwater 50
raspberries 30, 126, 161
red admiral butterflies 174
red spider mite 137
RHS gardens to visit 234–5
rhubarb 219
  rhubarb kombucha 76
Robinson, William 101

rocket 146
roe deer 21
root cuttings 219
rosemary 38
roses 11, 29, 103, 162, 213
rudbeckia 143, 175
runner beans 86, 145
rusts 137

S
Sackville-West, Vita 233
sage 228
salad leaves 48, 106, 164
salad onions 146
salvias 139
sauerkraut, traditional 172
scale insects 21
scent combos, winter 24
seascapes, potted 128
seed trays 220
seedlings 67, 84
seeds, collecting 145
September 160–77
shrubs 180, 200, 209
  planting bare-root 144, 201
  pollarding 10–11
  pruning 30, 112–13
  removing suckers 11
  watering 135
slugs and snails 59
snow 11, 219
snowdrops 9, 29
sowing, little and often 56
spare ground, covering 84
spinach 163
spring cabbage 126
Spry, Constance 141

staking plants 67
strawberries 48, 86, 181–2
suckers, removing 11
summer bedding 84–5
sunrise and sunset 15, 33, 51, 71, 89, 109, 129, 149, 167, 185, 205, 223
swallows 156
sweet peas 181
sweetcorn 86
Swiss cheeseplant 12

T
tarragon 134
tender plants 30, 32
thyme 75
tomatoes 48, 125, 126, 164
tools 220
topdressing 146
trees 208–9
  planting bare-root 201
  pollarding 10–11
  pruning 227
  removing suckers 11
  watering 135
  see also fruit trees
trellis 219
tulips 65, 80, 84, 200

V
vegetables: feeding 114
  hardy vegetables 11–12, 47
  tender vegetables 29–30
  topdressing 146
  what to grow and when 20, 38, 56, 74, 94, 114, 134, 154, 170, 190, 210, 228

  see also individual types of vegetable
viburnum 99
vine weevils 155
voles 194

W
waste, recycling garden 188–9
water shoots 227
watering 104
weeding 105
wild flowers 84
wildlife: making space for 148
  spring bulbs for 162
  wildlife hedges 18
  see also individual species
Willmott, Ellen 121
winter scent combos 24
winter moths 229
witch hazel 9, 23
woodpeckers 60
wreaths, autumn 184

Picture credits

Ali Cundy © RHS 127 (7); Andrii Tsynhariuk/Alamy 218 (1); Anna Brockman © RHS 154tr, 175mt; Andrew Halstead © RHS 21, 118, 138, 202b; Arterra Picture Library/Alamy 60, 194; Associated Press/Alamy 81; Barry Philips © RHS 69 (5), 157mr, 165 (6), 195t; blickwinkel/Alamy 156; Bryan Reynolds/Alamy 175t; Carol Sheppard © RHS 10 (1), 13 (5), 23l, 31 (3), 46 (1), 47 (4), 49 (3), 49 (6) 55t, 69 (3), 69 (5), 70 (3 (l)), 79br, 85 (2), 87 (10), 87 (11), 93, 107 (3), 107 (4), 115br, 125 (3), 139b, 147 (10), 162 (2), 165 (1), 165 (10), 165 (11), 174, 180 (1), 183 (6), 183 (10), 191 (3), 203 (8), 203 (9), 204 (1), 212, 221 (7), 230; Cecile Moisan © RHS 69 (1), 87 (1), 139ml; Christopher Whitehouse © Christopher Whitehouse 165 (7); Claire Campbell © RHS 157t, 157bl; Clive Nichols © RHS 31 (2), 107 (2), 190 (1); Craig Joiner Photography/Alamy 75 (2); Cyrustr/Shutterstock 199t; Deborah Vernon/Alamy 132; Duncan Coombs © Duncan Coombs 221 (3); Fiona Lea © RHS 87 (8), 127 (8), 147 (2), 157br, 175ml, 228 (1); GAP Photos 70 (1), 70 (2) 146 (6), 166 (1); Georgi Mabee © RHS 40, 59, 78, 94 (1), 97, 98, 145 (2) 164 (5); Graham Titchmarsh © RHS 67 (2), 75br, 99 mt, 134b, 147 (9), 175mb, 228 (2), 231tr; Hazrat Bilal/Alamy 106 (6); Helen Yates © RHS 28 (3), 86 (6), 125 (4), 135 (3), 181 (5); Hulton Deutsch/Getty 223; Janet Horton/Alamy 126br; Jason Ingram © RHS 49 (11), 54, 62, 127 (5), 135 (4), 158, 191 (2), 221 (4); Jerry Harpur © Jerry Harpur 99t, 191 (4); Joanna Kossak © RHS 13 (1), 13 (6), 31 (6), 31 (11), 49 (5), 69 (10), 87 (6), 107 (6), 107 (7), 119bl, 127 (2), 139mb, 147 (1), 147 (5), 147 (8), 165 (4), 165 (8), 183 (3), 183 (7), 195mb, 221 (8), 221 (11), 226, 227b; John Scrace © John Scrace 137, 211; John Trenholm © RHS 117; Julian Weigall © RHS 55b, 189t; Katy Prentice © RHS 107 (5), 171 (2); Keith Harris © RHS 39; Krzysztof Dzidek/Shutterstock 166 (2); Lee Beel © RHS 99br, 147 (6); lcrms/Shutterstock 31 (7); Lee Charlton © RHS 124 (2); Leigh Hunt © RHS 31 (8), 79tr; Les Gibbon/Alamy 22; Liz Beal © RHS 193; Liz Blyth © RHS 67 (3); Luke MacGregor © RHS 197; Mali lucky/Shutterstock 61tl, 61b; Mark Bolton © RHS 31 (1), 70 (3(r)), 147 (3); Mark Winwood © Dorling Kindersley Ltd 13 (9), 23mb, 41m, 41r, 49 (1), 66 (1), 69 (7), 69 (8), 87 (2), 99mb, 119br, 119mt, 157mt, 165 (5), 200 (1), 203 (6), 209, 213tm, 213bml, 221 (1); Mark Waugh © RHS 95 (2); Martin Hughes-Jones/Alamy 99; Mike Sleigh © RHS 13 (8), 23mt, 79bl, 135 (2), 139mt, 183 (1); Neil Hepworth © RHS 14 (1), 14 (2), 14 (3), 24, 29 (4), 31 (4), 31 (10), 32 (1), 32 (2), 32 (3), 38 (1) 50 (1), 50 (2), 50 (3), 50 (4), 57 (3), 75 (4), 80, 95 (4), 108 (1), 108 (2), 108 (3), 128 (1), 128 (2), 128 (3), 128 (4), 144 (1), 148 (1), 148 (2), 148 (3), 148 (4), 153r, 182r, 184 (1), 184 (2), 184 (3), 184 (5), 201 (4), 201 (5), 203 (1), 203 (11), 204 (2), 204 (3), 214, 220 (4), 222 (1), 222 (2), 222 (3), 222 (4); mizy/Shutterstock 231mr; Nadia Young/Shutterstock 166bl; Nicola Stocken © RHS 13 (7), 87 (3), 88 (3 (t), 127 (9), 147 (7), 165 (2), 171br, 183 (11), 195mt, 203 (4), 221 (10), 231tl, 231ml, 231b; Nigel Cattlin/Alamy 92; nnattalli/Shutterstock 61ml; Oliver Dixon © RHS 68r, 87 (5); Paul Debois © RHS 107 (1); Paul Harris © Paul Harris 107 (10); Paul Thompson Images/Alamy 145 (5); PeopleImages.com - Yuri A/Shutterstock 146bl; Peter Turner Photography/Shutterstock 213t; Philippa Gibson © RHS 13 (10), 13 (11), 23t, 31 (5) 49 (9), 113m, 127 (1), 139t, 147 (4), 195bl, 203 (3), 219 (2), 221 (6), 221 (9); photoPOU/Shutterstock 124 (1); Pictorial Press Ltd/Alamy 25; Quagga Media/Alamy 76; Raymond J. Evison © Raymond J. Evinson 61mr; Rebecca Ross © RHS 41b, 57 (4) 228br; RHS © RHS 13 (2), 49 (4), 77, 87 (1), 127 (11), 157m, 173, 229; RHS Lindley Collections 43, 63, 96, 116, 121, 136, 141; RHS Lindley Collections / Elizabeth Blackwell 192; RHS Lindley Collections / Ernest Bernary 58, 172; RHS Lindley Collections / Birket N Satterthwaite © Artist's Estate 101; RHS/Visions Pictures © Visions BV 107 (10), 126 (5), 191 br, 208t; Richard Bloom © RHS 31 (9), 41t, 42, 69 (9), 69 (11) 100, 120, 140, 176, 196, 203 (7), 232; Robert Murray/Alamy 41bl; Sarah Cuttle © RHS 183 (8); Sheila Dearing © RHS 13 (4), 127 (6); Simon Garbutt © RHS 203 (5); Stephen Parker/Alamy 159; Sylvio Dittrich/imageBROKER/Shutterstock 108bl; t.sableaux/Shutterstock 86br; The History Collection/Alamy 215; Tim Sandall © RHS 10 (2), 11(3) 11 (4), 12 (5), 19t, 19b, 20t, 20b, 28 (1), 28 (2), 28 (5), 28 (6), 36, 38b, 47 (2), 47 (3), 48t (5), 48b, 49 (7), 49 (8), 49 (10), 56 (1), 57 (2), 57br, 61tr, 67 (4), 68l (5), 74 (1), 75 (3), 75 (5), 84 (1), 85 (3), 85 (4), 85 (5), 87 (7), 87 (9), 88 (2), 88 (3 (b)), 95 (3), 95tr, 104 (1), 104 (2), 105 (3), 105 (4), 105 (5), 106 (7), 107 (5), 107 (9), 112, 113t, 113b, 114 (1), 114 (2), 115 (3), 115 (4), 119mb, 127 (3), 127 (10), 133, 134 (1), 135 (1), 135tr, 145 (2), 145 (4), 147 (11), 152, 153l, 154 (1), 155, 162 (1), 163 (3), 163 (4), 164t, 166 (3), 170 (1), 170b, 171 (3), 171 (4), 175b, 177, 180 (2), 181 (3), 181 (4), 181 (6), 182 (7), 183 (2), 183 (4), 183 (9), 188, 189b, 190b, 200 (2), 201 (3), 203 (2), 203 (10), 208b, 210 (1), 210b, 219 (1), 220r, 221 (2), 221 (5), 227t; VaDiBa/Shutterstock 195ml; Vera Petruk/Shutterstock 202 tr; Vicky Turner © RHS 69 (2); Volcko Mar/Shutterstock 183 (5); Washington Imaging/Alamy 12b; Wendy Wesley © RHS 23b, 49 (2), 165 (3), 165 (9); Wiert nieuman/Shutterstock 213b; Wilf Halliday © RHS 13 (3); Zebrina Rendall © RHS 69 (4), 79tl; Zoonar GmbH/Alamy 213bmr